IMAGES
of America

FOREST PARK

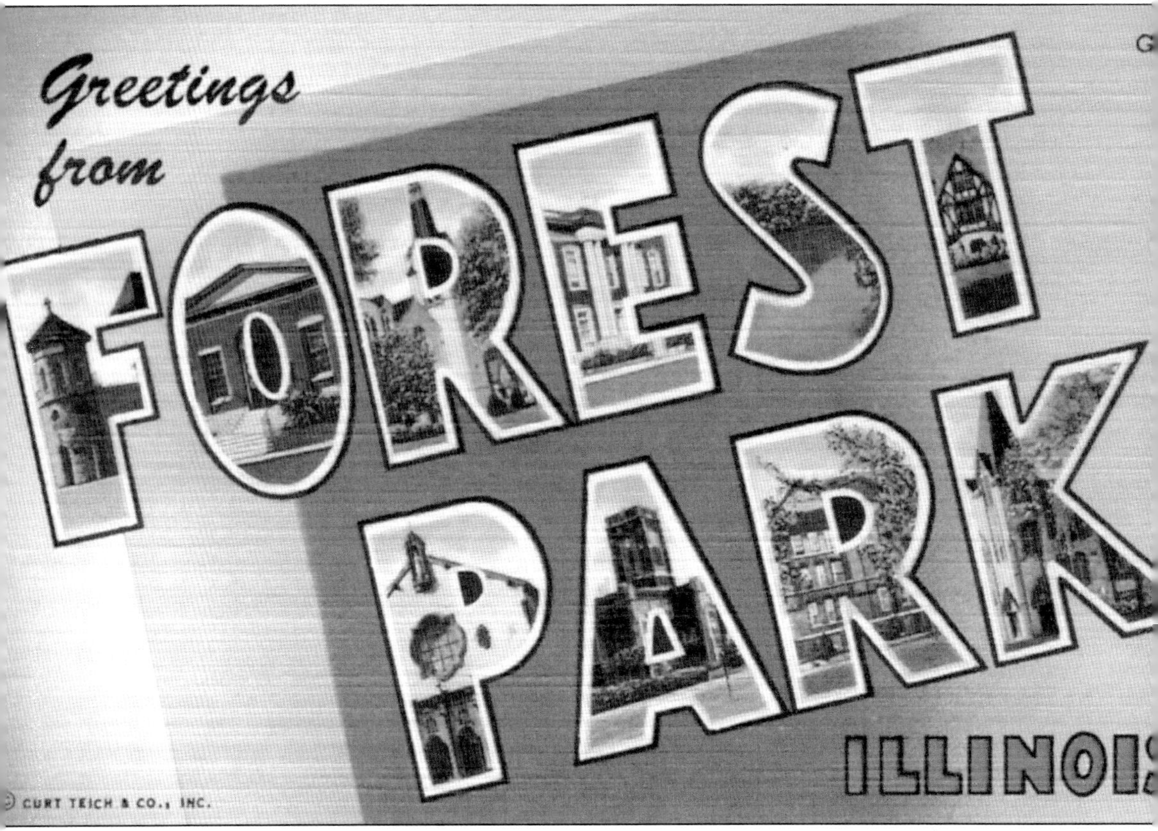

The large letter linen cards produced by the Curt Teich Company were a popular way to share civic pride. These letters display the following Forest Park images: (F) Waldheim Cemetery entrance, (O) the post office, (R) St. John's Church, (E) the village hall, (S) Des Plaines River, (T) Park District building, (P) St. Bernadine's Church, (A) Proviso East, (R) Altenheim, and (K) the Forest Park Baptist Church. (Courtesy of the author.)

ON THE COVER: Madison Street appears eerily quiet as Chicago and West Towns Railway car No. 136 approaches Circle Avenue and passes Zimmerman's Funeral Home and the Wolf brothers furniture store. The Wolf brothers, who owned many properties along Madison Street, constructed the building in 1919 and opened the store in 1920. Alfred Krader bought the business in 1960, and it continued as Krader-Wolf for many years. Both buildings are still in use. (Photograph by Robert W. Gibson; courtesy of Walter R. Keevil.)

IMAGES
of America

FOREST PARK

Kenneth J. Knack

ARCADIA
PUBLISHING

ISBN 978-0-7385-8326-6

Published by Arcadia Publishing
Charleston, South Carolina

Printed in the United States of America

Library of Congress Control Number: 2010934701

For all general information, please contact Arcadia Publishing:
Telephone 843-853-2070
Fax 843-853-0044
E-mail sales@arcadiapublishing.com
For customer service and orders:
Toll-Free 1-888-313-2665

Visit us on the Internet at www.arcadiapublishing.com

To my wonderful wife, Diane, my muse, who has not only tolerated my incessant ramblings about Forest Park for over 13 years, but has inspired me and kept me on track. Sorry this project broke our computer.

Contents

Acknowledgments		6
Introduction		7
1.	The Settlers	9
2.	The Days of Old Harlem	15
3.	Silent Cities	23
4.	Summertime Fun	33
5.	Education and Salvation	47
6.	A New Era Begins	61
7.	The Postwar Years	91
8.	Same Place, Different Time	115

ACKNOWLEDGMENTS

Although my own personal collection of postcards and other memorabilia served as the foundation for this endeavor, it would not have been possible without the help and support of the following people—many of whom entrusted irreplaceable family or institutional photographs to my care. While all helped in some way or another, some went beyond the call, and without them this book would have been impossible. Those people are Jan Grover (Licht family), Walter R. Keevil, Jeff Oswalt, my editors Jeff Ruetsche and Michael Stafford (Arcadia Publishing), and Tim Shanahan.

I would like to thank the following individuals for contributing photographs: Tony Bale, Jim Hall, Kevin Johnson, Tom Krenek, Virginia Marischler, Bruce G. Moffat, the Mohr family (Mike, Steve, and Marlene), Jim Papa, Jerry Parichy, Dixie Quitsch Paugh, Frank Petrovic, Al Reda, Gail Roos, Richard and Wayne Schauer, Susan Schierstedt, Harold Stover, Loretta Woeltje, the family of Thomas A. Walsh Jr. (who dedicate their photographs to his memory), and Herman Ziebell.

Additionally, I would like to thank the following people, institutions, and organizations for contributing photographs: Marcus Berry of the Chicago Public Library; Gary Neubieser of Concordia Cemetery; Mary Gosmire of Ferrara Pan Candy Company; Richard Vitton of the Historical Society of Forest Park; Pastor Dr. Dean Kucera of First United Church of Christ; Jim Peters of Forest Home Cemetery; Pastor David Steinhart and Lauren Woodruff of Forest Park Baptist Church; Frank Lipo of the Historical Society of Oak Park and River Forest; David Penzell of the Waldheim Cemetery Company; Jeanette Barnes and Joanne Leber of School District 91; Chris Richards of the Park District of Forest Park; Pastor Audree Catalano of St. Peter's and St. Paul's Churches; Chris Winters of the University of Chicago Library; Mayor Anthony Calderone and Sally Cody of the Village of Forest Park; and John Isaacson of Woodlawn Cemetery.

I would like to sincerely thank the Forest Park Library and staff, which includes Rodger Brayden, Ben Haines, and Kate Niehoff, for making the *Forest Park Review* archives accessible online and free of charge.

Others who provided stories, resources, or encouragement are Mark Bishop, Dianne Howard, Mary Flanagan, Dan Licht, Marge Moskos, Duke Olliges, Andy Plummer, Linda Shrader, Bob Sullivan, Frank Troost and, finally, my family, coworkers, and friends. I thank you all.

Additionally, I would like to posthumously thank Dr. Frank Orland, who helped save and preserve Forest Park's history and heritage. All photographs and images that are not credited are from my own personal collection.

Introduction

Those of us raised on the south side of Forest Park were often prohibited from crossing the busy streets of Harlem Avenue and Roosevelt Road. That exile forced my brother Eric and me to explore the Jewish and Woodlawn Cemeteries. Those early excursions led to my lifelong fascination with history, specifically the history of Forest Park.

My maternal grandparents, Luciano and Millie Petrone, moved to Forest Park in 1948, while my mother was still in high school. My father's family had already set down roots in the community. My great-granduncle Leo Knack had a music shop at 7316 Madison Street. My father, Richard Knack, was sworn in as a reserve police officer on September 22, 1956, which inspired my brother Steve to join the police department when he grew up. Steve served 29 years, retiring as a lieutenant. My mother, Virginia, kept a copy of the 1956 centennial book, and I remember being fascinated with the photographs at an early age. I spent hours reading the original *Chronicles of Forest Park*. Over the years, I have collected many items of Forest Park memorabilia, including postcards and artifacts, and have taken many photographs of the area.

Several years ago, I found the Arcadia series of local history books and noticed the lack of a Forest Park edition. Knowing a great deal about the history of Forest Park, I knew that it needed to be included in the series. I have attempted to be as complete and as accurate as possible in telling the history of Forest Park, although many conflicting facts and versions of stories have surfaced during the research.

Forest Park is usually known for one of two things. The first is for being the watering hole of the nearby suburbs. While neighboring villages Oak Park and River Forest remained dry, Forest Park quenched the thirst of the area's locals. Forest Park's other claim to fame is that of being a "city of the dead." Forest Park is home to more deceased people than those alive—some say by as much as a 30 to 1 ratio, or well over 450,000.

Forest Park, or Harlem as it was previously known, is located just 4 miles outside of the city limits of Chicago. It is bisected by the Eisenhower Expressway and is the terminus for both the blue and green lines of the Chicago "L" system. The village is bordered by Maywood to the west, North Riverside to the south, Berwyn and Oak Park to the east, and River Forest to the north.

The village has long served as a respite from the hectic life of the inner city. In the earliest days, picnic groves attracted huge crowds to enjoy fresh air and relaxation along the Des Plaines River. A racetrack along Twelfth Street (Roosevelt Road) offered gamblers a chance to bet on a racehorse or an early race car. The Harlem Golf Club gave the public a chance to enjoy the sport without country club dues. Forest Park was also home to an amusement park that rivaled Riverview. The amusement park opened against the wishes of several Lutheran organizations who thought it was inappropriate to have an amusement venue located literally next door to the final resting place of their dearly departed.

The cemetery business built Forest Park. Taverns and restaurants opened to serve mourners, who would often stay after funeral services for food and drink. Several monument companies, including Troost, S. Berliner, Otto Reich, and Kistenbroker, along with florists like Klimmers and Quitsch, relied upon the steady stream of internments and visitors.

Many notables, including royalty, are interred in the town's cemeteries. Among them are the Haymarket riot martyrs, Elizabeth Taylor's husband Michael Todd, Billy Sunday, and victims of the SS *Eastland* disaster, the Iroquois Theatre fire, and the Hagenback-Wallace circus train crash of 1918. Ernest Hemingway's parents are among those buried in Forest Home, along with gypsy kings and queens.

Forest Park was widely regarded as being a haven for gamblers from its earliest days well into the late 1960s. Gorke's place, located at Harlem and Circle Avenues, was raided several times early on in Forest Park's history. Slot machines, poker tables, roulette wheels, and boards with racing odds were all found in the second floor gambling room. In the 1960s, the FBI wiretapped a back room that used as an "office" by reputed mob boss Sam Giancana at the Armory restaurant.

Madison Street from Harlem to Des Plaines Avenues is, and has always been, the main street in Forest Park. Despite the urban-renewal phase of the 1960s and 1970s that destroyed the character of many small-town business districts, Madison Street was able to retain much of its charm and personality. Many of the buildings date back to the late 1800s and early 1900s. The building located at the southwest corner of Madison Street and Harlem Avenue was at one time the tallest building between Chicago and St. Louis.

Forest Park has endured many changes, beginning with its name. Harlem had been using neighboring Oak Park's post office, but when Harlem sought a post office of its own, it was discovered that there was already a town named Harlem located near Rockford. A contingent was sent to try to convince the other Harlem to change its name, to no avail. Several names including Forest Home were considered, but in the end, the name Forest Park was selected.

Prohibition closed Forest Park's bars for the first time in its history. In all, 39 taverns were closed. Many became soft drink parlors, and a few became speakeasies. In the 1950s, the town was literally sliced in half when the Congress Expressway was built.

In 1998, the Living Word Christian Center purchased the Forest Park Mall. With over 12,000 members, the congregation built a new auditorium at the southwest corner. More recent changes include the replacement of the pool with a new aquatic center and the opening of the Proviso Mathematics and Science Academy in 2005 at First Avenue and Roosevelt Road. Two five-story buildings and 60 townhomes replaced the Abell Howell plant on Van Buren Street. Other large building projects include Madison Street Commons, located between Elgin and Marengo Avenues. Townhomes replaced Donna's Meat Plant and the Kneip facility on the north side and the Moose Hall on south Des Plaines Avenue. A rejuvenation of the Madison Street business district has made it a popular destination for dining and shopping.

I hope the images found on the following pages bring back some fond memories and inspire further research and preservation.

One

The Settlers

The land now known as Forest Park was once home to many Native American tribes, including the Ojibwa, Menominee, and Potawatomie. Of these, the Potawatomi were the last to inhabit the area. They settled along the banks of the Des Plaines River upon the high ground, which is geologically known as the Oak Park spit. The spit is a natural sandbar that marks the ancient shoreline of Lake Michigan. This high ground was perfect for trails, villages, and burial grounds. The Potawatomie tribe had a substantial settlement in the area known today as Forest Home Cemetery.

Leon Bourassa was the first settler to lay claim to this land. In 1839, he secured a land grant for 160 acres, signed by President Van Buren. He married a native Potawatomi named Mnitoqua (Spirit Woman) and built a small cabin, in which he raised a family. Legend has it that when Mnitoqua's tribe moved west across the Mississippi, she stayed behind to care for the ancestral burial grounds.

The area that encompasses Forest Park has known many names. In 1839, most of the area was known as Oak Ridge, but the post office was called Noyesville. The early settlers of the era included Ashbel Steele and Joseph Kettlestrings, of River Forest and Oak Park fame, respectively. Still the area was sparsely populated in 1851, when Bourassa sold 40 acres to a German immigrant named Ferdinand Haase. In the 1850s, others moved into the area as well, including Peter Carney and John Henry Quick. Legend has it that Quick named the area Harlem after his birthplace in New York. Haase gradually acquired additional land, until he eventually owned 248 acres between what is now Madison Street and Roosevelt Road.

Haase raised cattle and built a New Orleans–style mansion on his property. In the 1860s, he decided to open a picnic grove on the grounds. Wisely, Haase convinced the Chicago and Galena Union Railway to build a spur line on his property in exchange for gravel. The building of a roundhouse by the railroad in 1856 is widely regarded as being the birth of Harlem.

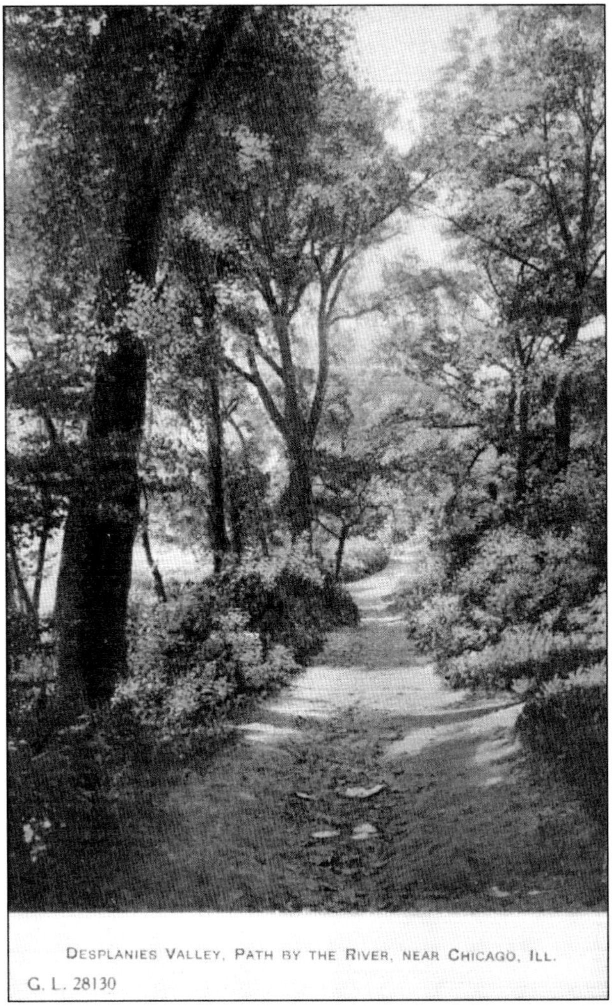

The postcard at left features one of the many paths along the Des Plaines River. These well-worn paths may very well be the same ones used by the Native American tribes that called this area home. In addition to the village and burial ground in the Forest Home area, there were many others along the river.

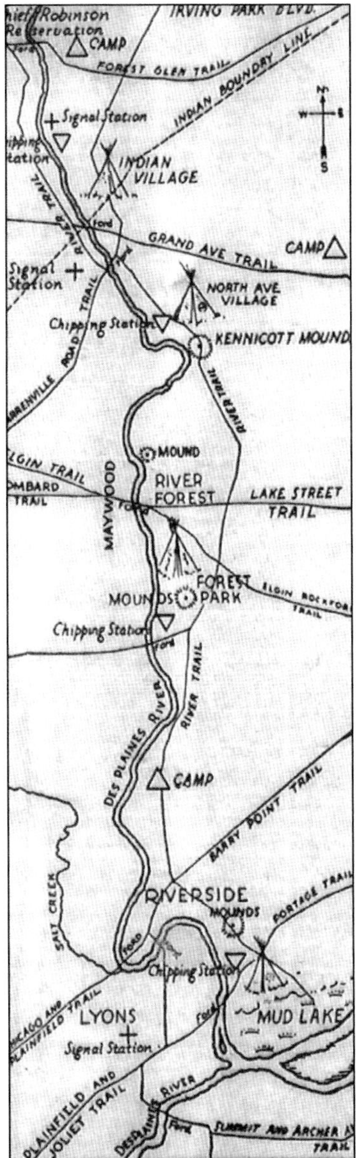

INDIAN TRAIL
Leading Through Forest Park

The old map at right shows the extensive presence Native Americans had in the area along the Des Plaines River. The map shows the approximate location of their villages, chipping stations, and burial mounds. Many exquisite artifacts uncovered in Forest Home Cemetery are housed in the Forest Park Library.

In an effort to preserve local history, the owners of Forest Home dedicated a monument on Indian Hill in 1941. Local artist and historian Paul Strayer designed the relief on the monument, and the carving was done by Arthur Kistenbroker III. The monument marks the location of the cabin of Leon Bourassa and the burial site of Carl Zimmerman, who died in 1854. (Courtesy of the Kistenbroker family.)

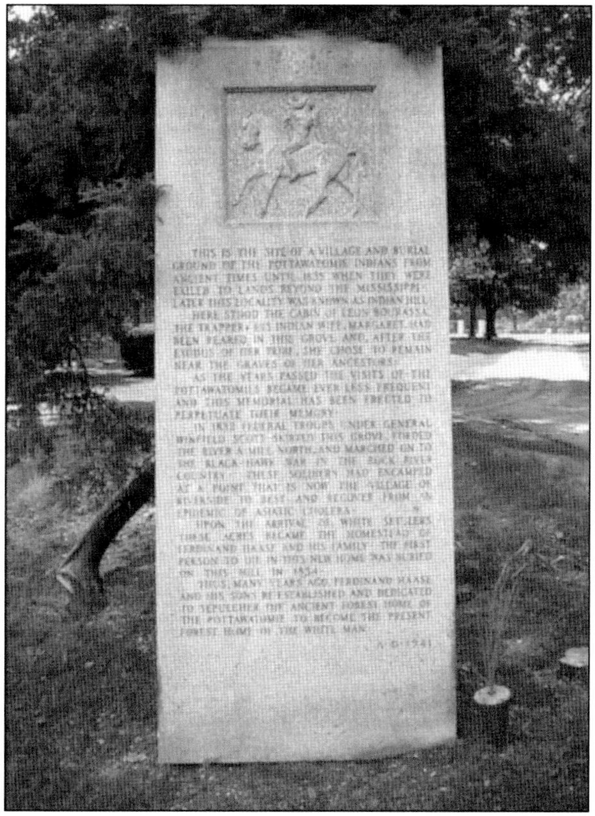

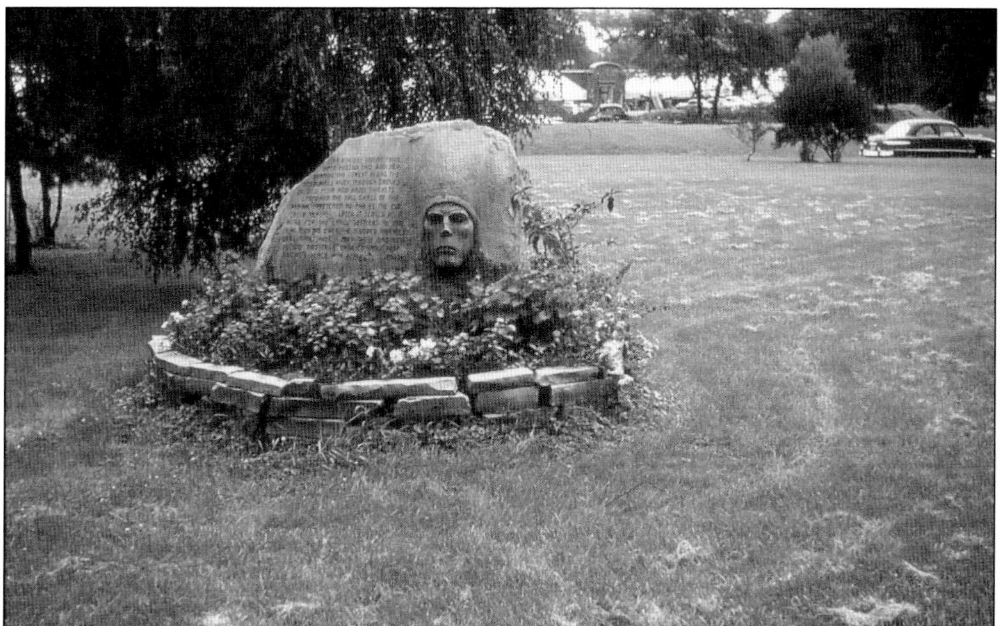

Continuing their effort to preserve the history of the area, the owners of Forest Home commissioned this monument, carved by Arthur Kistenbroker III in 1942. The boulder is shown here in 1958, sometime before vandals broke off the tip of the nose. (Courtesy of Forest Home Cemetery.)

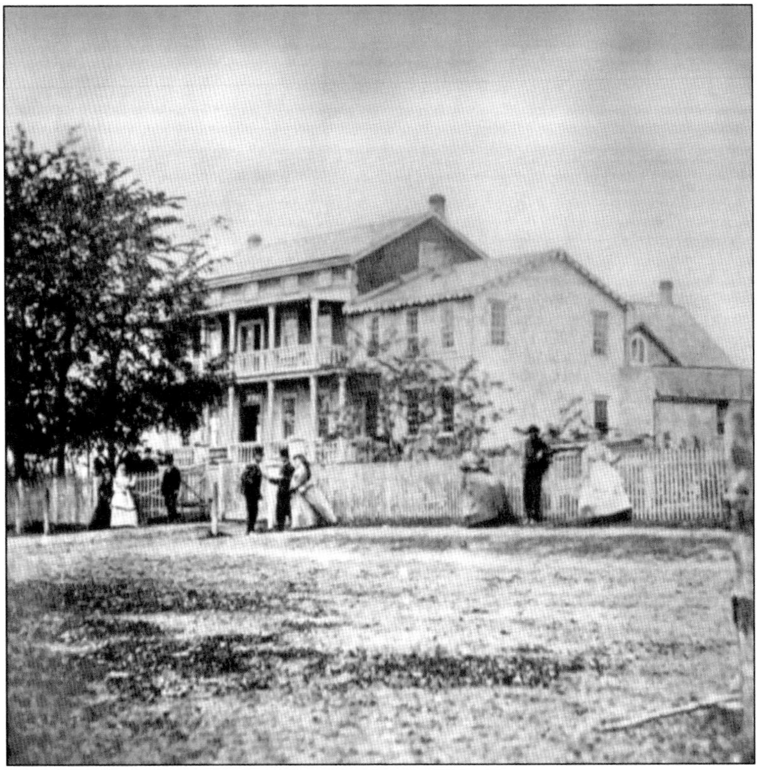

This photograph from the late 1800s shows the 30-room New Orleans–style mansion that was built by Ferdinand Haase. After a stint as a farmer and cattle rancher, Haase opened a picnic grove on his land. Crowds of 5,000–15,000 people were not uncommon. Attractions included boat races, bands, dancing, and contests, and on July 4, 1872, guests enjoyed a hot air balloon and a tightrope walker. (Courtesy of Forest Home Cemetery.)

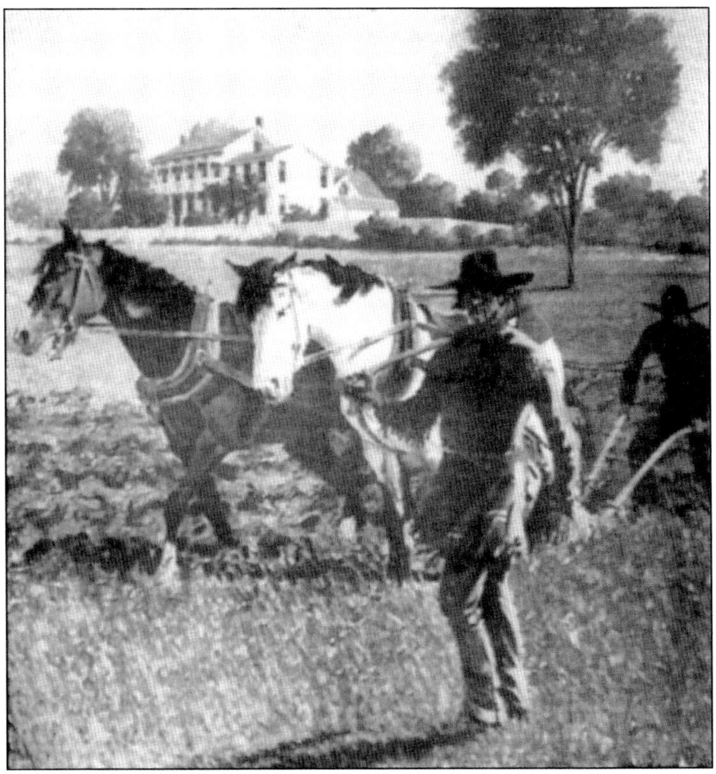

This mural, created by Paul Strayer in the 1940s, depicts what life may have looked like at the Haase homestead in the 1850s, prior to its use as a picnic grove. Strayer was also the designer of the monument on Indian Hill in Forest Home Cemetery on page 11.

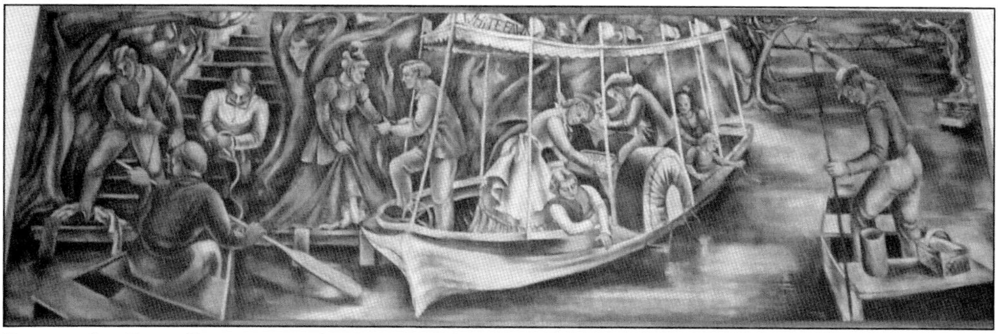

During the Great Depression, the Section of Fine Arts commissioned Miriam McKinnie to create a mural for the Forest Park Post Office. *The White Fawn* mural depicts visitors to Haase's Park in the 1860s, boarding the excursion boat that bears the same name as the mural. The mural was removed in the 1960s during some post office redecorating and stored at the library, where it was subsequently forgotten for nearly 30 years. It was later found and underwent a seven-month restoration. The mural was rededicated and replaced in the post office on February 25, 2005.

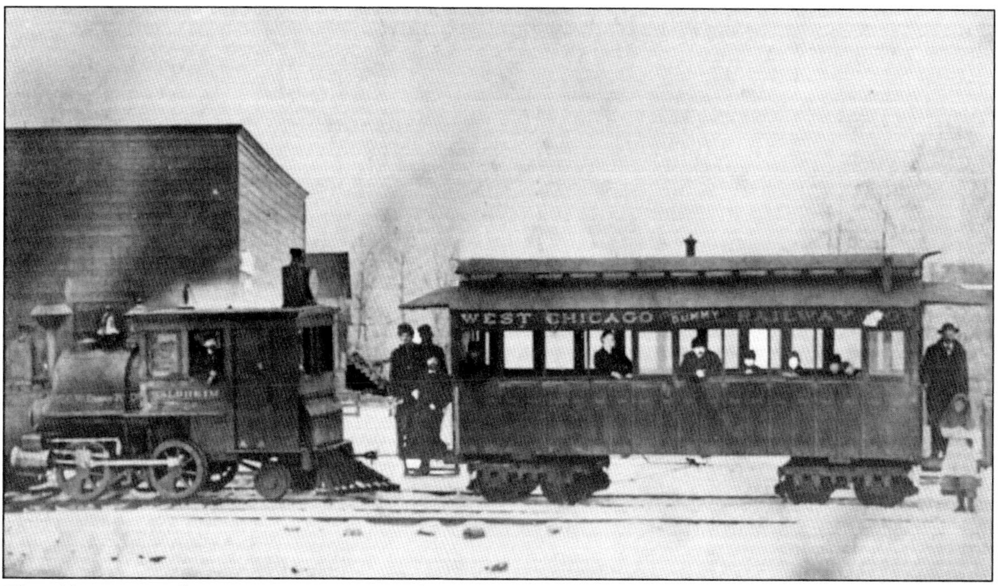

The Chicago and Western Dummy Railway served as the precursor to the streetcar. The small steam locomotive in this mid-1800s photograph bears the name Waldheim, which is referring to the stop it made at Waldheim Cemetery. The photograph was taken from Randolph Street and Harlem Avenue on a cold winter day. (Courtesy of Chicago Public Library, Special Collections and Preservation Division, CCW 1.395.)

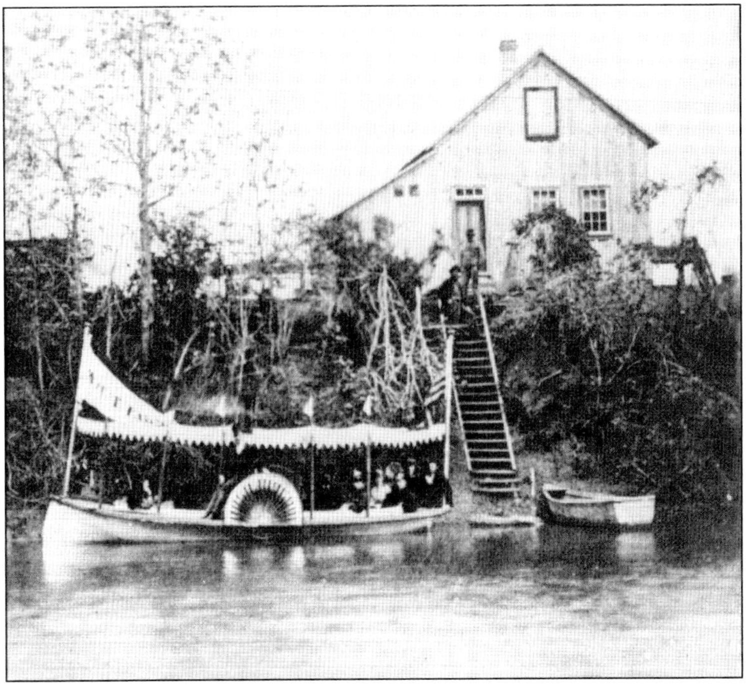

A voyage on the *White Fawn* must have been a thrilling experience. Just getting down to the boat appeared to be challenging. The small, steam-powered boat carried passengers on excursions along the Des Plaines River during the days of Haase's Park. The name may have been inspired by a stage drama that was in production in the late 1860s. (Courtesy of Historical Society of Forest Park.)

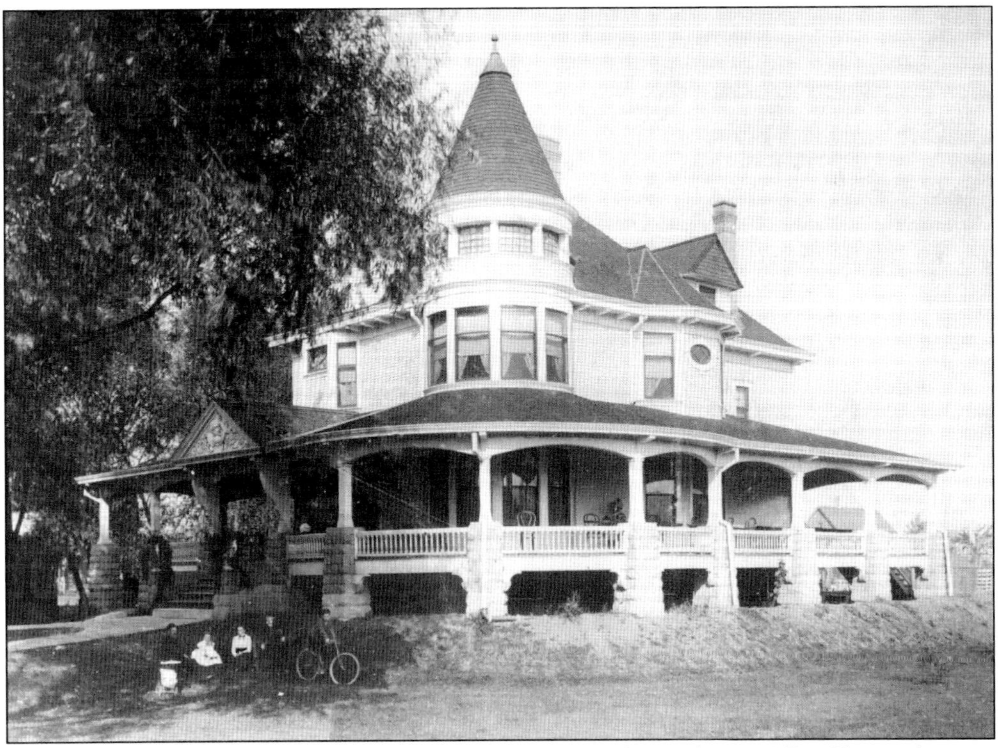

Arthur Kistenbroker built this magnificent Victorian home, located at 1020 Des Plaines Avenue. The home was located just south of and adjacent to his monument company. It was demolished sometime in the late 1960s and was replaced by a large apartment complex. (Courtesy of the Kistenbroker family.)

Two

The Days of Old Harlem

In 1880, the residents of the northern section of Harlem voted to separate and incorporate as the Village of River Forest. The remaining portion of Harlem would not incorporate for another four years. In the early days of Harlem, most of the town existed north of Madison Street. The village hall stood in the northeast corner of Circle Avenue and Randolph Street. The first schoolhouse within the current boundaries of Forest Park was located on the west side of the street, which is now the playground of the current Grant White School. The first fire department was made up of volunteers in 1890 and was also located at Circle Avenue and Randolph Street.

By the time the village was incorporated, the Concordia, Waldheim, Forest Home, and the Free Sons of Israel Cemeteries had been opened for years. The trip to the cemeteries in those days was a long journey over bad roads, and people would need food and refreshments before heading back home. Not surprisingly, many saloons and restaurants opened near the cemeteries, catering to the large groups of mourners. The cemeteries also created a demand for monuments and grave markers. Several monument companies opened along Des Plaines Avenue and Madison Street. Other businesses opened to supply the growing number of people moving to the community. These businesses included butcher shops and grocery, dry goods, and clothing stores.

The proximity to the rail yards north of Franklin Street provided for a wealth of goods to be shipped directly into town. Lumber, coal, and even ice were commodities that were readily accessible to the area residents. Ice was cut from Lake Geneva and transported by rail to icehouses. By 1894, the year the racetrack was built, Harlem had 51 saloons—one for every 30 people.

With all things considered, Harlem seemed to be an up-and-coming community that was well poised for continued growth and development. This growth would foster a desire for a post office of their own; however, to get that post office, Harlem would ultimately need to change its name.

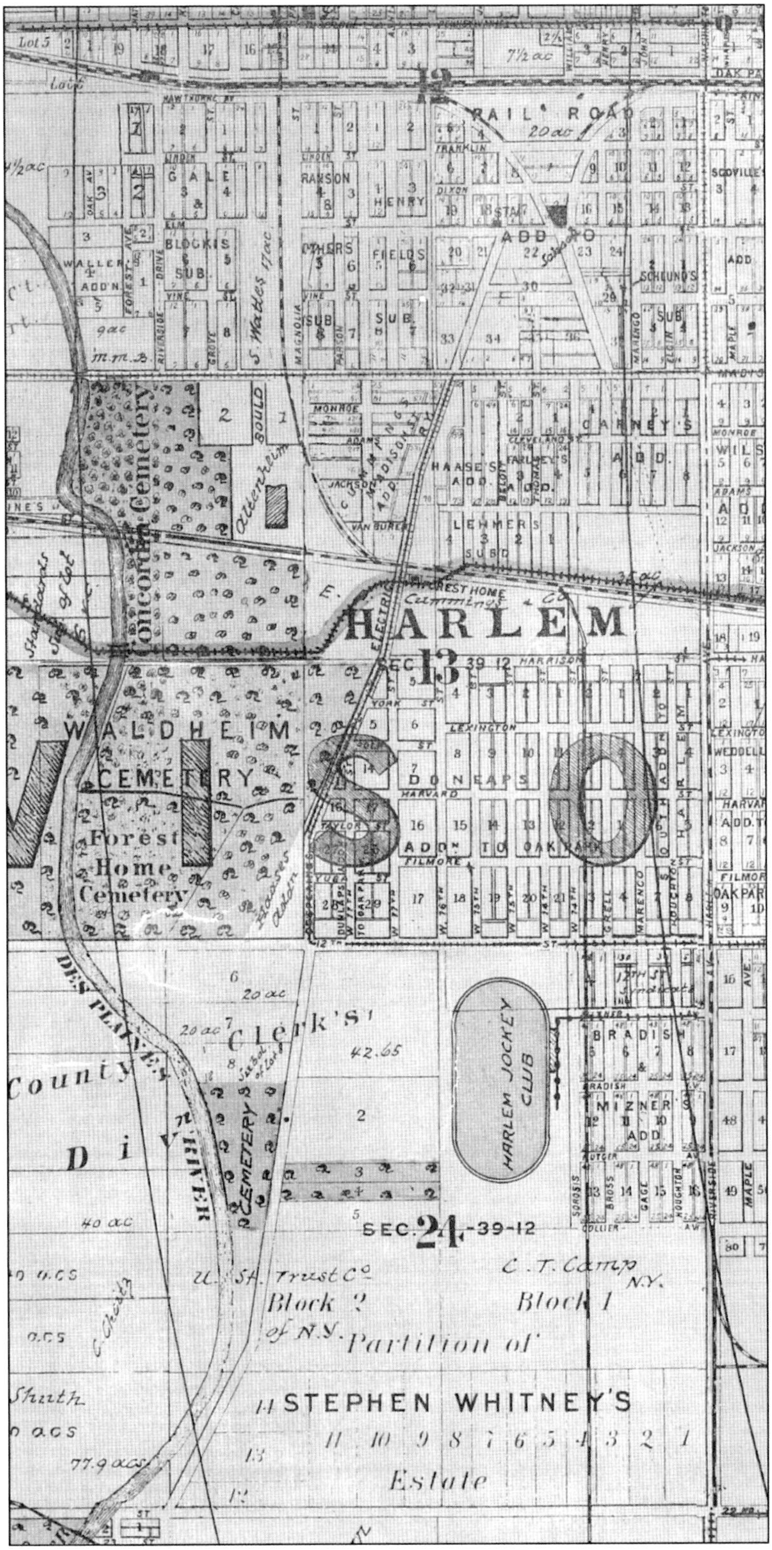

This is a map of Harlem from 1903. It is interesting to note the large holdings of Haase, Carney, and Cummings. The Harlem Jockey Club also owned a large parcel. With the number of railroads and surface lines, it is easy to see how convenient the early transportation system was. It is also interesting to note that the streets on the south side of Twelfth Street bore different names than the same street to the north. (Courtesy of University of Chicago Library.)

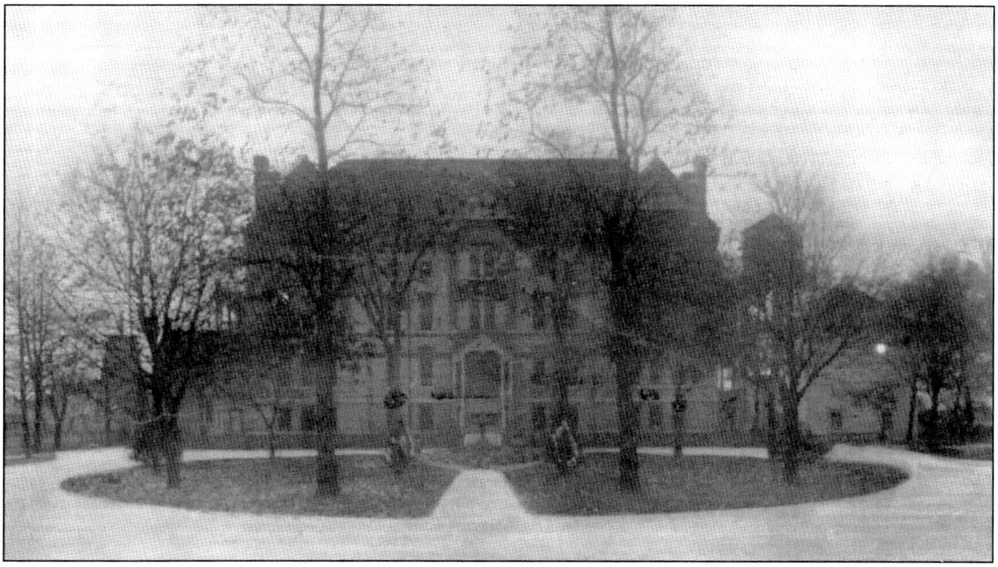

This early postcard view features the main building of Altenheim as it appeared before its many subsequent additions. Altenheim (which translates to "home for the elderly") was founded by the German community and was nearly a city unto itself. It had a farm, a chapel, and even its own cemetery. The main building at Altenheim was constructed in 1885. There were reportedly 4,000 people at the dedication and formal opening on June 4, 1886.

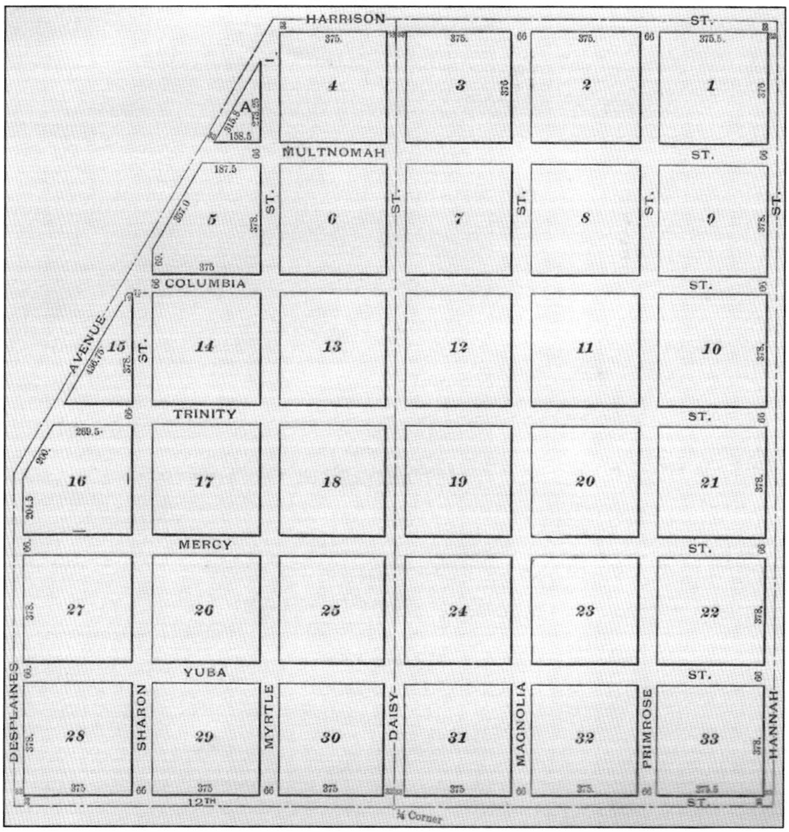

This c. 1874 map shows the section of town that is still referred to as Dunlop's addition to Oak Park in zoning cases today. Note the original names of the streets. The street now known as York Street was called Multnomah on the map. (Courtesy of Forest Home Cemetery.)

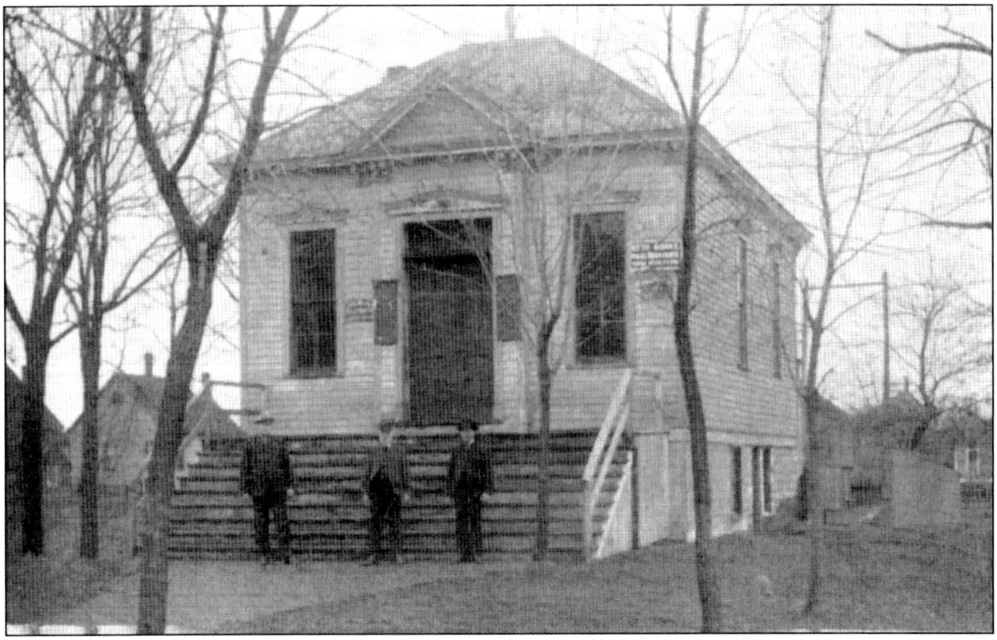

Harlem's first village hall was built in 1885 at the northeast corner of Randolph Street and Circle Avenue. This building was used until 1915, when a new municipal building was constructed at 517 Des Plaines Avenue. In 1917, this building was moved to 7318 Randolph Street. In 1947, it was moved to the front of the lot, which was where it survived until it was replaced with a condominium complex. (Courtesy of Forest Park Baptist Church.)

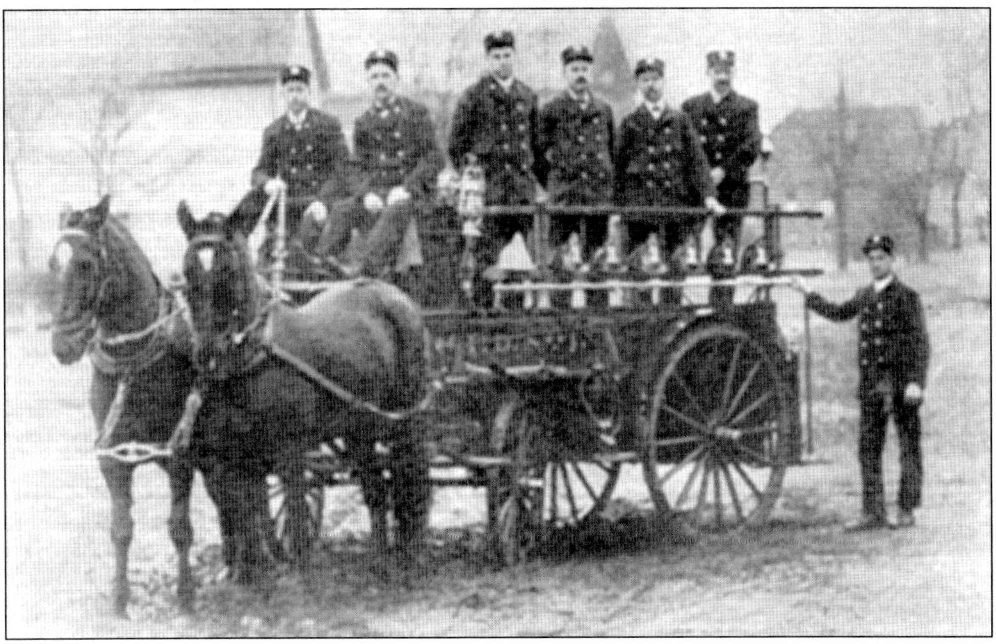

The Harlem Fire Department in 1906 is seen here with the hose wagon led by horses Tom and Jerry. John Condon, who owned the racetrack, donated the horses along with $500. The horses served the fire department faithfully until the first motorized truck arrived in 1920. Rather than retiring, they were transferred to the street department. (Courtesy of Forest Park Baptist Church.)

Madison Street House, established in 1873, was one of the early restaurants and saloons that catered to mourners. Here they could stop for a meal and refreshments before returning to the city after a funeral. Henry Licht was the proprietor for many years. This magnificent structure was located at 147 Madison Street, approximately where Schauer's Hardware is today. (Courtesy of the Licht family.)

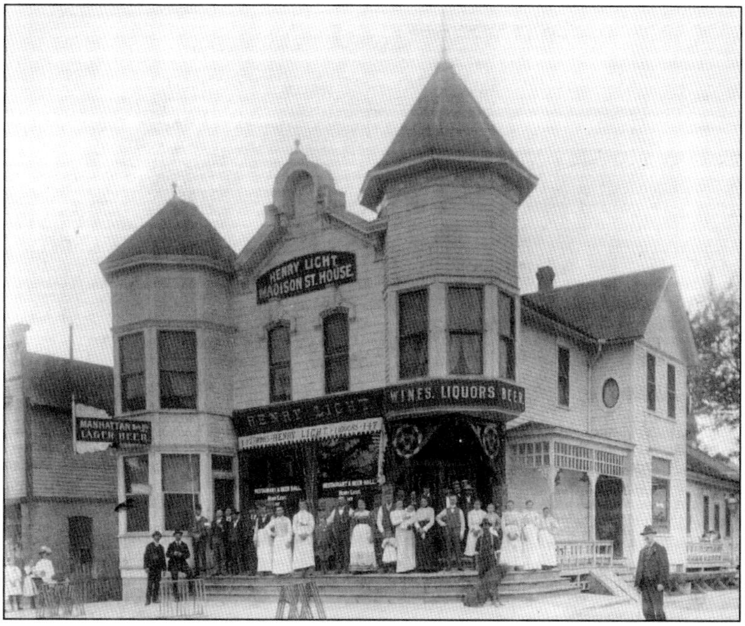

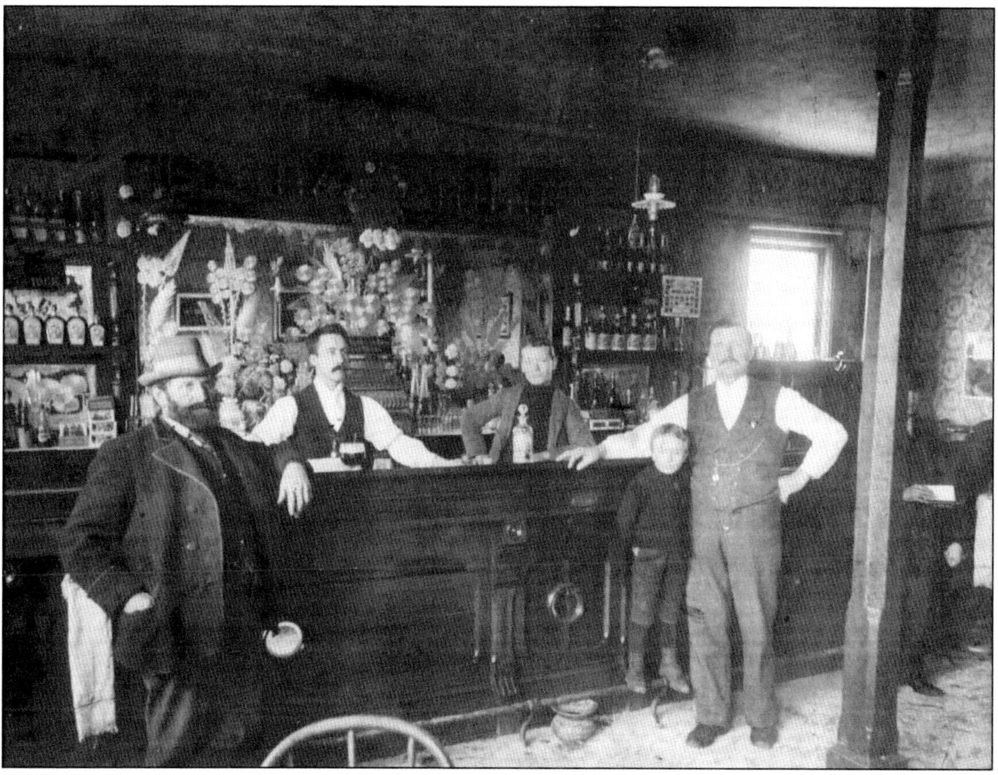

Saloons and taverns were family-run affairs, and all members of the family were expected to do their part. This image of the inside of Madison Street House shows, from left to right, an unidentified patron, a bartender, young Fred Licht, his brother Henry Jr., and proprietor Henry Licht Sr. Fred would go on to become one of the village's longest-serving police chiefs. (Courtesy of the Licht family.)

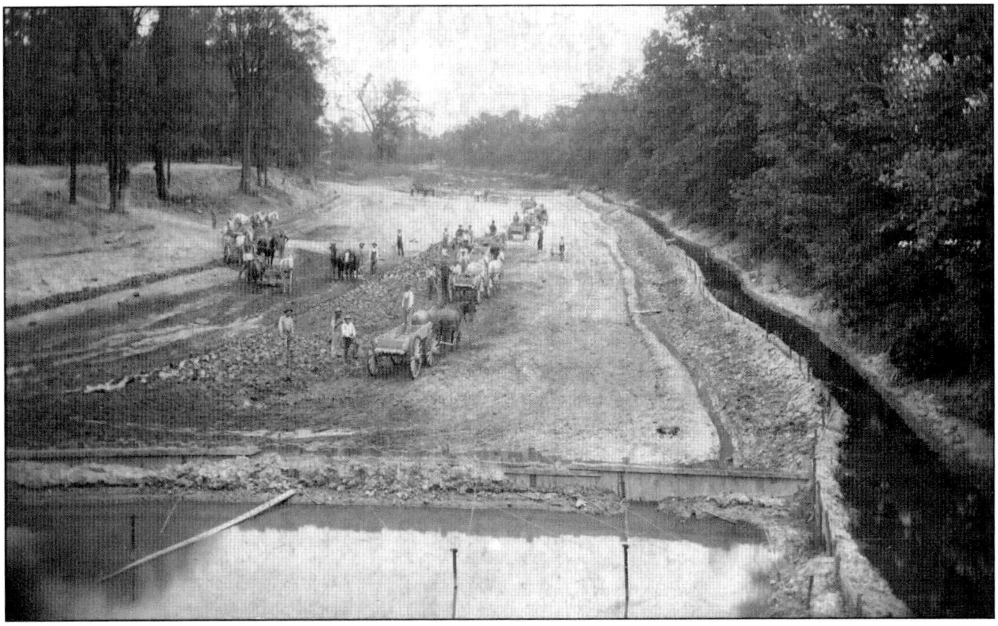

The Aux Plaines River, known later as the Des Plaines River, was prone to seasonal flooding. A bad storm on August 2, 1885, during which 5.58 inches of rain fell, may have inspired the work shown here, which is described as "the deepening of the Des Plaines River c. 1892–1897." The photograph was most likely taken from the cemetery bridge facing south. (Photograph by W. F. Arnold; courtesy of Forest Home Cemetery.)

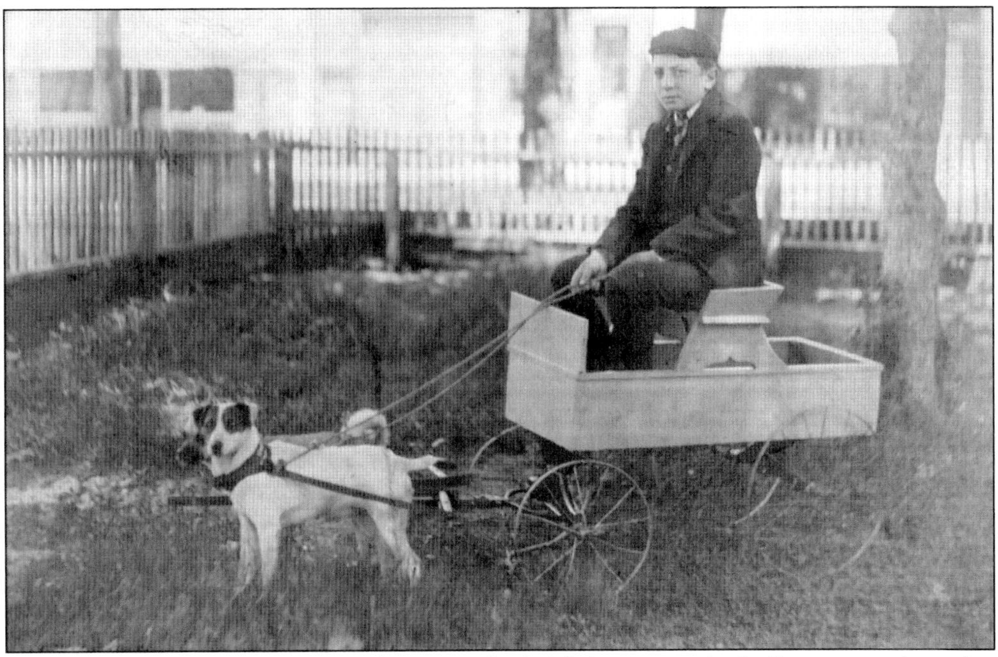

Based on the small statures of his dogs, it is doubtful that Henry Licht Jr. got very far in his dog-powered wagon. Henry's love of the outdoors and animals would serve him well later in life, as he became a groundskeeper and eventually the manager of the Harlem Golf Course. While working there, he even had a pet raccoon. (Courtesy of the Licht family.)

G. Kunz Confectionery at 7513 Madison Street was built in 1892. It was possibly the first building made of brick constructed on Madison Street, and it is the oldest surviving structure on the block. Kunz was the first business in town to sell ice-cream sodas. The building is now home to Duffy's Tavern, known for a different type of refreshment. Note the wooden sidewalks.

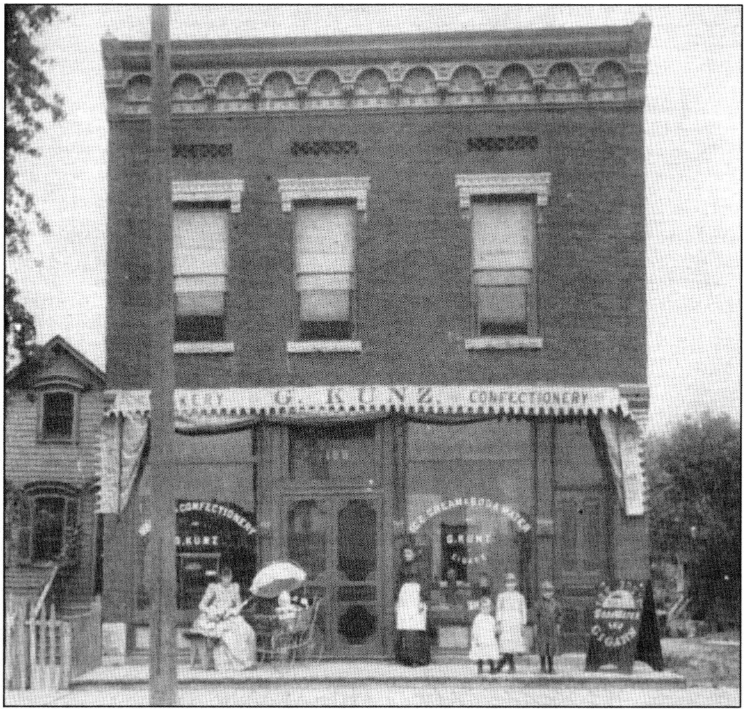

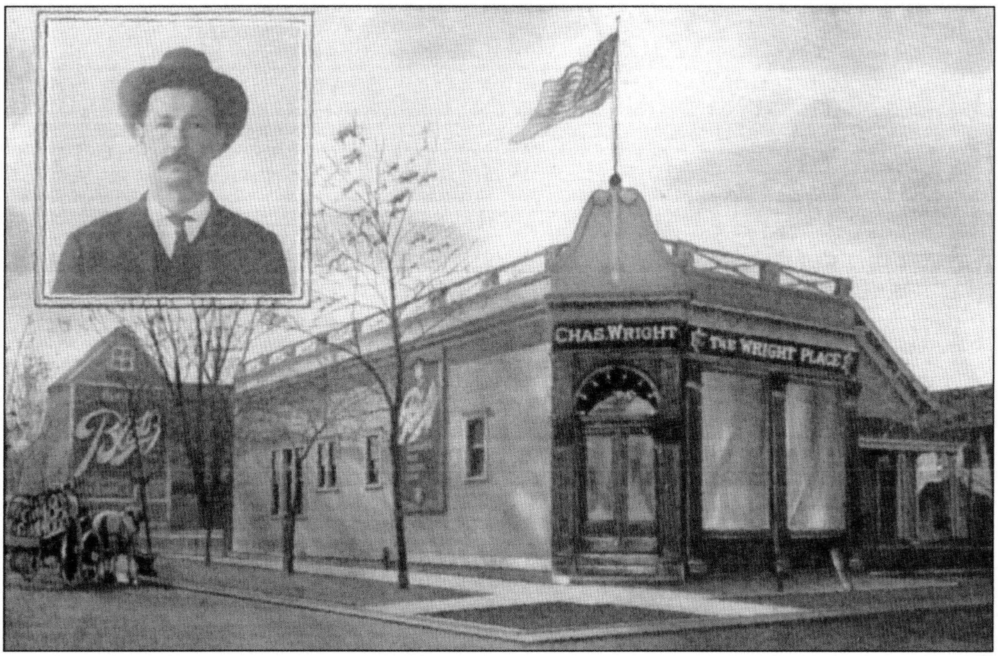

The Wright Place, shown here in 1906 with proprietor Charles Wright pictured in the inset, has a long and colorful past. Now home to Kevil's at 7228 Circle Avenue, it has also been known as Set Back North and the Canteen. The tavern was the site of the double murder of racketeers Barney "Murphy" McCone and Herman "The Kid" Diehn on July 16, 1931. Two slot machines were confiscated from the Canteen in a 1949 gambling raid. (Courtesy of Forest Park Baptist Church.)

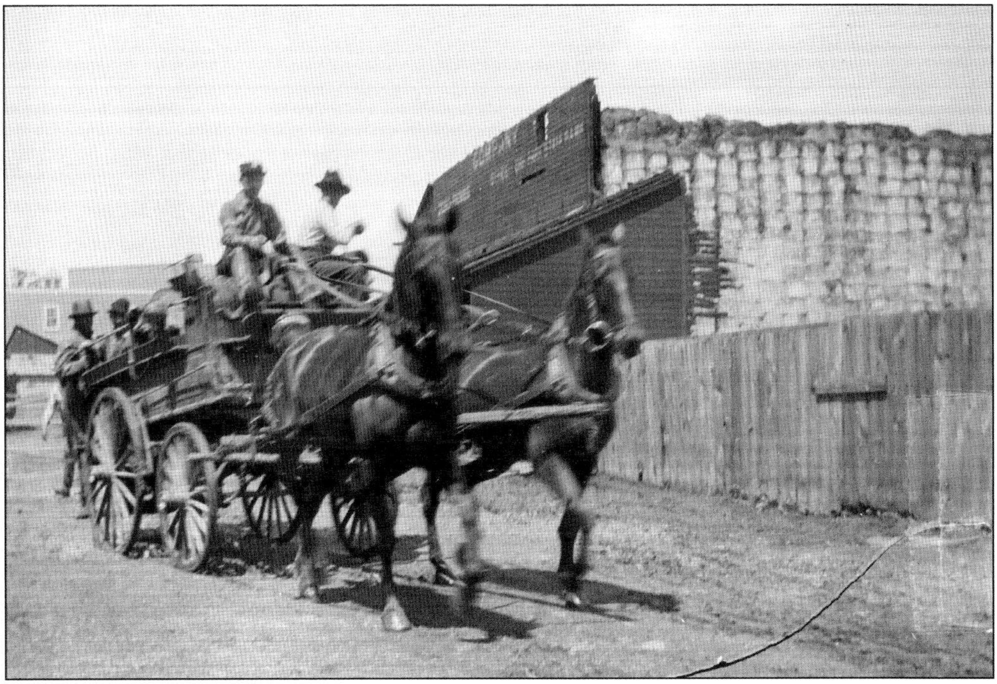

This 1903 photograph shows the Harlem volunteer fire department leaving the scene of a fire at the George Nordenholt icehouse located near Franklin Street and Marengo Avenue. The blocks of ice can be seen in the partially destroyed building. Icehouses were prone to fires because they often used straw or sawdust as insulation. (Photograph by Philander Barclay; courtesy of Historical Society of Oak Park and River Forest.)

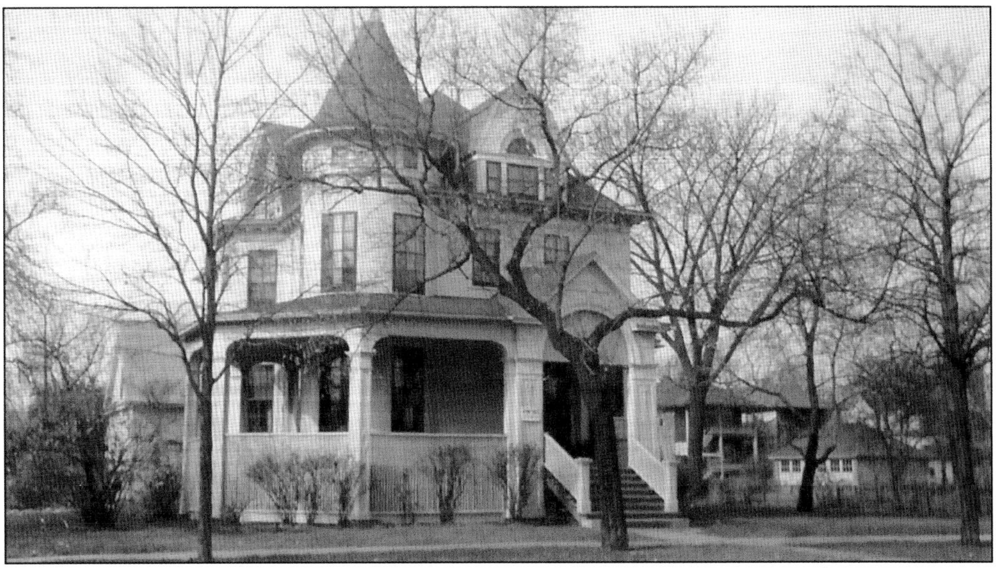

Forest Park has many homes that were built in the 1800s; however, few remain that can compare in style and elegance with the house at 905 Elgin Avenue. The home, built in the late 1800s by John Lobstein, is seen in this photograph from 1939. It has long been reputed to be haunted and has appeared in many books and articles about the paranormal or ghostly locations in and around Chicago. (Courtesy of the Thomas A. Walsh Jr. family.)

Three

SILENT CITIES

When Carl Zimmerman was laid to rest in 1854 upon Indian Hill on the homestead of Ferdinand Haase, it was a solemn, yet unexceptional, event. Native Americans had been burying their dead upon those lands for generations. It was significant in that he was the first person of European descent to be interred in what is now called Forest Park—but he was certainly not the last.

In the 1860s, Ferdinand Haase began to look for new uses for his land. His picnic grove often attracted seedy characters from the city, including pickpockets and prostitutes. There were occasionally fights, and even stabbings, amidst the rowdiness. It was around this time that the City of Chicago closed the City Cemetery located in what is now Lincoln Park. The city also prohibited any new cemeteries from opening within the city limits.

In 1871, Haase sold off the northern section of his land to a Lutheran organization for the formation of what would become Concordia Cemetery. In 1873, he sold off another portion, which became Waldheim Cemetery. In 1876, Ferdinand began Forest Home Cemetery, which would eventually merge with Waldheim. Today one can tell the difference between the two by noting the more parklike setting of Forest Home, versus the more European style of Waldheim. The Waldheim section had high curbs and narrow pathways lined with concrete and stone.

In 1876, the Free Sons of Israel Cemetery Association formed on several acres on both sides of Des Plaines Avenue, near Sixteenth Street, and established the largest of the original Jewish cemeteries. Other congregations purchased lots and established their own cemeteries—over 300—each with their own gate.

In 1912, the Woodlawn Cemetery Association formed. They took over the land that had been developed as a cemetery by the Des Plaines Avenue Cemetery Association, which began in 1907 on the old Stephen Whitney estate.

There is one other cemetery in Forest Park that is often overlooked, and that is the graveyard behind Altenheim. This cemetery has around 750 graves, consisting mostly of former residents and a former superintendent. Most of the headstones are simple concrete markers that were made on site. With over 300 cemeteries, nearly a half million burials, and a living population of 15,688, Forest Park could certainly be called more dead than alive. Forest Park is the final resting place for both the famous and infamous.

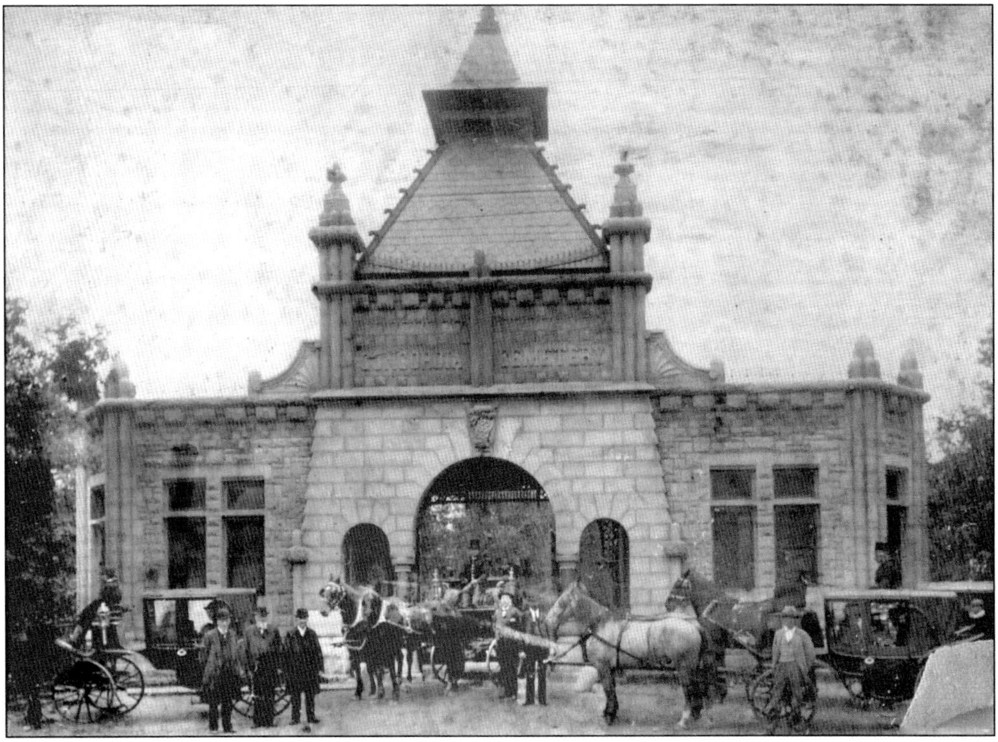

Concordia Cemetery's original entrance was located about 600 feet west of the current entrance, where Madison Street meets Gale Avenue. The entrance was designed in the days of the horse and carriage and constructed in 1889. This entrance was demolished when the new one was built. The safe inside the building was strong enough to survive at least nine attempts to break into it. (Courtesy of Concordia Cemetery.)

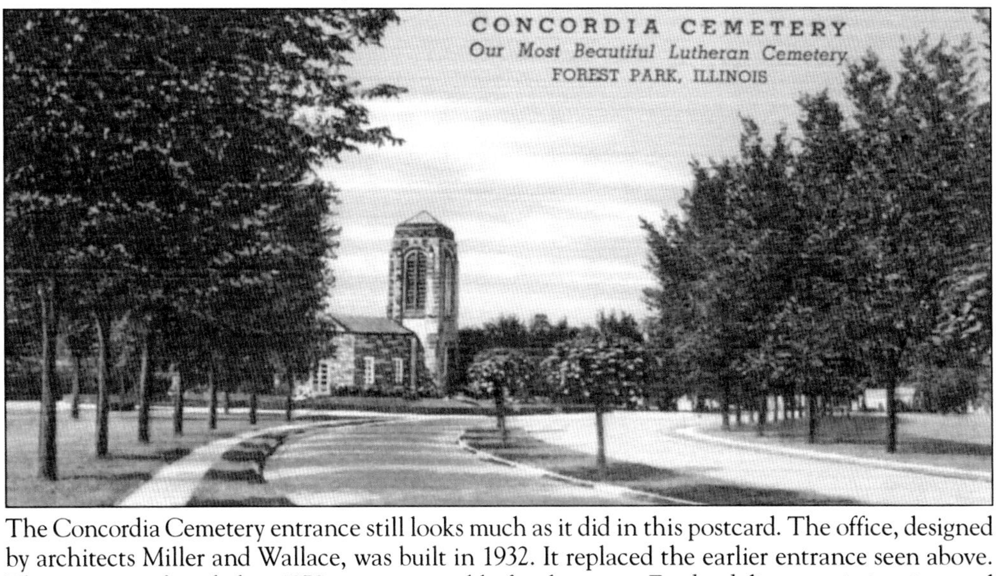

The Concordia Cemetery entrance still looks much as it did in this postcard. The office, designed by architects Miller and Wallace, was built in 1932. It replaced the earlier entrance seen above. The cemetery, founded in 1872, is most notable for the many *Eastland* disaster victims interred there. In 1908, a group of Lutheran ministers vehemently protested the building of the amusement park because of the proximity to the cemetery.

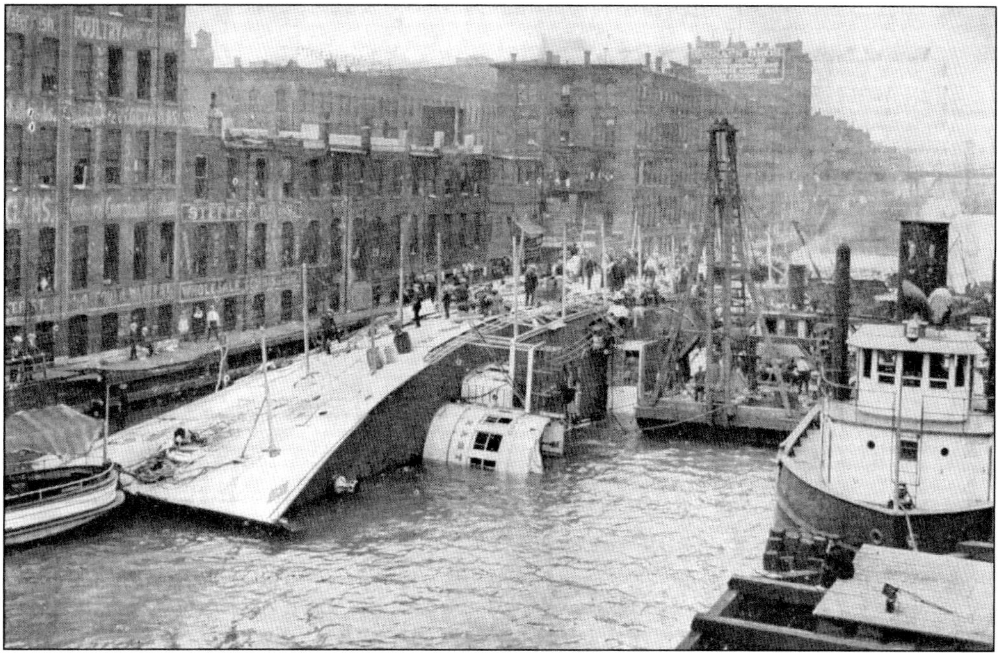

This postcard shows the *Eastland* disaster, which occurred at 7:40 a.m. on July 24, 1915. Some 844 people died when the ship capsized at its moorings at Clark Street on the Chicago River. The outing for Western Electric employees and their families ended in disaster, and 22 entire families lost their lives. There were 63 people interred in Concordia, 41 in Forest Home, 26 in Waldheim, and 3 in the Jewish Waldheim.

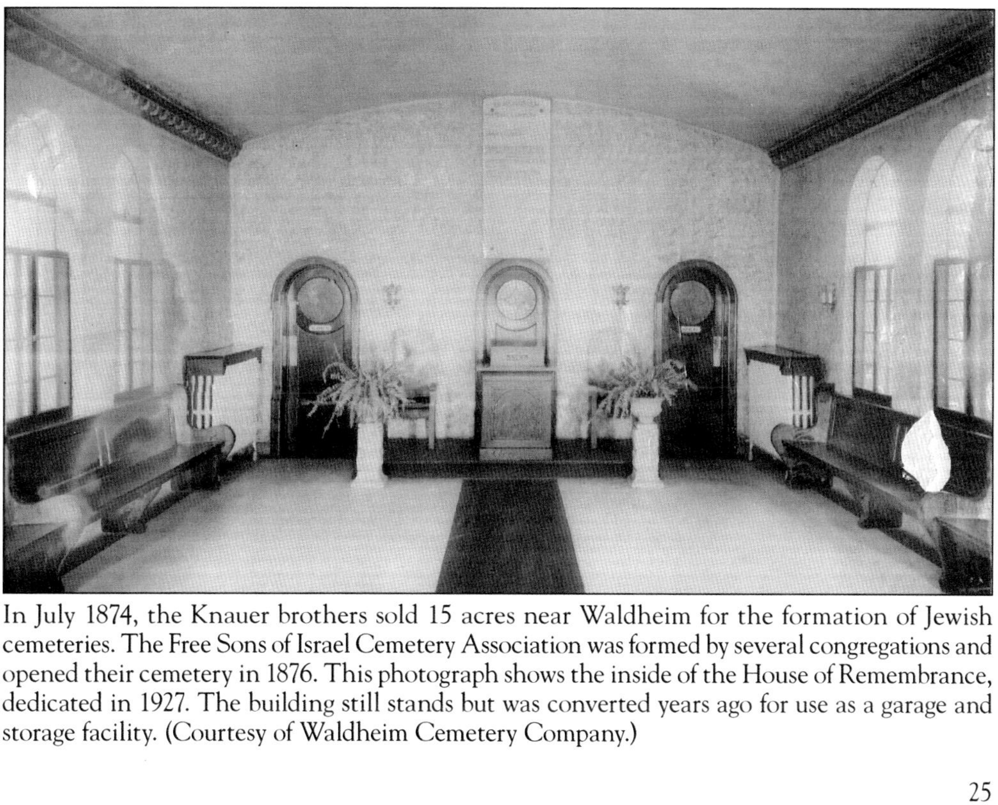

In July 1874, the Knauer brothers sold 15 acres near Waldheim for the formation of Jewish cemeteries. The Free Sons of Israel Cemetery Association was formed by several congregations and opened their cemetery in 1876. This photograph shows the inside of the House of Remembrance, dedicated in 1927. The building still stands but was converted years ago for use as a garage and storage facility. (Courtesy of Waldheim Cemetery Company.)

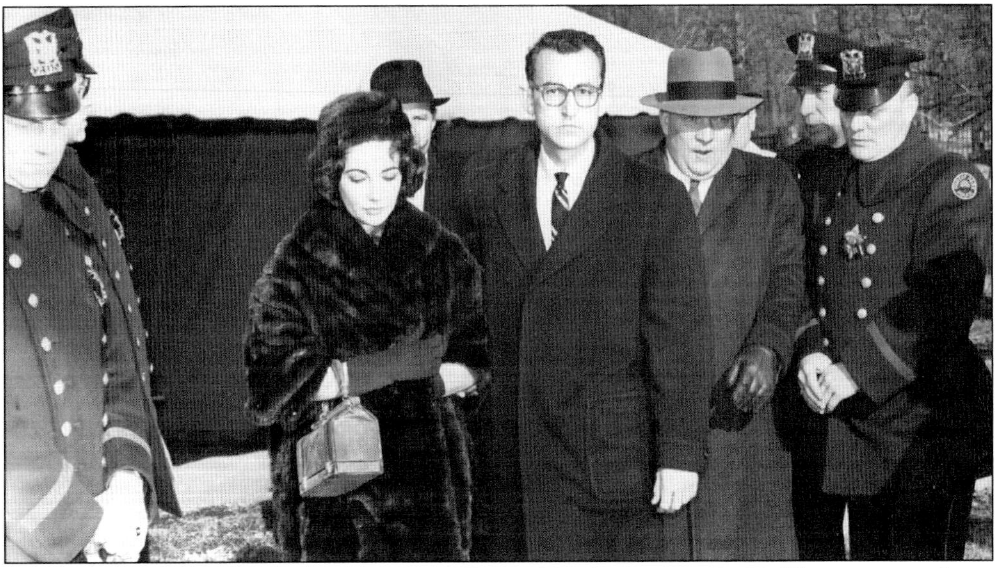

Elizabeth Taylor's husband Avrom Hirsch Goldbogen (also known as Mike Todd), a movie producer, was killed March 22, 1958, when his plane the *Lucky Liz* crashed in Grants, New Mexico. This photograph was snapped at his funeral, which was held in the Beth Aaron Dorsche Tov Cemetery (now part of Jewish Waldheim). In the photograph from left to right are officers Howard Sawusch and Dick Triebes; Elizabeth Taylor; her personal physician, Dr. Rexford Kennamer; Lt. Moe Schnurstein; and officers Edward Shultz and James Hornsby. (Photograph by Arnold Walderson; courtesy of Jeff Oswalt.)

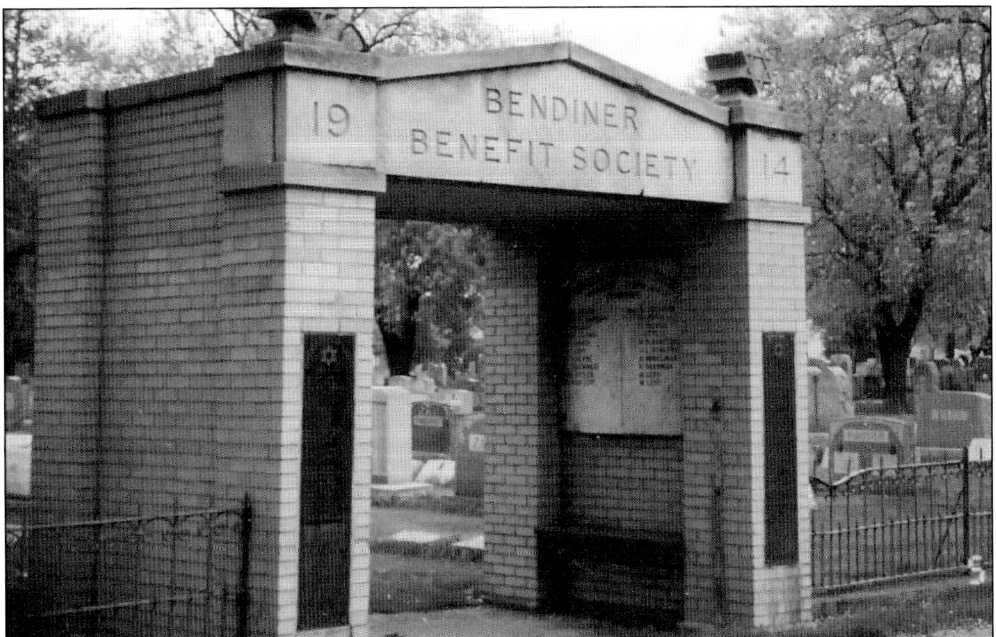

This photograph shows an example of the one of the many gates belonging to different congregations within the Jewish Waldheim Cemeteries. Some, like the one shown, were substantial brick structures that included seating, while others were much simpler wrought iron gates. Many have deteriorated to the point that they had to be removed for safety considerations.

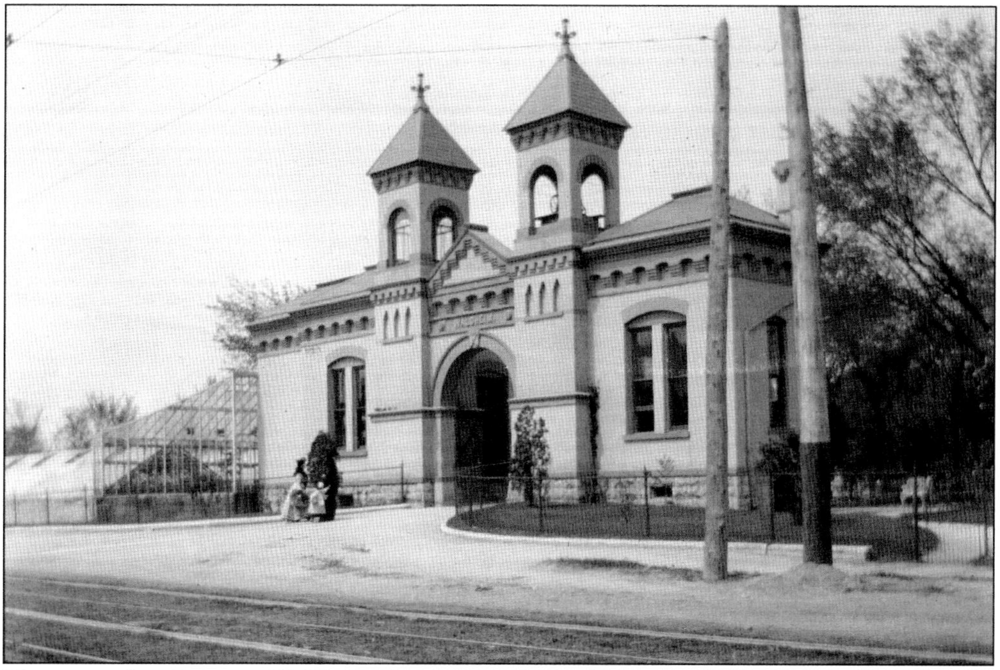

The original entrance to Waldheim Cemetery, seen in this image from 1890, was replaced by a second entrance, which was itself replaced around the time Forest Home and Waldheim merged in 1968–1969. A portion of the greenhouse wall survives from the second entrance and is connected to the current office at 863 Des Plaines Avenue. (Photograph by Philander Barclay; courtesy of Historical Society of Oak Park and River Forest.)

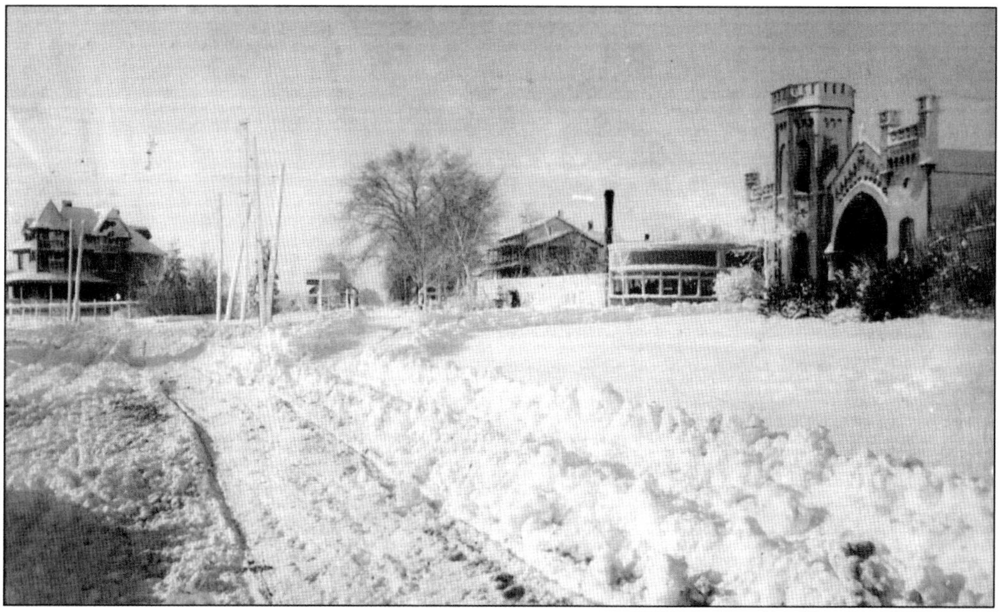

This photograph, taken sometime prior to 1905, shows the original entrance to Forest Home Cemetery on the right. In the middle is the home of Ferdinand Haase, and the house to the left may have been that of the Zimmerman family. This photograph would have been taken in the area of Des Plaines Avenue and Harvard Street, looking south. (Courtesy of Forest Home Cemetery.)

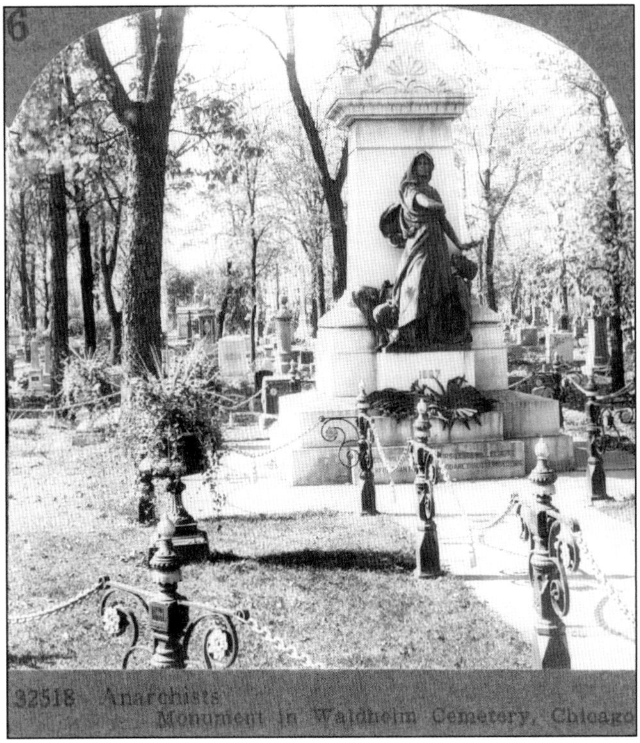

One of the most visited sites in Forest Home Cemetery is the burial site of the Haymarket martyrs, which was adorned with a magnificent monument in 1893 by sculptor Albert Weinert. The Haymarket riot occurred at a Chicago labor movement rally on May 4, 1886. A bomb was thrown into the crowd, killing seven policemen and injuring more than a hundred people. The monument has suffered from vandals and thieves, but a restoration has been planned. This 1930 stereograph shows the original grandeur of the monument. On February 18, 1997, the site was declared a National Historic Landmark. (Courtesy of Library of Congress, LC-USZ62-61671.)

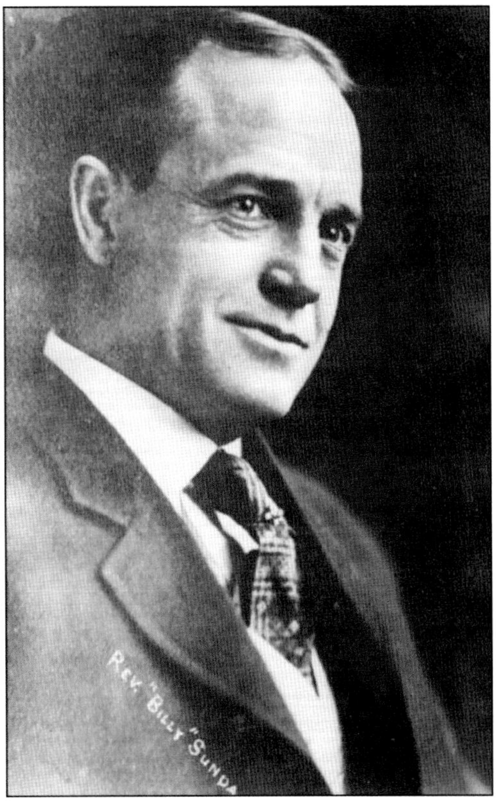

William Ashley Sunday was a former professional baseball player turned evangelist, who fought the good fight for Prohibition. The Reverend Billy Sunday was known for throwing off his jacket and for jumping on tables. His tent revivals along "the Sawdust Trail" attracted thousands of people, and he is immortalized in the Frank Sinatra classic "Chicago (That Toddling Town)." He is among the many noteworthy people buried in Forest Home Cemetery.

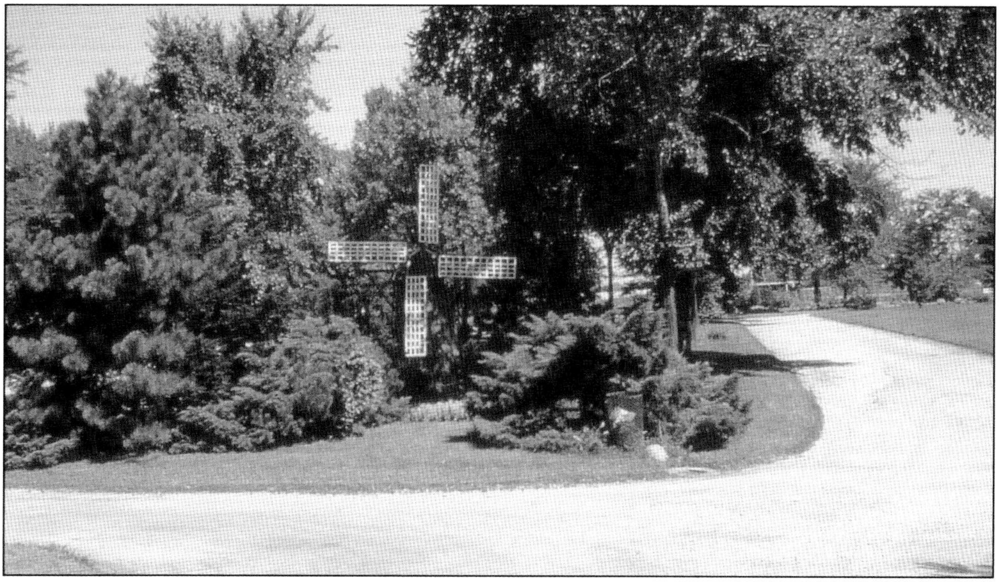

True to the nature of the parklike design, Forest Home featured a bit of whimsy with the installation of the miniature windmill, which is shown in this photograph from 1958. The structure, located in section 75 on the west side of the river, lasted until the 1980s but eventually succumbed to the ravages of nature and vandalism. (Courtesy of Forest Home Cemetery.)

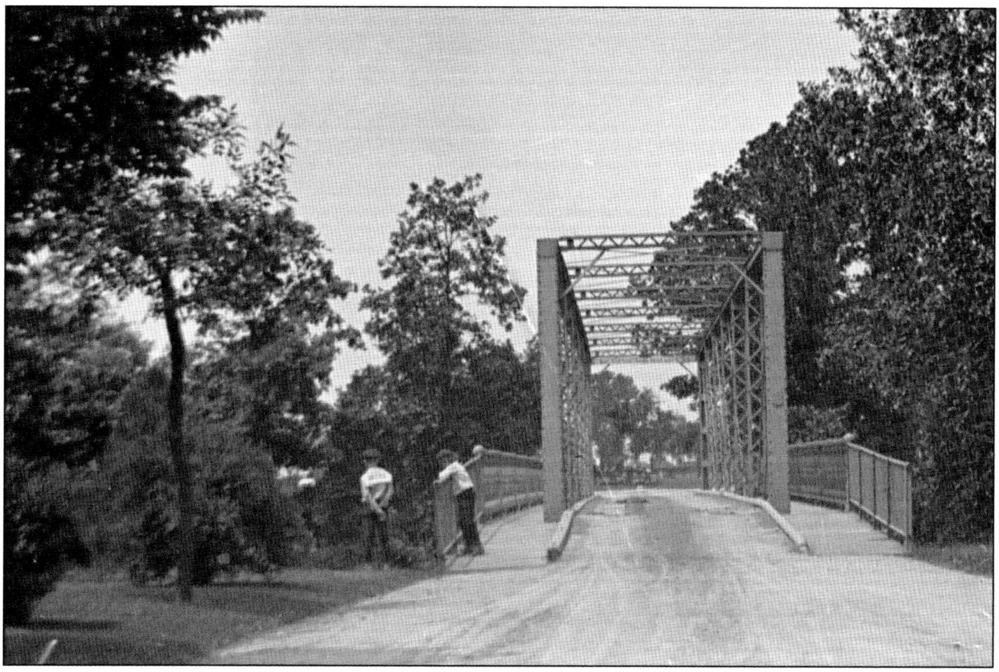

Many people will recall holding their breath as the crossed the Des Plaines River in the final days of the old Massillon Bridge in Forest Home Cemetery. The bridge, built in 1895, is pictured here in 1903. A second bridge was built alongside several years later. They served until 1997, when the village condemned them. A new, single-lane bridge was built using some of the same concrete supports in 2000. (Photograph by Philander Barclay; courtesy of Historical Society of Oak Park and River Forest.)

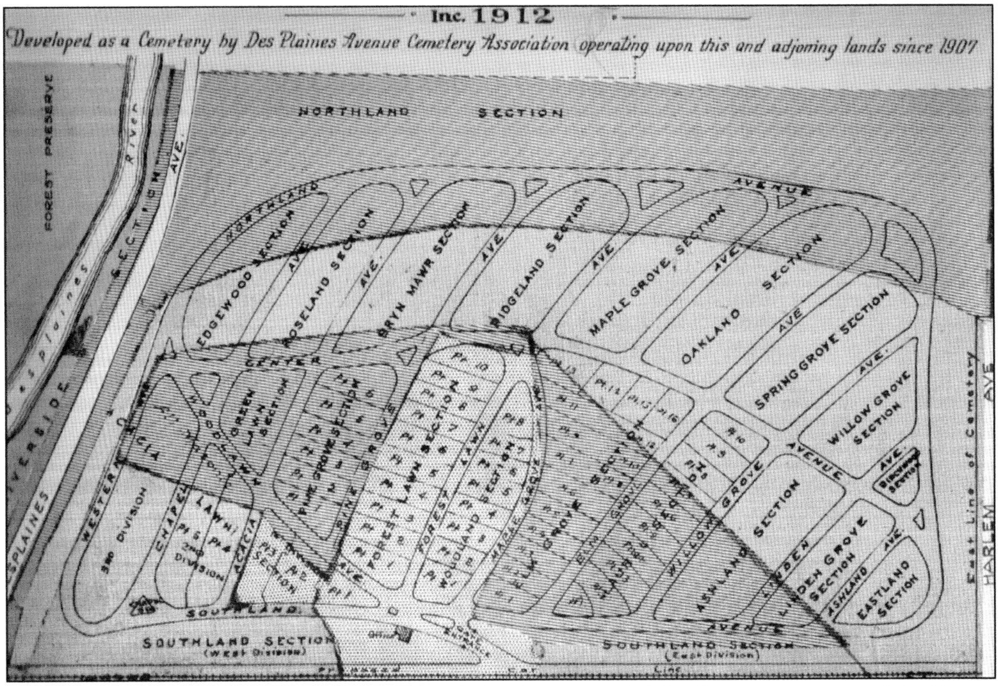

This map dating to 1913 shows the plan and development of Woodlawn Cemetery. Woodlawn, the newest of the cemeteries, was developed in 1907 under the Des Plaines Avenue Cemetery Association. It became officially incorporated as Woodlawn Cemetery in 1912. Only a small section was in use at the time this map was made. (Courtesy of Woodlawn Cemetery.)

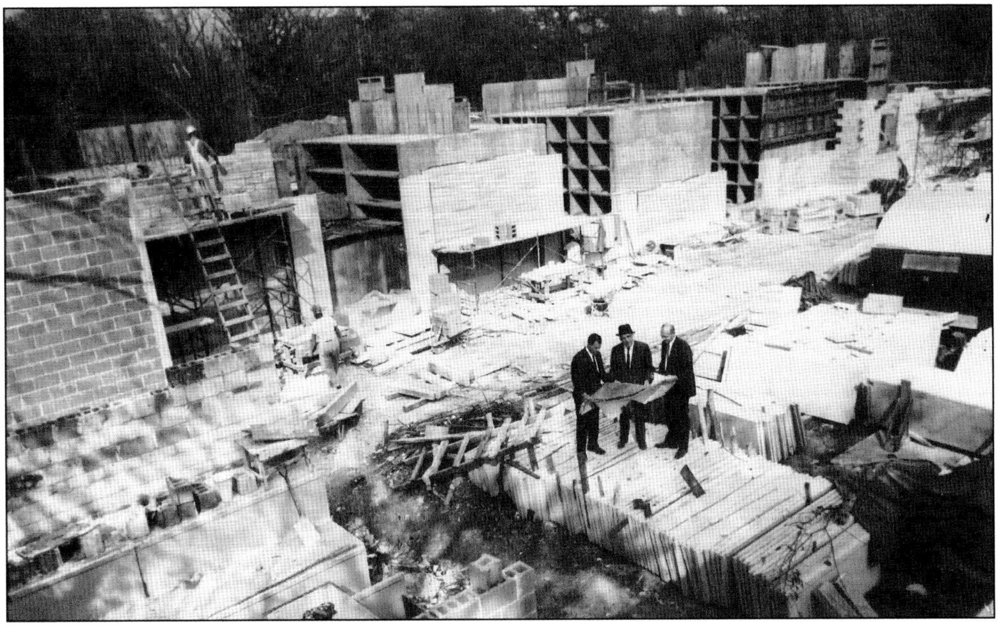

In the early 1960s, Woodlawn Cemetery erected a large mausoleum and crematory on the west side of Des Plaines Avenue. This area was once the site of a twin-gabled, Danish-style peasant home, built by the renowned landscape architect Svend Lollesgard. Lollesgard also helped design Woodlawn and Chicago's Graceland cemeteries among others. (Courtesy of Woodlawn Cemetery.)

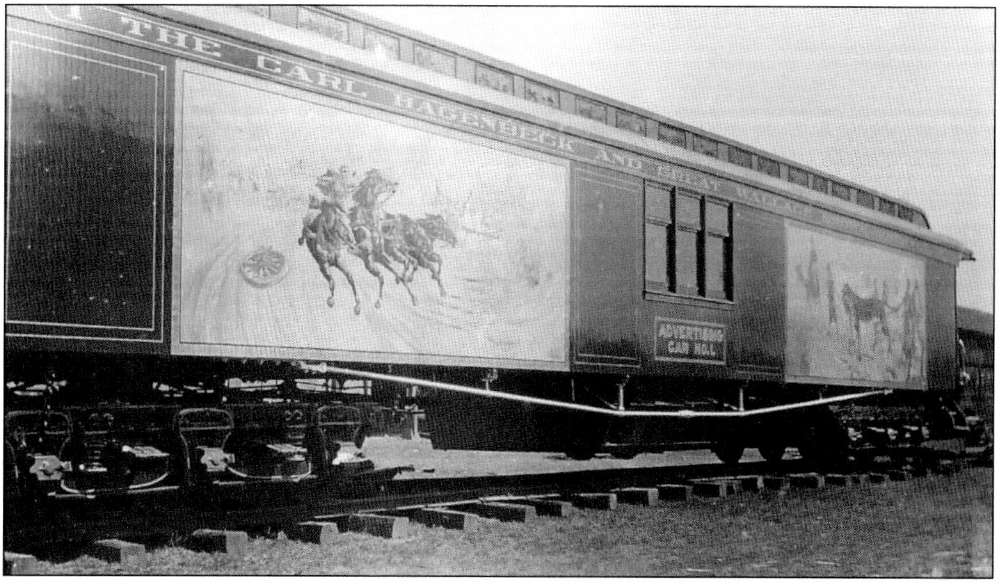

The most famous spot in Woodlawn Cemetery is the "Showman's Rest" section, which is noted for the five elephant monuments marking the boundaries. The Showman's League of America purchased the plot less than a year before the train disaster that took the lives of an estimated 86 people on June 22, 1918. The photograph above shows a train car from the Hagenbeck and Wallace circus in 1907, much like the ones involved in the accident. An empty troop train crashed into the circus train, causing oil lamps to ignite the wooden cars. Over 1,500 people attended the mass funeral, where 53 coffins were buried on the same day in a mass grave. In all, 56 victims were buried at Woodlawn. Contrary to local legend, no animals were killed in the accident or buried in the cemetery.

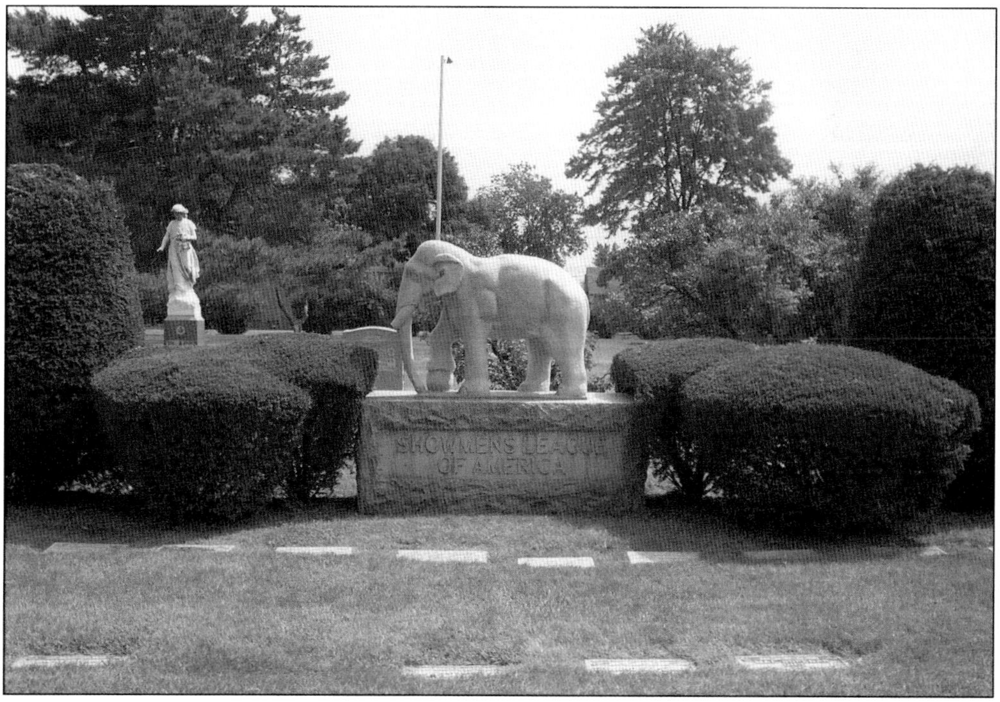

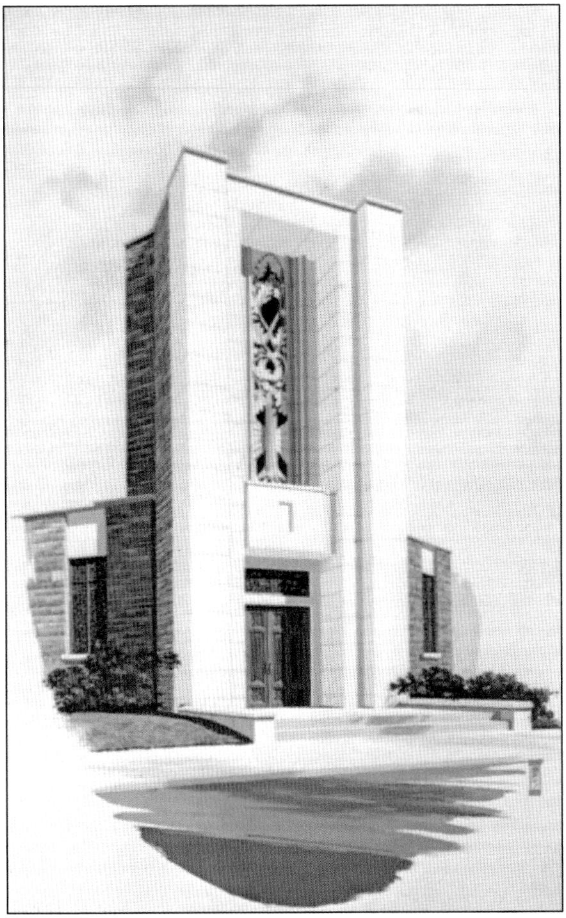

The Woodlawn Mausoleum on the west side of Des Plaines Avenue is the largest in Forest Park, with an estimated 2,500 interments. The grand and distinctive entrance has been a landmark on Des Plaines Avenue since it opened October 11, 1964. Visitors find that it is much larger than it appears, as it stretches back along the river.

This postcard view gives a rare glimpse inside of the tranquil and serene Woodlawn Mausoleum. This seating area features the "Tree of Life" window. The mausoleum was actually constructed in three phases over several years, yet featured the most modern design elements in both the architecture and decor of the period.

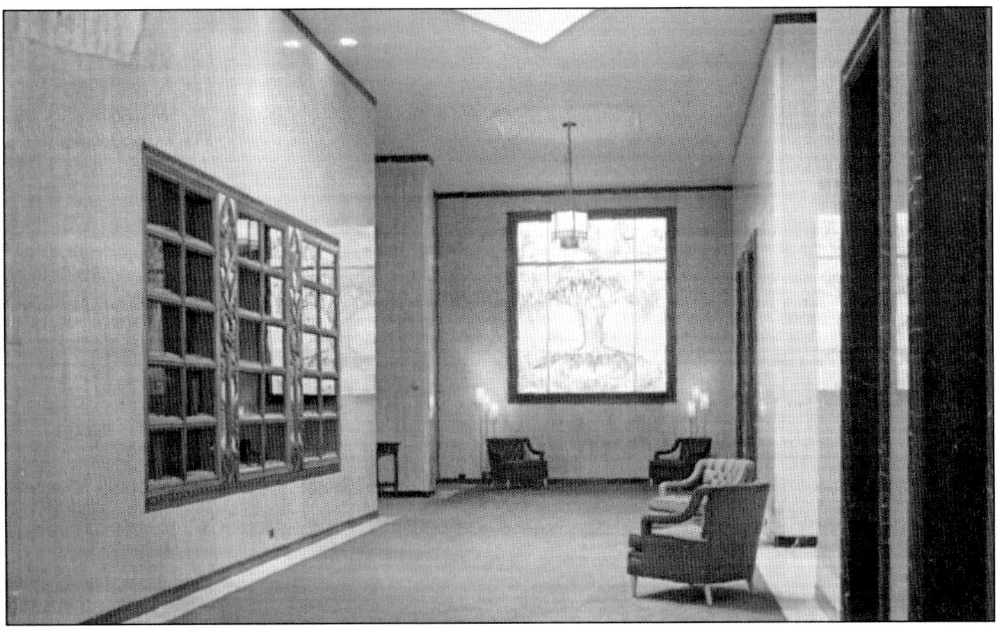

Four

SUMMERTIME FUN

On May 31, 1908, Theodore Roosevelt was in the White House. A loaf of bread cost a nickel. The average income was $915 a year, which would still only be around $21,000 by today's standards. Air conditioning was still in its infancy. On hot summer days and nights, the residents of the Chicago area would seek pleasure and excitement wherever they could find it. The world's fair of 1893 was still vivid in the minds and hearts of Chicagoans seeking relief from the daily toils of modern city living. Many found that relief in a wonderful amusement park, named Forest Park and located in the former village of Harlem, which had only a year earlier adopted that very same name.

On that glorious day in May, Forest Park opened its gates to the public. For 15 seasons, tens of thousands would pour through the gates to enjoy time with their families. A devastating fire on July 25, 1918, destroyed numerous attractions, including the swimming pool, the skating rink, the Leap the Dips, and 400 feet of the Giant Safety Coaster. The park closed for good in 1922.

Forest Park was already an entertainment mecca of sorts. Thousands attended the races held at the Harlem Jockey Club, formerly the Harlem Race Track. A fire destroyed the grandstand on May 22, 1899, but the track quickly reopened. Horse-racing was banned in 1905, and the track began hosting automobile and motorcycle races.

In 1901, the golf course opened on the infield of the racetrack. It was one of the first and finest public courses in the area. The golf course survived until the government needed the land for a torpedo factory.

In the 1940s and 1950s, Emery Parichy's baseball stadium at Harlem Avenue and Harrison Street was the home to his Bloomer Girls of the National Girls Baseball League. The stadium would also host other events like wrestling and boxing matches until the expressway was built.

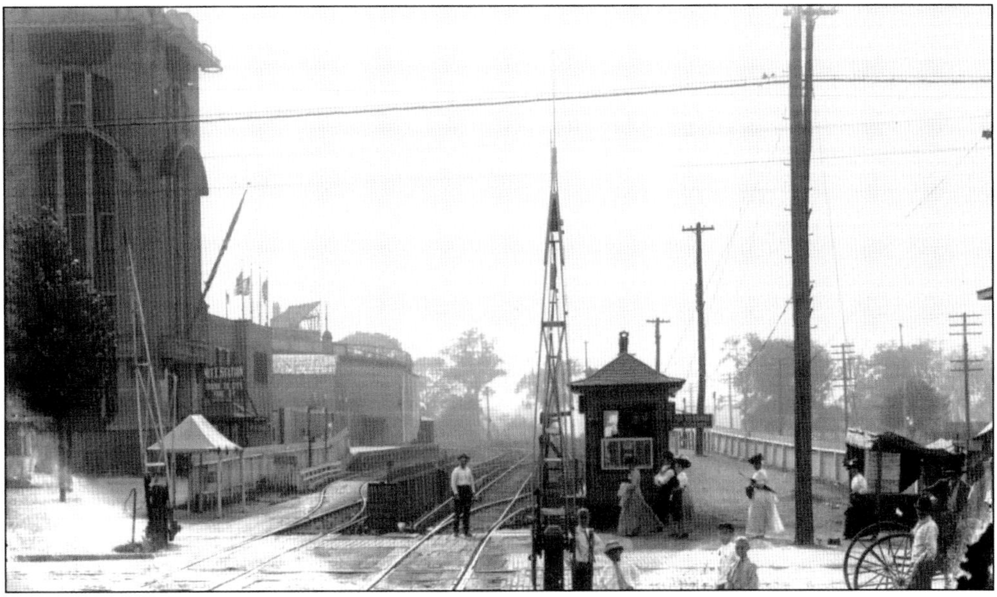

This 1910 photograph, taken from the east side of Des Plaines Avenue, shows the bustling activity near both the "L" tracks and the Chicago, Aurora, and Elgin tracks. The north tower of the amusement park entrance is seen on the left. The crossing gates were manually raised and lowered until the 1950s. (Fred Lonnes collection, courtesy of Walter R. Keevil.)

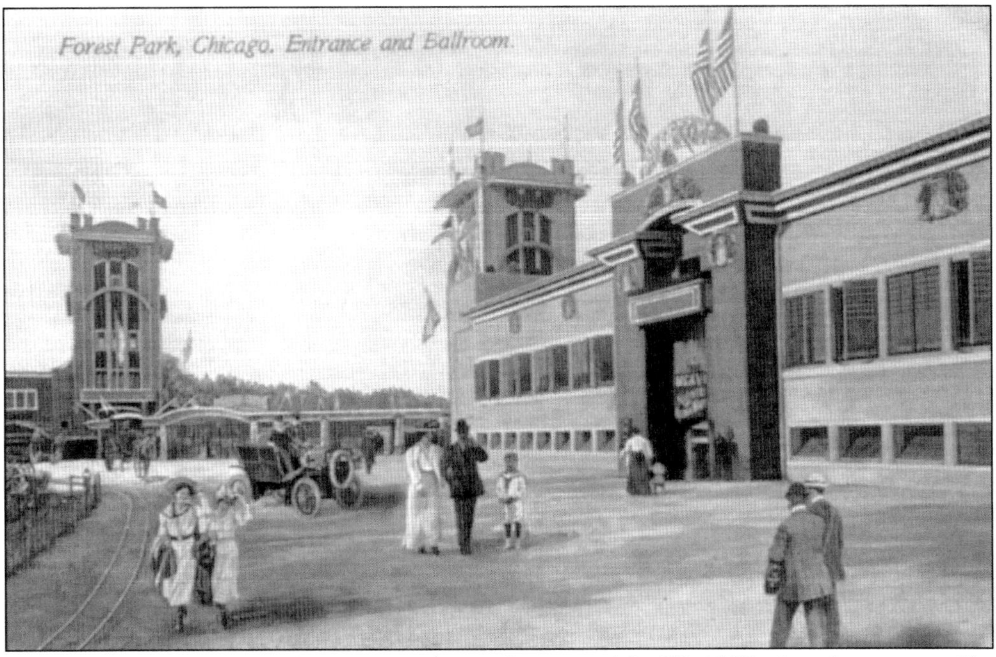

Forest Park was bedecked with patriotism during the years of the World War I, as demonstrated by the abundance of flags shown in this postcard rendering. Notice the various modes of transportation of the day. There are autos, horse-drawn vehicles, and train tracks. Although the park closed in 1922, the ballroom remained in use for several years afterward.

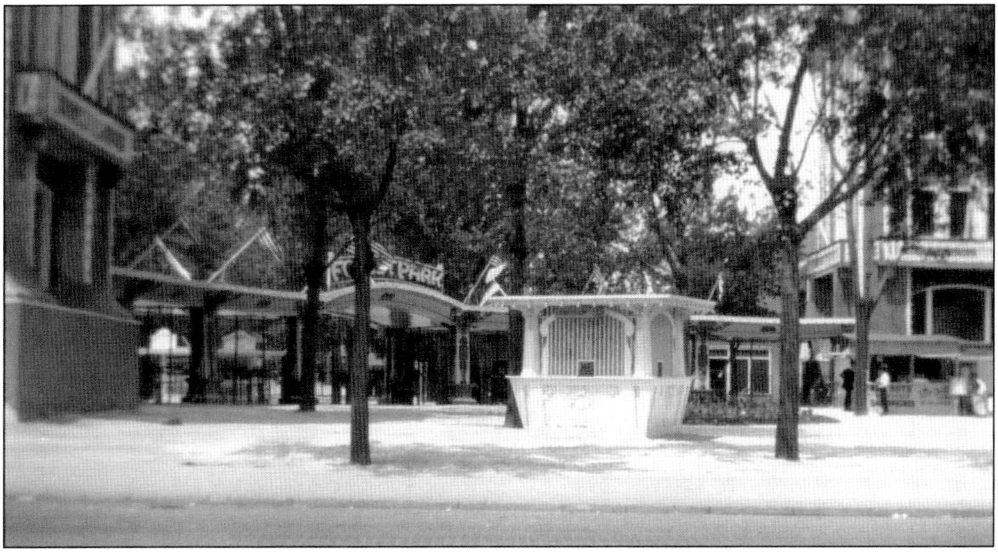

The city folk who visited the amusement park would often seek relief from the hot summer sun under the many trees that inhabited the park. This image shows that even the entrance was well shaded and validated the aptly named venue. Note that Des Plaines Avenue was paved with bricks at the time. (Photograph by Fred Borchert; courtesy of Bruce G. Moffat.)

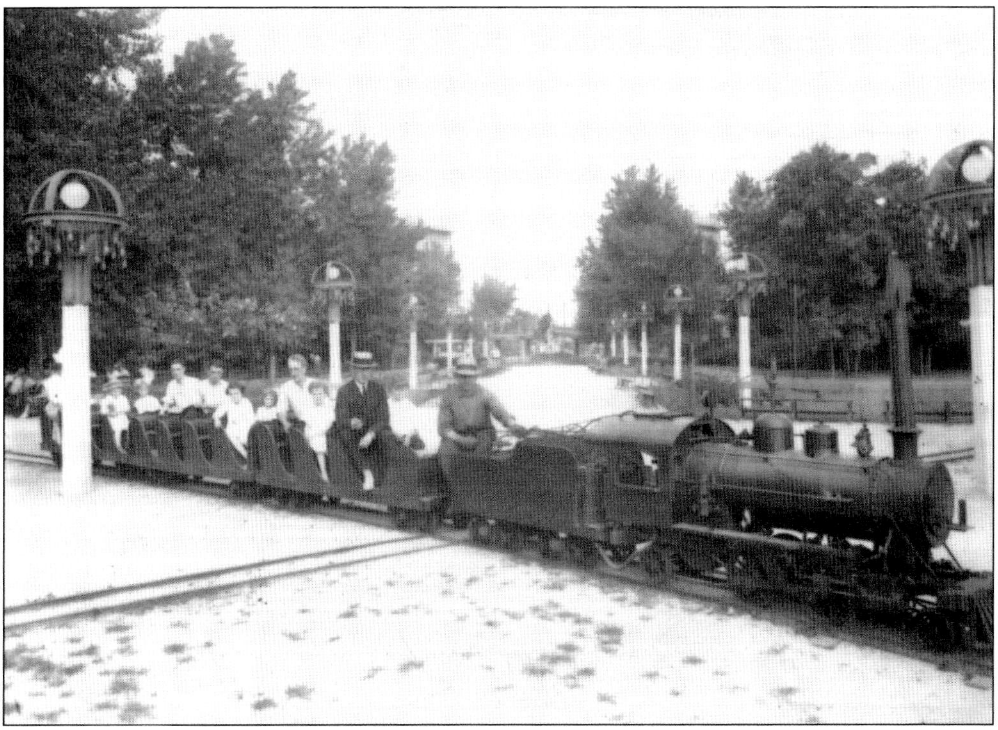

No amusement park of the day would be complete without a miniature railroad. When the park closed in 1922, the rides were sold off to parks throughout the country. The 1909 Dentzel carousel went to the Mid-South Fairgrounds in Memphis in 1923. It stayed there until 1975, when it was moved to Libertyland, which closed in 2005. The carousel is currently in storage awaiting a new home. (Courtesy of Bruce G. Moffat.)

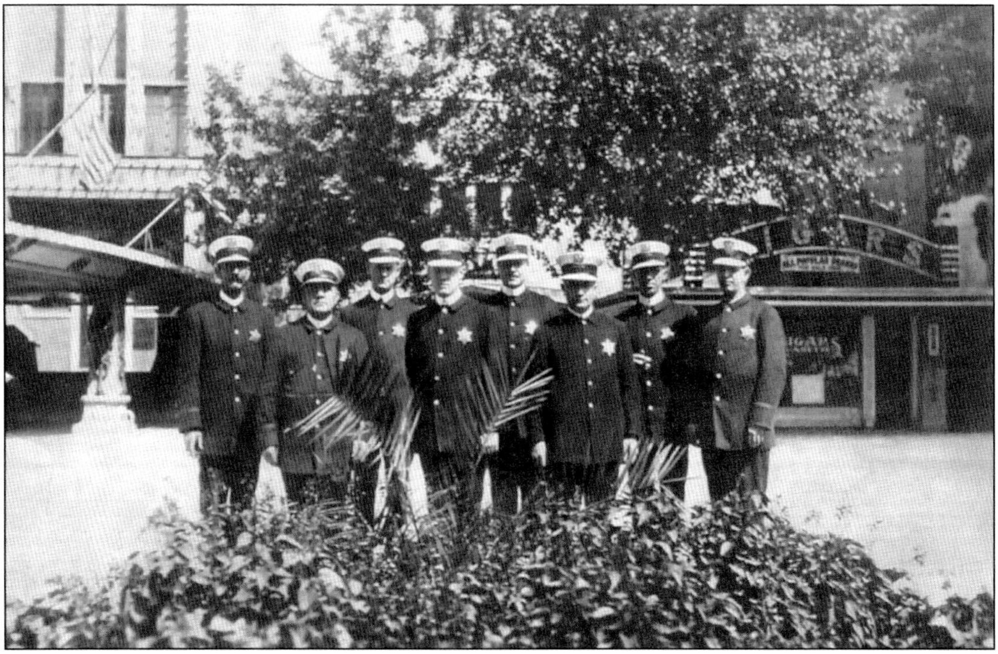

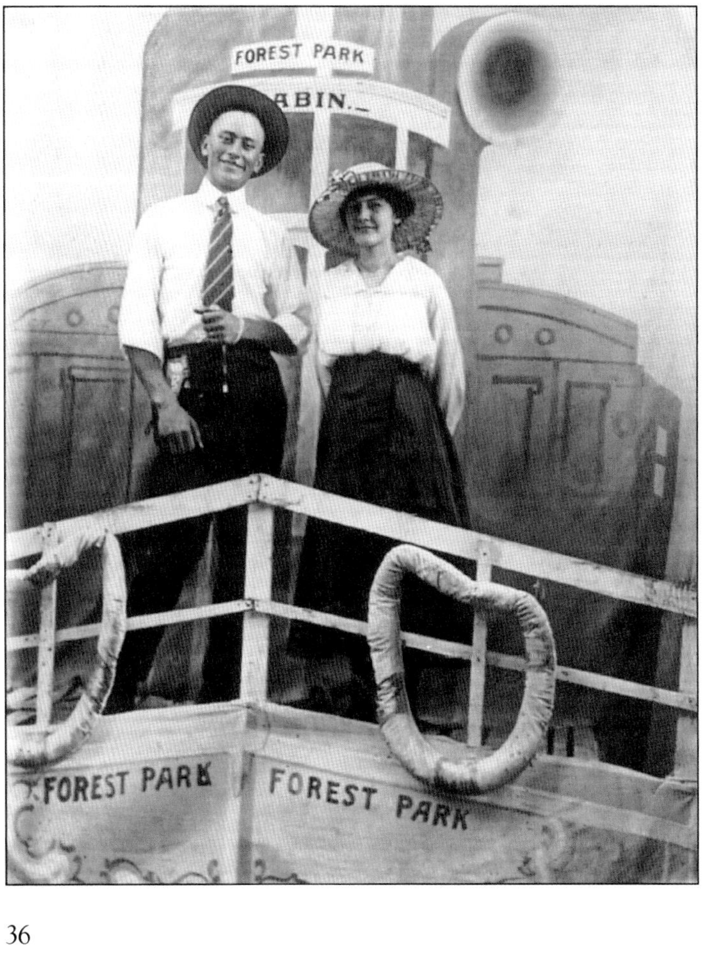

The amusement park kept the Forest Park police busy during its heyday. The village hired seasonal police officers to supplement the department and patrol the park. Above is a group of officers at the park near a cigar and cigarette shop. (Courtesy of the Licht family.)

Visitors to the amusement park would often pose for pictures with whimsical themes and costumes that would be turned into postcards. They would send them to friends and family across the country or just save them as a memento. Here is a charming couple aboard the rather unseaworthy-looking SS *Forest Park*.

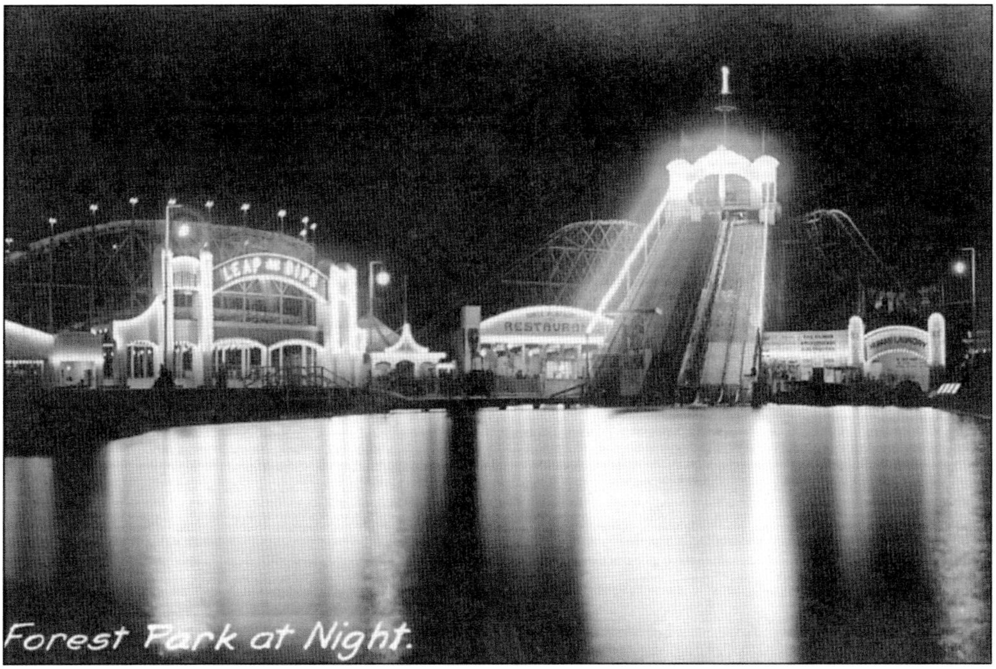

The amusement park was a dazzling sight at night. The Leap the Dips ride, featured here, was the most dangerous of the three major coasters in the park. It featured a very steep drop, which was reputed to fling a rider out occasionally. Also seen are the Kaffe Klotsche Restaurant, the Human Laundry, and the Chutes.

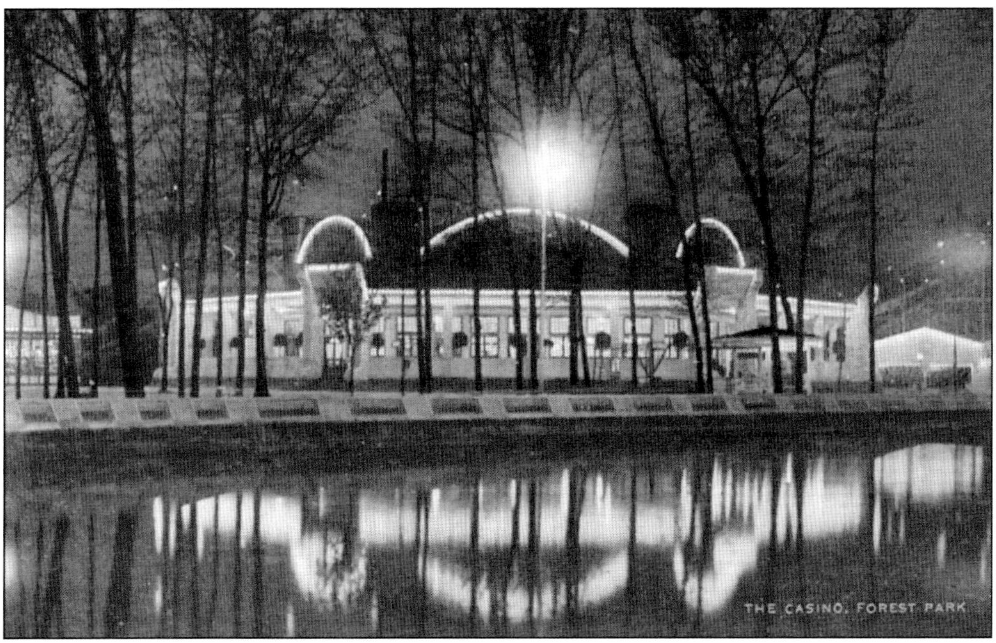

A casino is a public building used for social activities, not to be confused with the gambling halls of today. The casino at the amusement park held United Service Organization (USO)–type shows during the war years and was the setting for several graduations. Gambling, however, was a problem at the park, and many a visitor left with less money than they had anticipated.

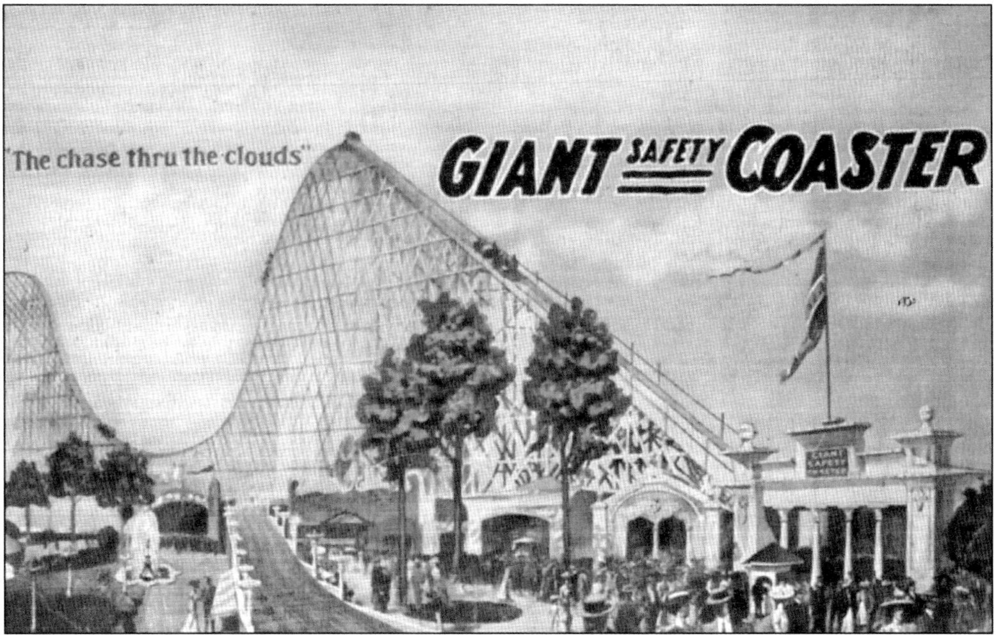

"The Chase thru the Clouds," also known as the Giant Safety Coaster, was one of the major roller coasters at Forest Park, along with the Grand Canyon and the Steeple Chase. The ride was renamed after safety concerns were raised due to some injuries that occurred. It was boasted that the coaster was the "most elaborate and largest" roller coaster in the United States. The first drop took riders 76 feet in the air; by comparison, the American Eagle coaster at Great America is 127 feet tall. A section of 400 feet of the coaster was damaged in the July 25, 1918, fire that devastated the park.

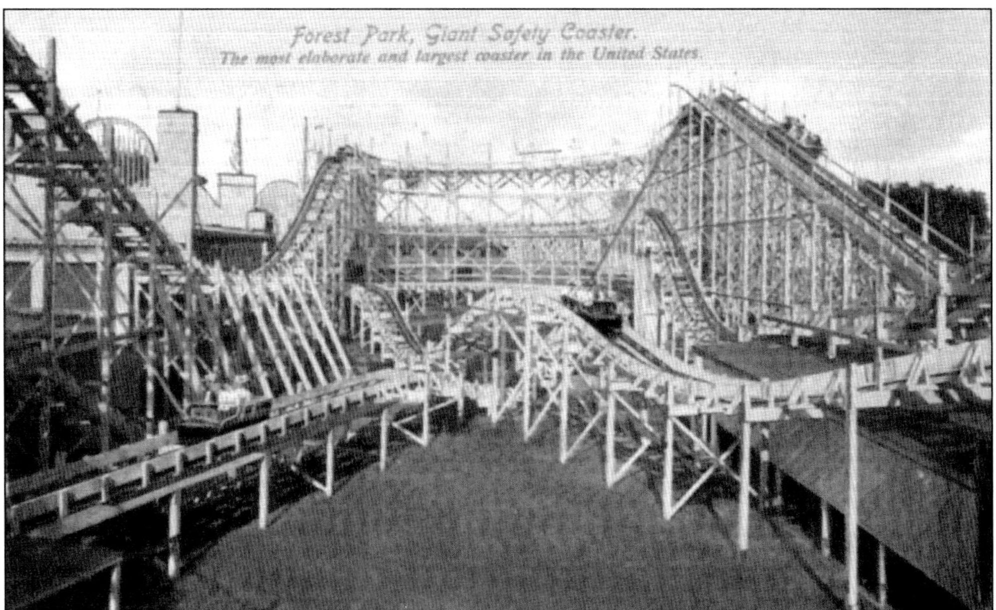

A popular attraction at many amusements parks of the period was the fire show. Much like the stunt shows presented at modern amusement parks, these shows would feature daring rescue scenes. In this *c.* 1910 postcard view from Forest Park, a woman is being "rescued" from a burning high rise. This one attraction employed 30 to 40 "firemen."

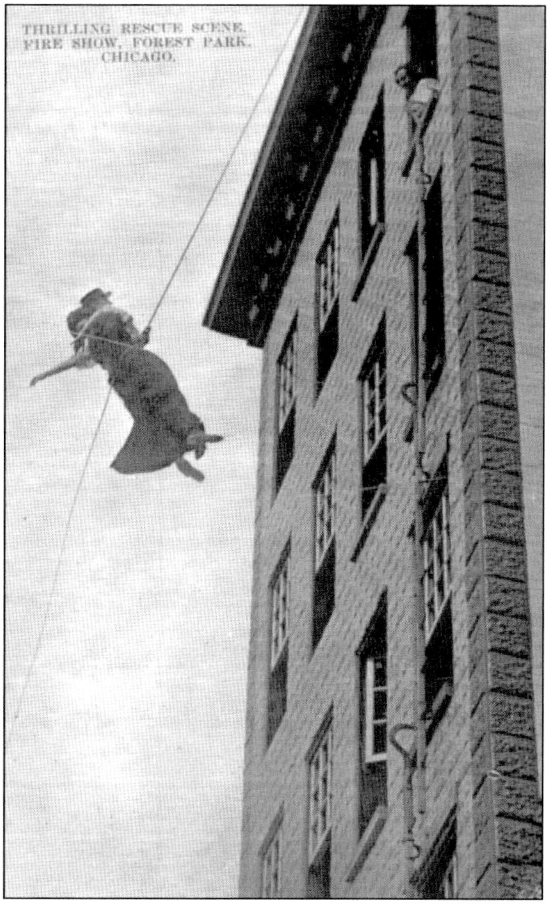

A momentary pause atop the chutes would provide a bird's-eye view above the spacious grounds before making the plunge into the lagoon. This 1910 postcard view is facing east towards the entrance, along Des Plaines Avenue. The Steeple Chase ride is just to the left of the lagoon.

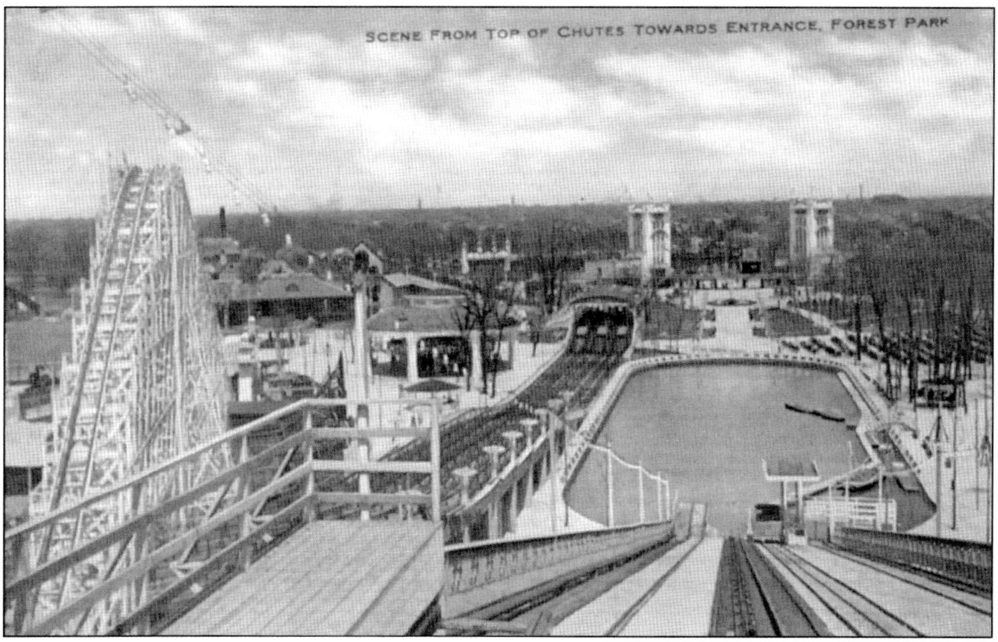

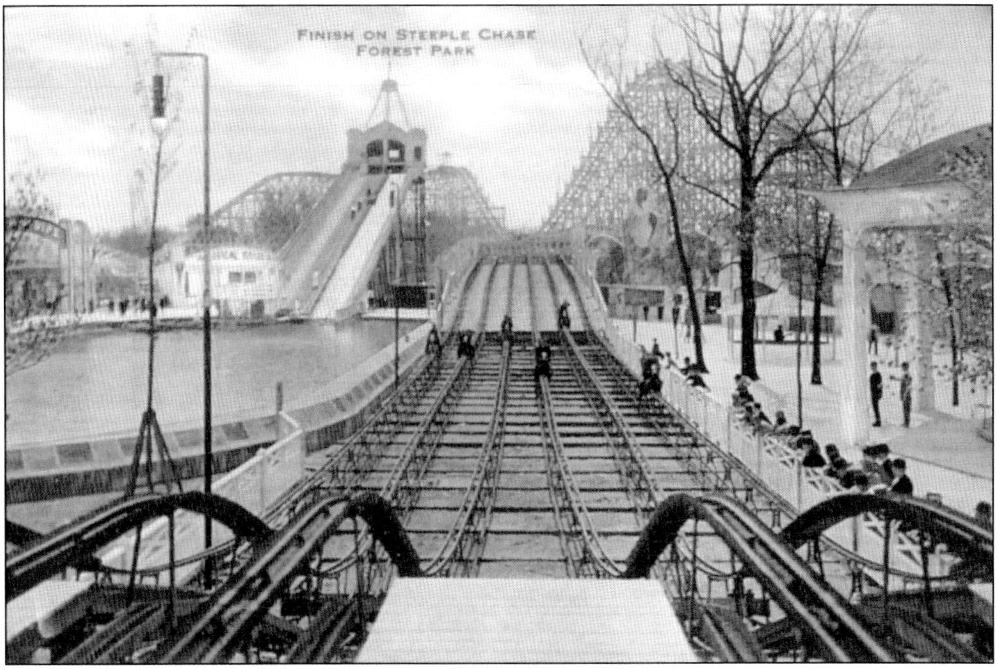

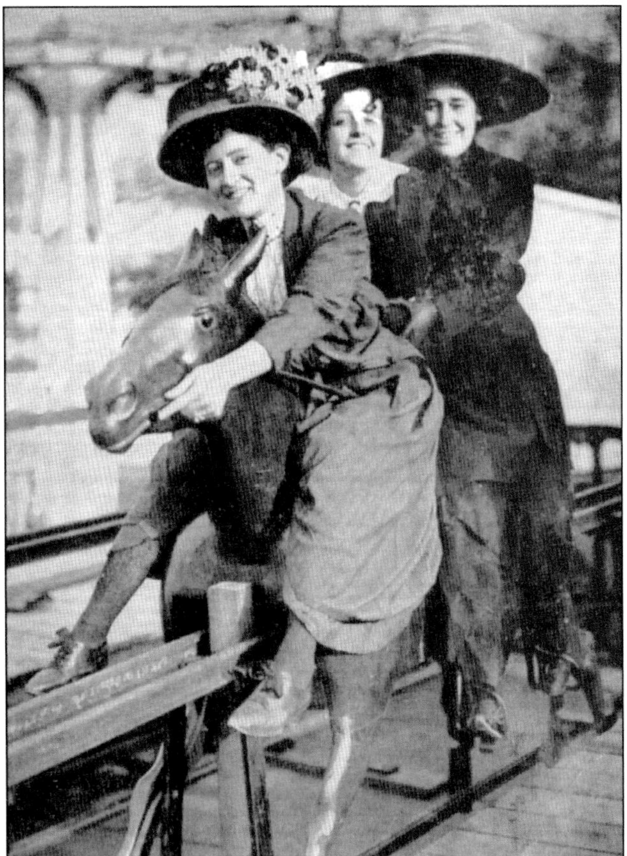

The postcard above features the Steeple Chase ride at Forest Park. This popular ride simulated a horse race, with riders mounting wooden horses that rode along an undulating steel track. With gambling being such a popular activity in Forest Park, it is easy to imagine money being exchanged among the spectators. The photograph of the women appears to be staged, as there are only two sets of stirrups, and the women would need chinstraps to hold those hats on. (Left, courtesy of Tom Krenek.)

This assortment of tickets from 1915 shows the wide variety of attractions at the amusement park. Those 10¢ tickets today would roughly be the equivalent of about \$2.20. The abandoned 150-foot-by-48-foot pool was refurbished in 1927 and used for two years before being demolished in 1929.

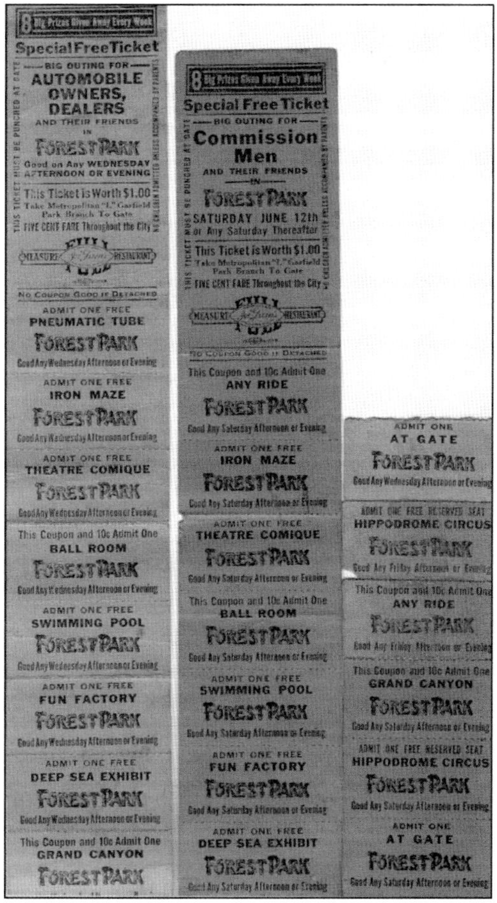

People are dressed in their finest Sunday outfits for a day at the amusement park in 1910. It appears that almost everyone wore a hat, including children and their dolls. Holding onto their hats would not be their only concern, as these folks would be well advised to watch their valuables. Pickpockets and con men would often separate a visitor from their cash.

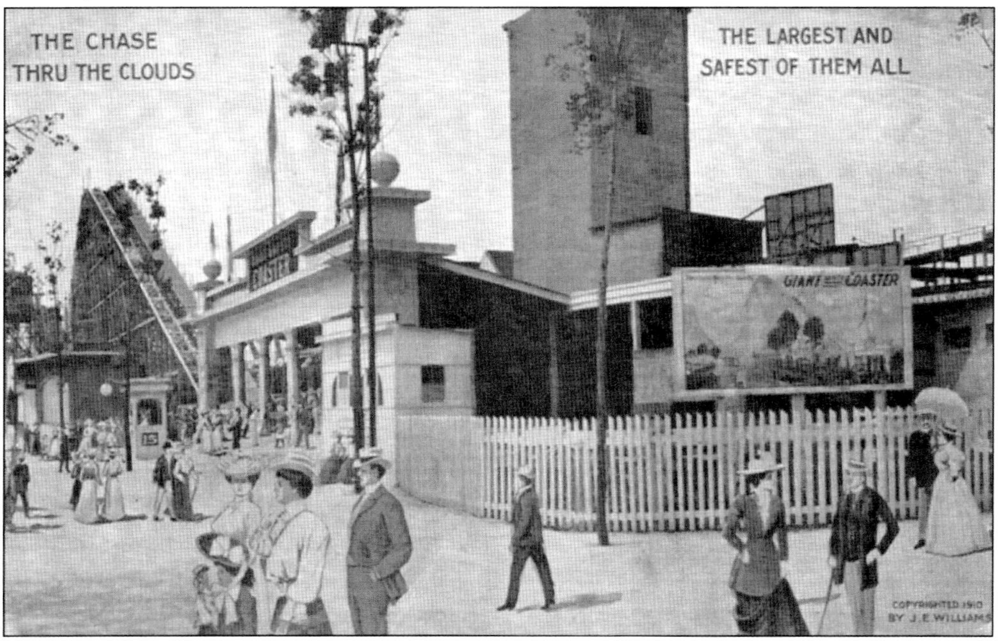

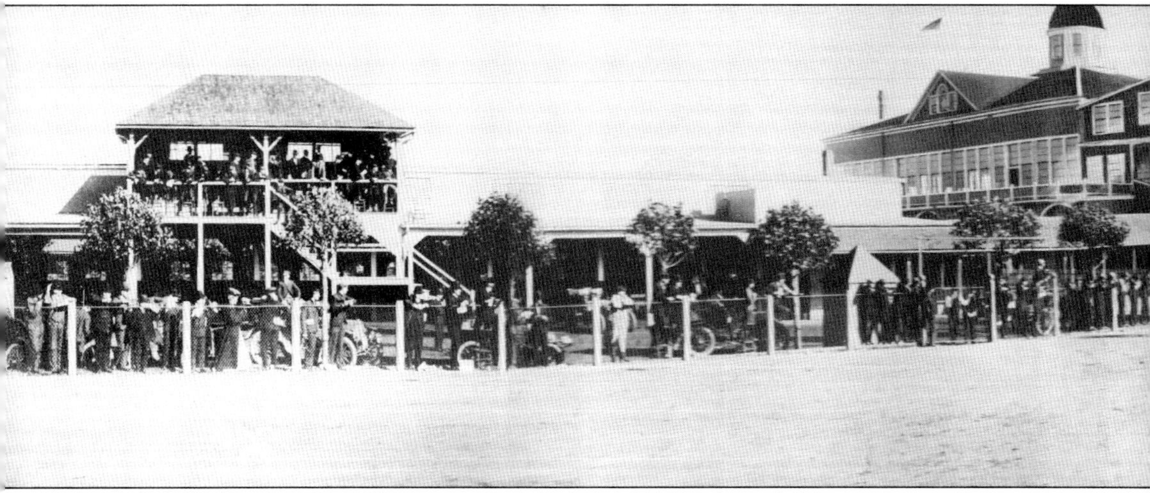

The Harlem racetrack was opened July 30, 1894. The 1-mile track was 80 feet at the widest and 70 feet across at its narrowest. The photograph was taken sometime between 1905 and 1910. A ban on horse-racing began in 1905, and the track began hosting automobile and motorcycle

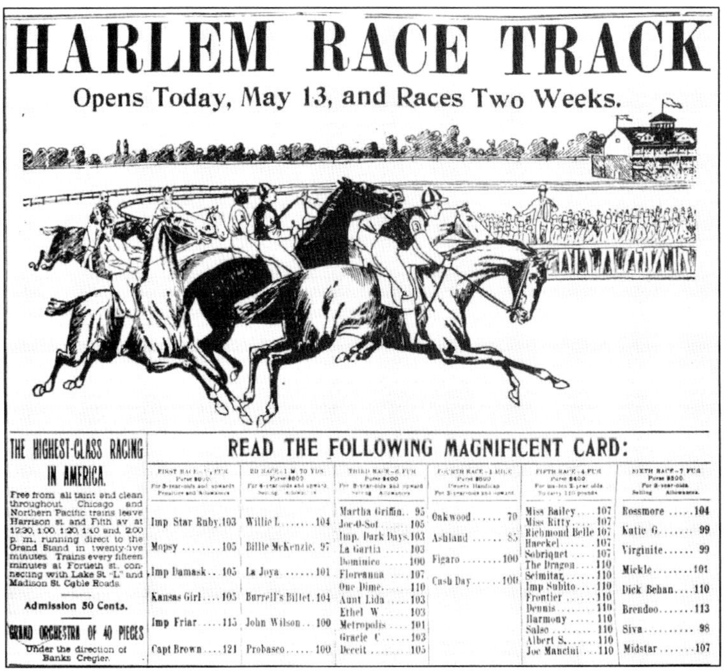

A day at the races on May 13, 1895, not only featured a fine race card, but for only 50¢ the patrons were treated to a 40-piece orchestra, according to this advertisement from the *Chicago Inter-Ocean* newspaper. The track was quite popular, as it was affordable and readily accessible by several trains. When the track opened, it was criticized because the grandstand faced west into the afternoon sun. Large awnings were later installed to shield the patrons. (Courtesy of Bruce G. Moffat.)

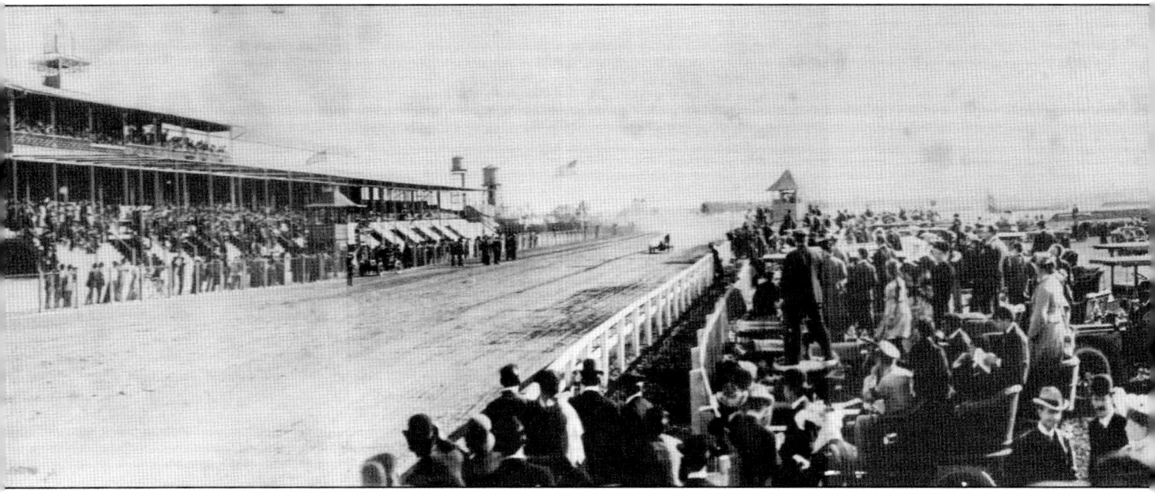

races. The track survived a devastating fire on Thanksgiving Day 1910, although hundreds of stables burned. There was a move to reopen the track in the late 1920s and 1930s, but it never happened. (Courtesy of Tim Shanahan.)

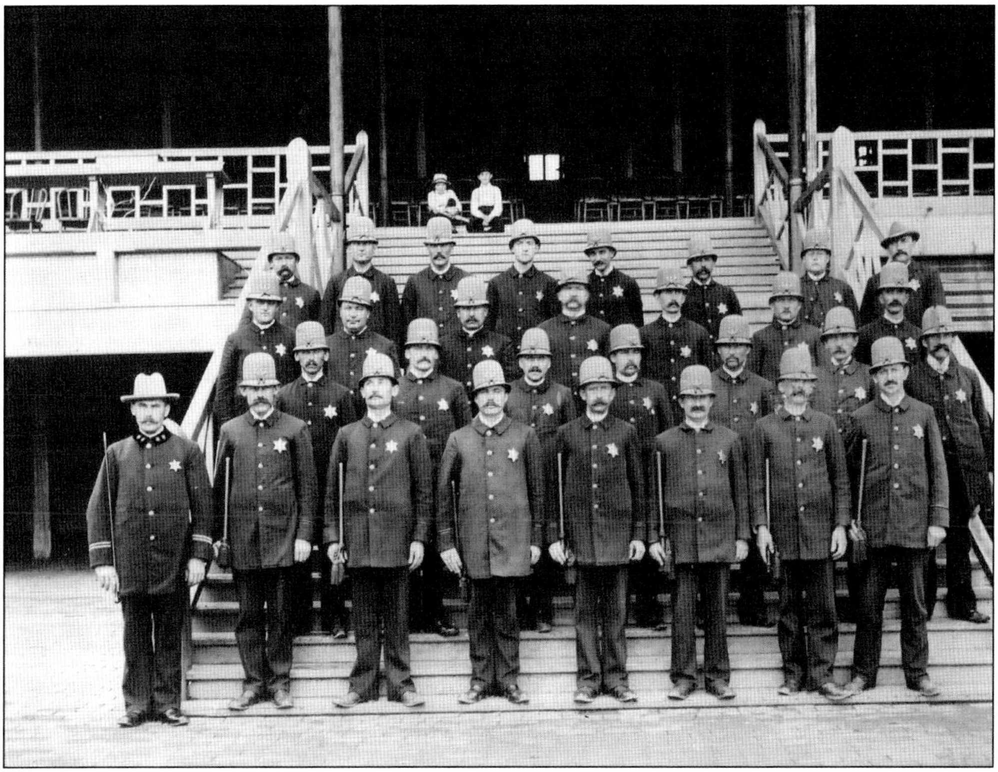

This undated photograph shows the police force on the steps of the Harlem racetrack grandstand around 1898. It is unclear whether this was the entire police force of Harlem or a special unit for the racetrack. This mostly wooden structure would succumb to a fire on May 22, 1899. The grandstand was quickly rebuilt, and a large clubhouse was added in 1903. (Courtesy of Tim Shanahan.)

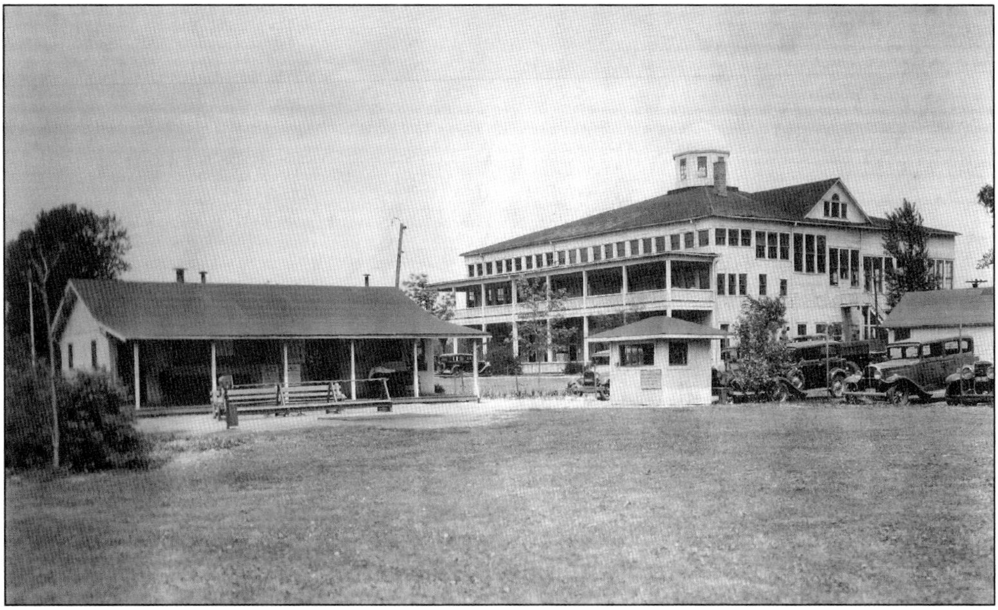

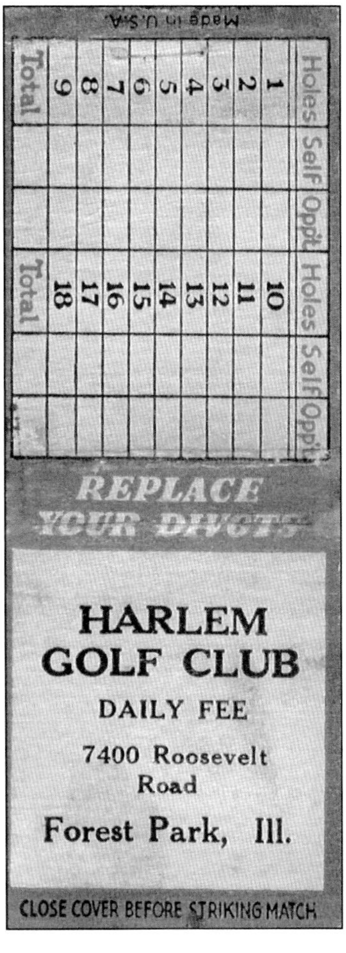

The Harlem Golf Course began in 1901 as a nine-hole course in the infield of the racetrack. It was later expanded to 18 holes. After the track closed, the grandstand was converted to a clubhouse. The course operated through 1940, but the government took control of the land in 1941, after a proposal to build a Studebaker airplane engine plant on the site fell through. (Courtesy of the Licht family.)

This matchbook cover would have been better at holding matches than used a scorecard, but as noted, the Harlem Golf Club was a daily-fee course. It was the first public daily-fee course in the Chicago area at a time when most courses were either private country clubs or municipal courses. In 1936, it cost 50¢ to play 18 holes, and to play all day was just 25¢ more.

In this aerial photograph from 1938, the outline of the racetrack is clearly visible as are the bunkers of the golf course. The famous statue of Cleopatra undoubtedly sat in the middle of the track. It is interesting to note all the vacant lots along the east side of Circle Avenue and the west side of Marengo Avenue, as well as along the north side of Roosevelt Road. (Courtesy of HistoricAerials.com.)

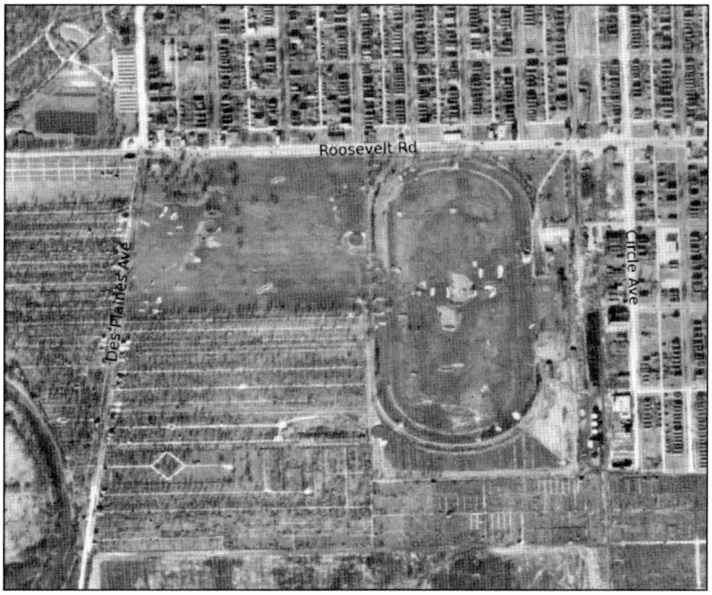

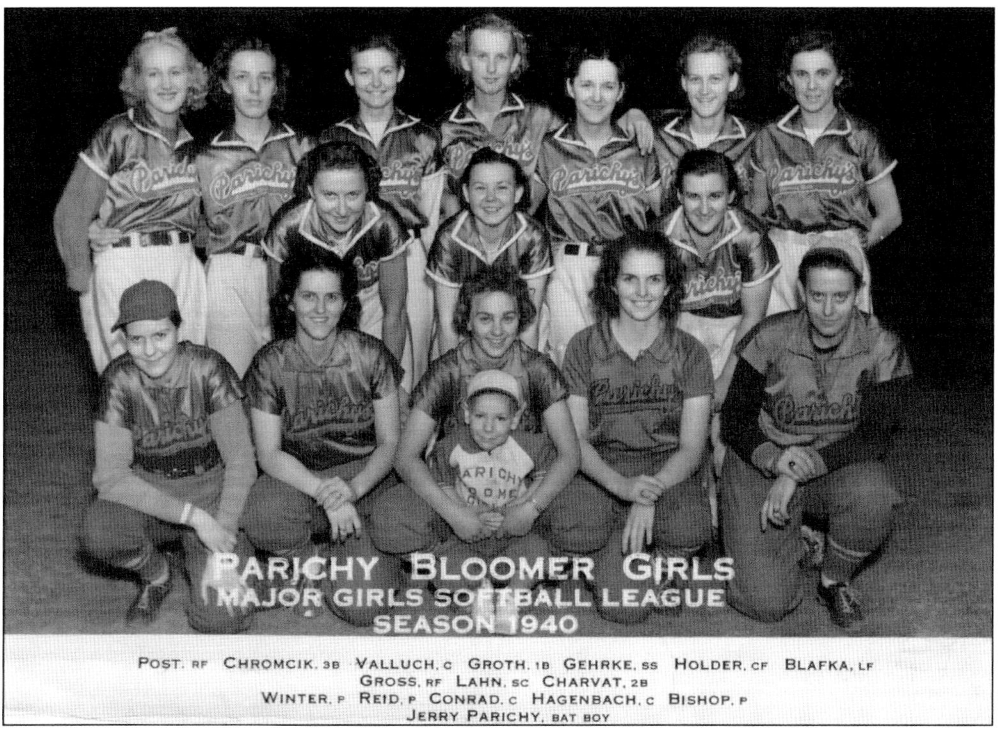

The Bloomer Girls were known as the Vogel Bloomer Girls until Emery Parichy sponsored them in 1936. He purchased the team in 1939. The Bloomer Girls were an original team of the National Girls Baseball League, which formed in 1944 and lasted until 1953. They played before crowds of thousands at Parichy Stadium, located at Harlem Avenue and Harrison Street. (Courtesy of Jerry Parichy.)

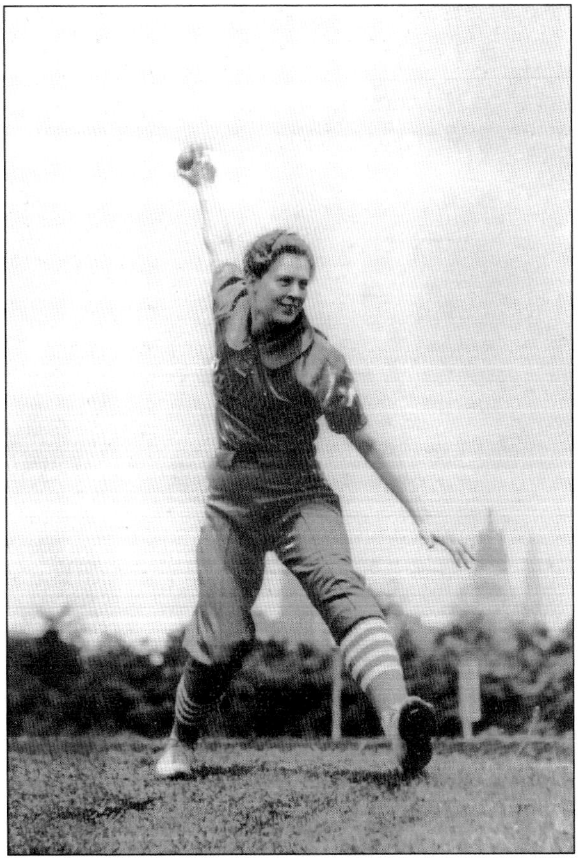

National Girls Baseball League player and star pitcher of the Parichy Bloomer Girls, Lonnie Stark shows her stuff in an undated photograph. Lonnie also pitched for the Bluebirds and was featured in a 10-minute 1947 newsreel about women's baseball. Lonnie pitched several no-hitters in her career that spanned nearly a decade. Lonnie passed away in 2003. (Courtesy of Frank Petrovic.)

Parichy Memorial Stadium was rededicated in 1945 in honor of Parichy's son, Emery William, who died on D-day, as well as the 80 other Forest Park residents who lost their lives during the war. The ballpark also featured a restaurant and baseball museum. Note St. Bernadine's Church over the third base wall. (Courtesy of SportsArtifacts.com.)

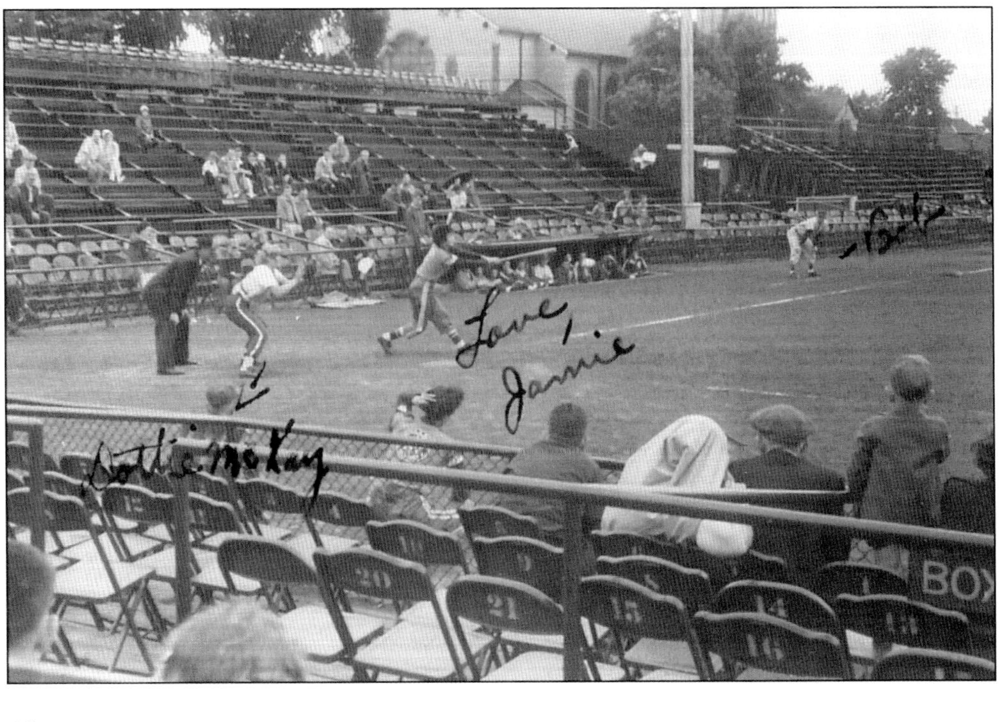

Five

EDUCATION AND SALVATION

Those who immigrated to the United States in the 19th century valued hard work and education and shared a faith that things would be better here for themselves and their families. The first public school in the area, built by Ashbel Steele, was located on Lake Street in River Forest and is still standing today. In 1877, a public school was erected on the northwest corner of Circle Avenue and Randolph Street. This school became known as Harlem School No. 1. The original building survived, albeit greatly modified, until the 1950s. Four other public school buildings would be added over the years. The second was the Farley School, later renamed after President Garfield.

As the village grew, so did the need for schools. The next two schools were built just a couple of years apart. First the Eugene Field School was built on the 900 block of Beloit Avenue. Named for the American writer of children's poetry, it was joined a few years later by a twin building named after Scottish author Robert Louis Stevenson. The Stevenson School faced Ferdinand Avenue. The two buildings were joined and eventually became home to the middle school for seventh and eighth graders. The final public school was Betsy Ross, which is the only school located south of Roosevelt Road. Proviso Township High School was built in 1911 and is the public high school that serves the village.

Forest Park has always been a melting pot where people of all races and religions have been able to coexist. The village has housed three Lutheran churches, St. John's, St. Paul's, and St. Peter's. Additionally, there are churches built for people of the Baptist, Methodist, Presbyterian, Catholic, and other Christian faiths. As the population changed, so have the congregations. A Filipino group called the Presbyterian church home for a time, and a Thai group now calls St. Paul's Church home. Many of the churches built their own schools, and with so many parochial schools, children often knew each other only from playing sports together at the park.

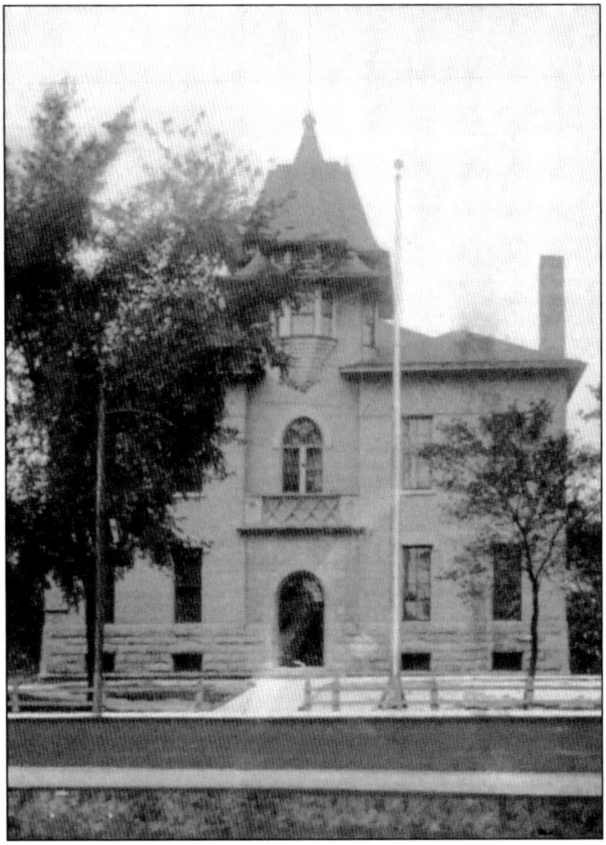

Harlem School No. 1, seen here in a 1909 postcard, was built in 1877 as a four-room affair that housed 200 students at Randolph Street and Circle Avenue. The building was enlarged in 1893 and renamed Grant School after Pres. Ulysses S. Grant. A 1928 addition was named for a beloved teacher, Elizabeth White. In 1958, the two earliest sections were demolished and a new section built.

The Robert Louis Stevenson building was constructed in 1909 and joined to the Eugene Field School, which opened September 8, 1907. Both are shown here prior to the construction of the Curtis Auditorium. In 1910, the Field School was the first school in town to have drinking fountains installed. (Courtesy of School District 91.)

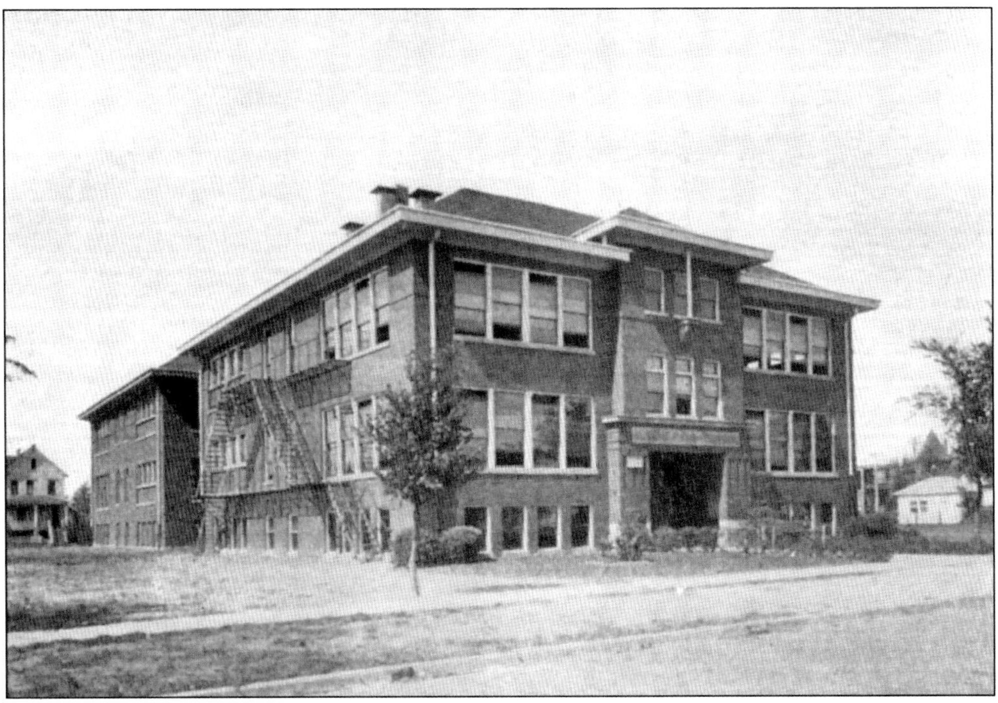

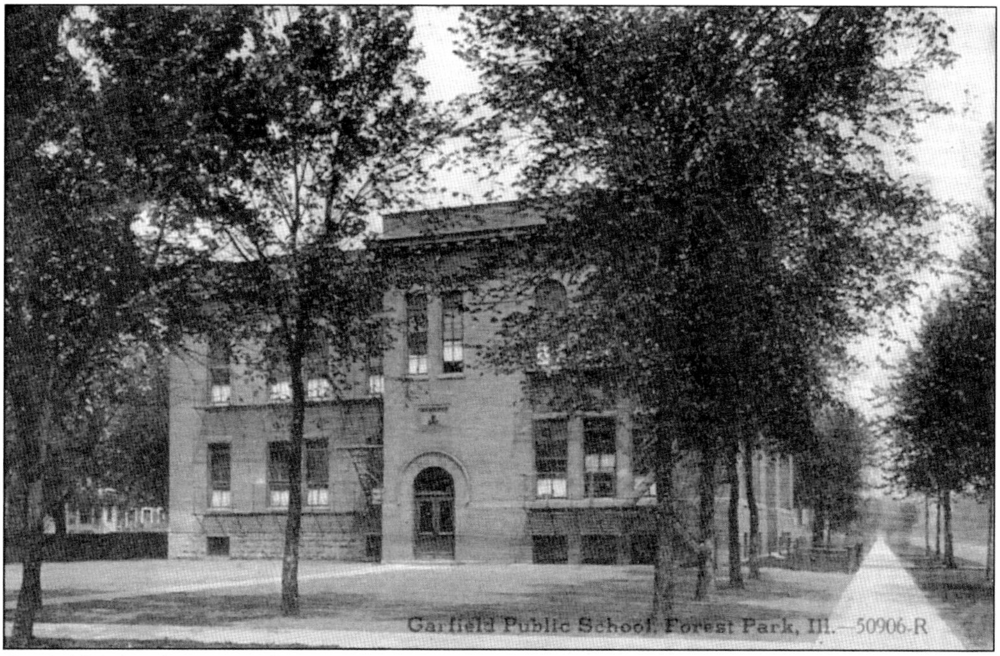

Garfield School, seen in this postcard, was situated a bit north of Jackson Boulevard, fronting Hannah Avenue. The two-room school was built in 1890, on land donated by Peter Farley, and named in his honor. The name was later changed to Harlem School No. 2, and additions were made. In 1913, the school was renamed to honor President Garfield. The building was razed in 1956 and replaced by an entirely new school.

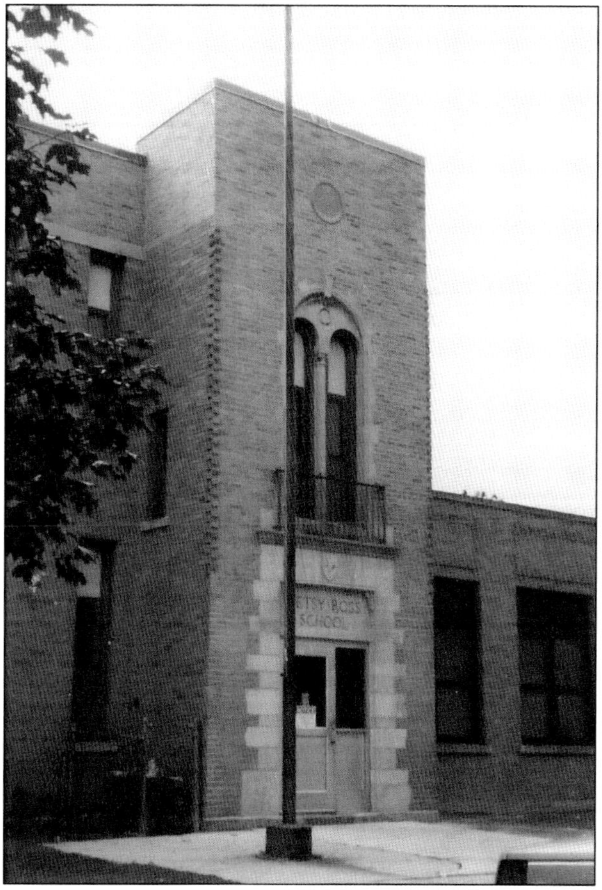

Betsy Ross School, the last of the original public schools, is located at Thirteenth Street and Marengo Avenue and was built in 1925. In 1957, a gymnasium was added. By the early 1970s, it was evident that the school needed more room, so in 1974, a portable building was brought in for use as a library. A permanent library was later added to the north side. The temporary structure was also replaced with a permanent addition.

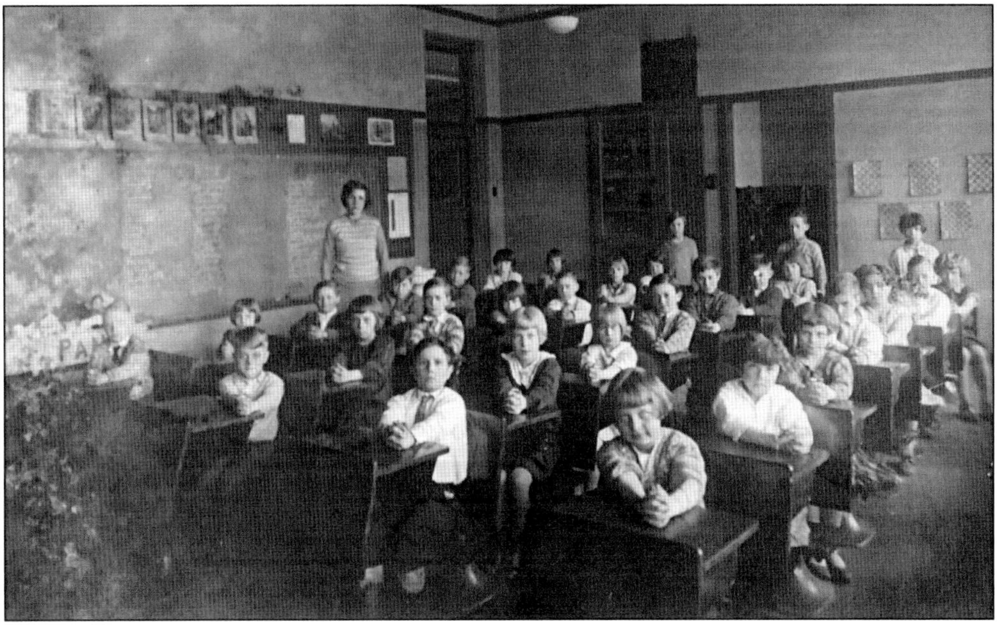

Betsy Ross School was built to serve the southernmost section of Forest Park and opened in 1926. The name of the school was chosen in a contest the previous year. A Garfield School sixth grader named Marian Taylor submitted the winning entry. This 1926 classroom photograph features a well-disciplined group of children, which includes Annamarie Herman, who is seated in the fourth row, second from left. (Courtesy of Jeff Oswalt.)

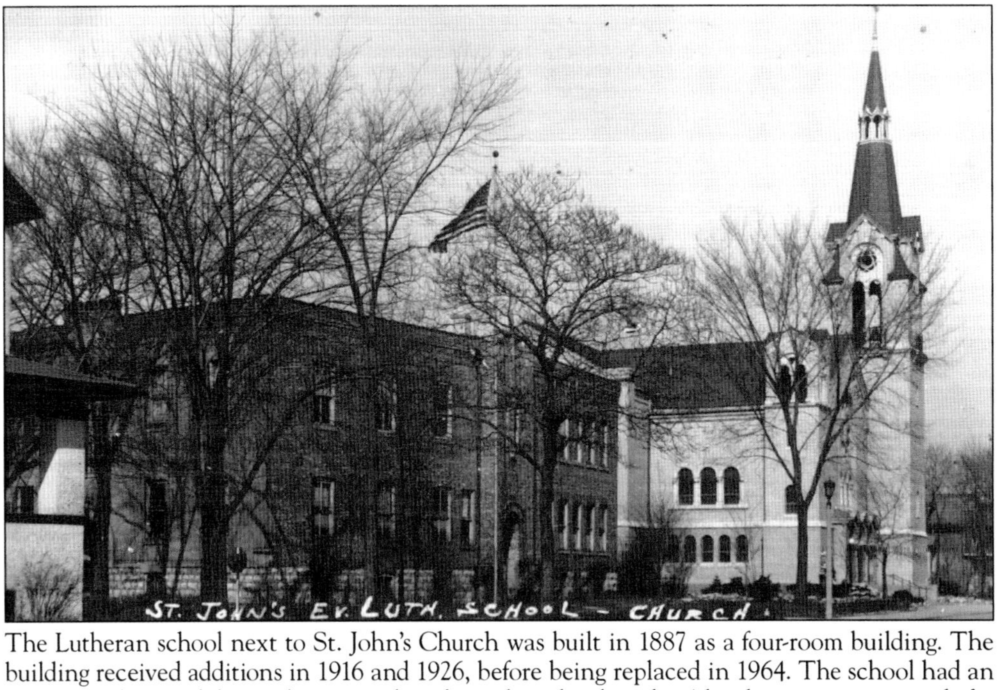

The Lutheran school next to St. John's Church was built in 1887 as a four-room building. The building received additions in 1916 and 1926, before being replaced in 1964. The school had an annual tradition of the students parading from the school to the Altenheim picnic grounds for a picnic, which should not to be confused with the all public schools parade and picnic. (See page 101.)

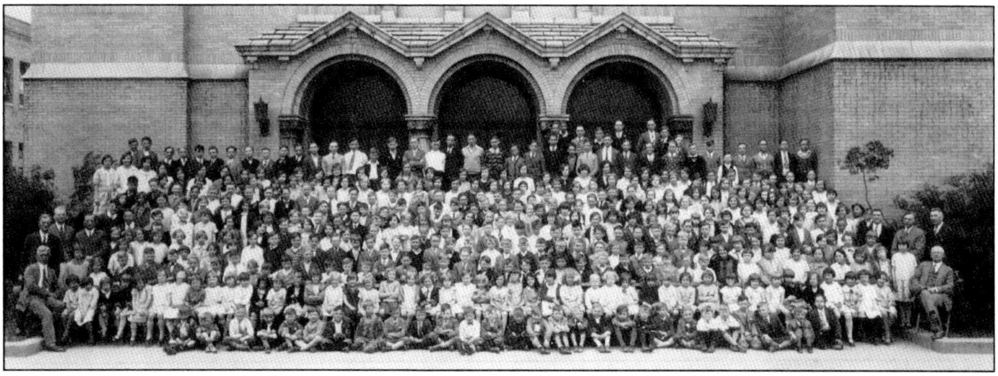

In 1939, there were 560 children attending St. John's Lutheran School. The faculty consisted of 11 teachers. In this photograph from that era, the children pose before the doors of the church, and the windows of the school can be seen on the far left. The large enrollment would eventually necessitate the construction of a larger school in 1964. (Courtesy of Harold Stover.)

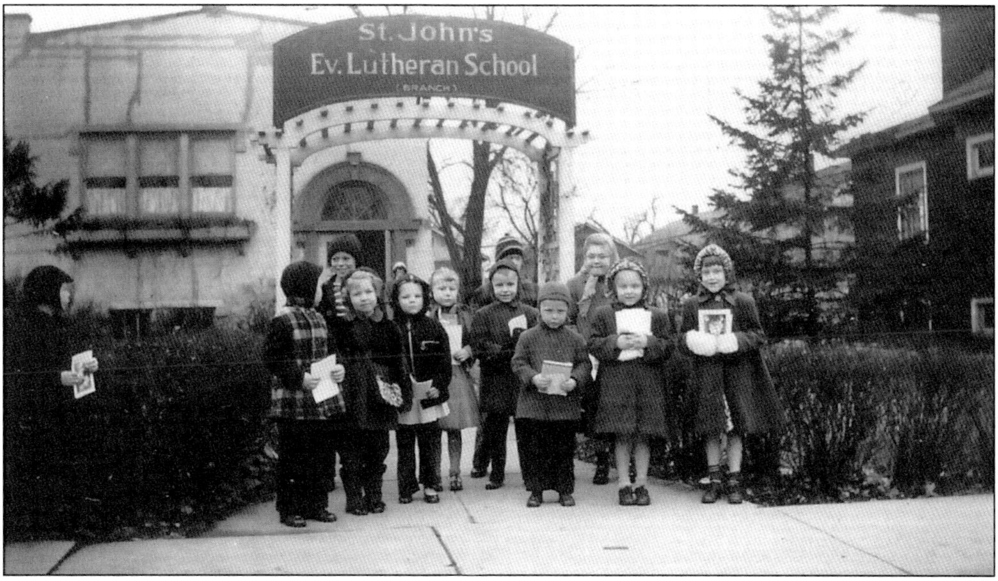

Harold Stover and his younger brother Lawrence are among the students of the south branch of St. John's Lutheran School. The school, located at 1037 Marengo Avenue, was dedicated in 1928 and continued to be used until 1959. The building still stands as a private residence, although a brick addition was added to the front several years ago. (Courtesy of Harold Stover.)

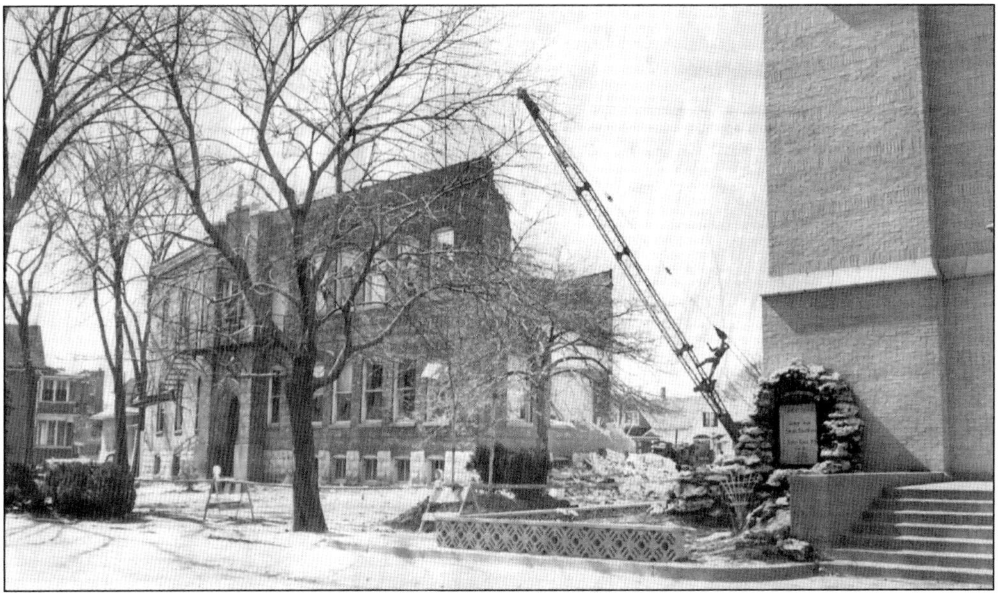

In 1964, St. John's opened a new school building on the north side of the church, and the old school became a parking lot. In 2007, the church closed the school, but the 1964 building stayed in use. The Walther Lutheran High School Association began operating the Walther Lutheran Academy at Forest Park for children from the age of three through the eighth grade. (Courtesy of Village of Forest Park.)

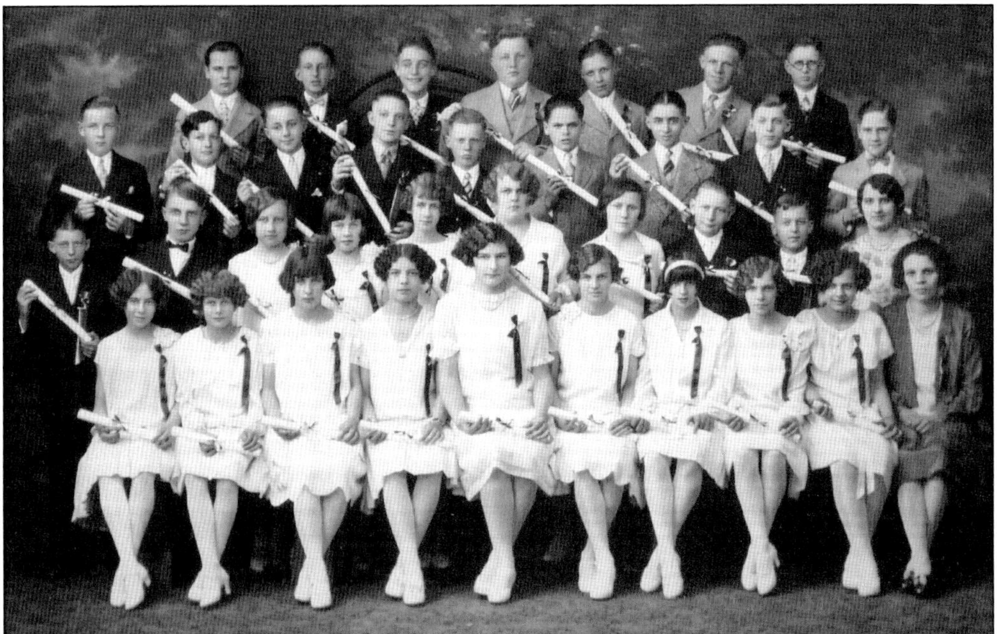

The girls of the 1927 Garfield School graduating class, in white dresses with waved, bobbed hairdos, are much more coordinated in their appearance than the boys were, but all proudly display their hard-earned diplomas. This class included a young Elmer Licht (second row, third from the right). (Courtesy of the Licht family.)

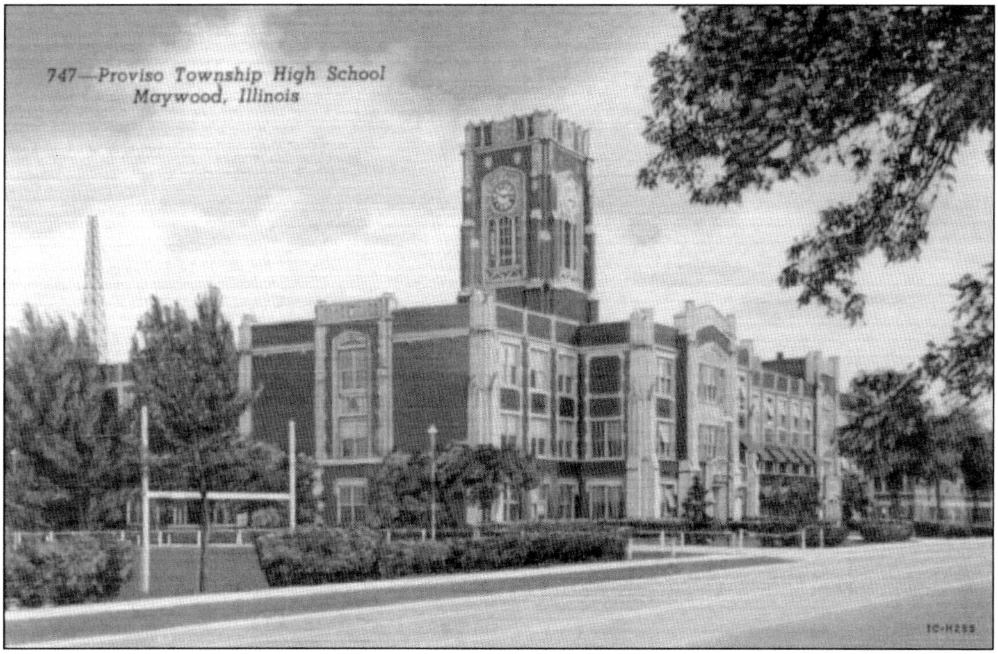

Although located in Maywood, Proviso East is the public high school that serves Forest Park residents. The building at Madison Street and First Avenue opened in 1911 on 5 acres of land. The original building is still use, but has been added to and remodeled several times. This 1950s postcard view shows the northern section with the stately clock tower, part of a major addition in the early 1930s.

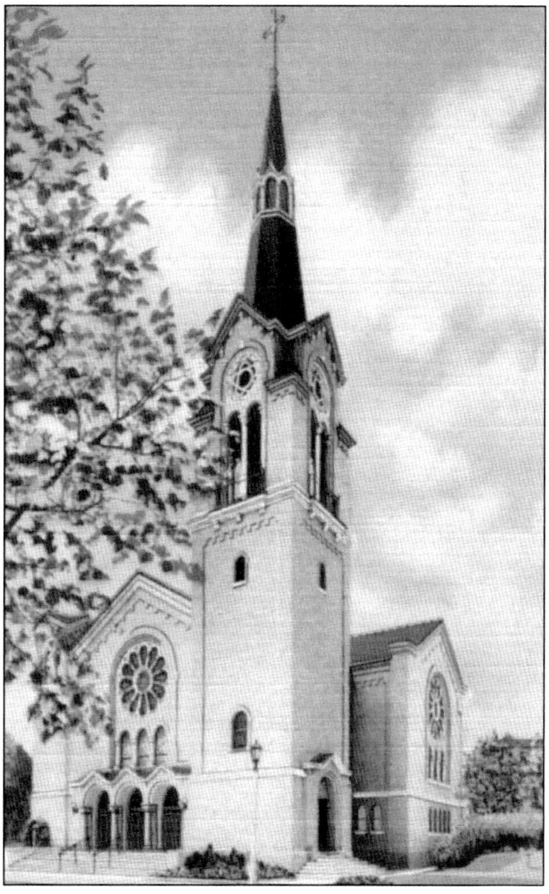

This postcard is an artist's rendering of St. John's Lutheran Church as it would have appeared prior to the 1964 addition of the school building. This landmark structure at 305 Circle Avenue opened May 3, 1914, with a seating capacity of 1,200 and features a 150-foot tower topped with a 10-foot-tall gold leaf cross.

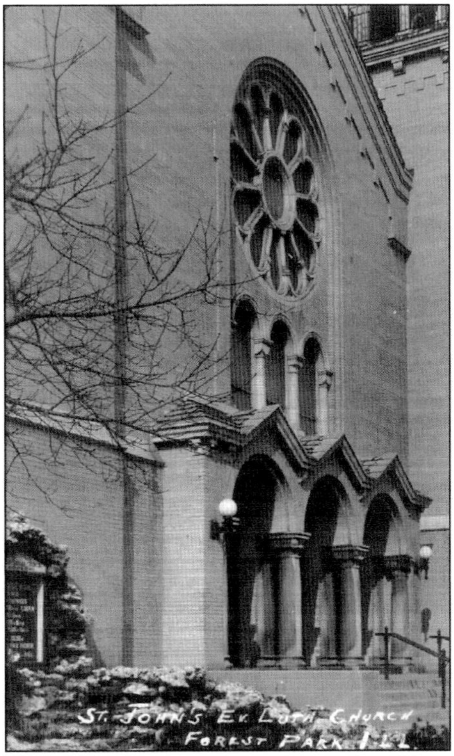

This 1940s postcard features St. John's Lutheran Church, as seen from the Circle Avenue sidewalk. The stone landscaping in the foreground has been removed, but little else has changed. This landmark structure is the third building to house the congregation. The first church was located at Marengo and Franklin Avenues.

This unidentified group, perhaps the choir, poses in the chancel of St. John's Lutheran Church. The Romanesque-style church featured a reproduction of Coletti's *Ascension*. The crucifix, adorned with mosaics, stands 14 feet tall. A baptismal font, carved from a single piece of Carrara marble, is hidden from view by the faithful. (Courtesy of Harold Stover.)

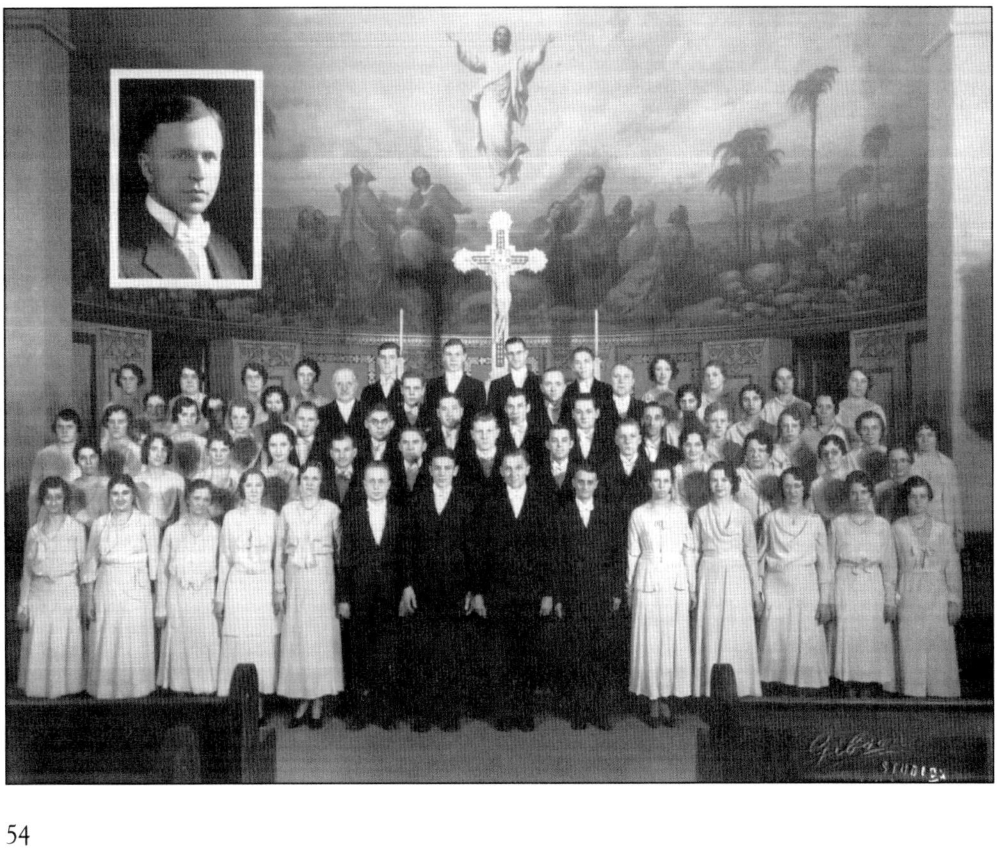

St. Paul's Lutheran Church at 7416 Dixon Street had two separate entrances when constructed in 1899, as seen in this 1908 postcard view. For reasons unknown today, they were sealed, and a single central entrance was created. Due to a declining congregation, the church held its last service on March 28, 2010. As of April 11, 2010, the church is now known as the St. Paul Thai Lutheran Church. A Thai congregation had been sharing the church since 1982.

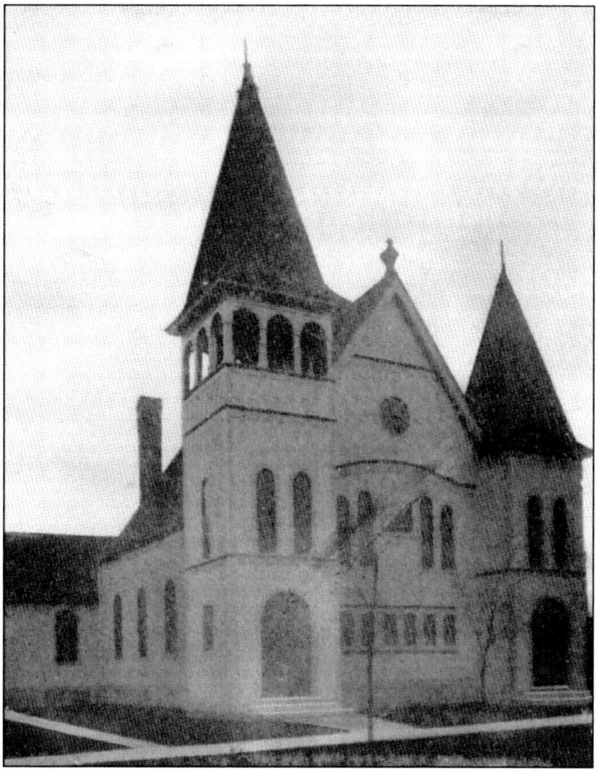

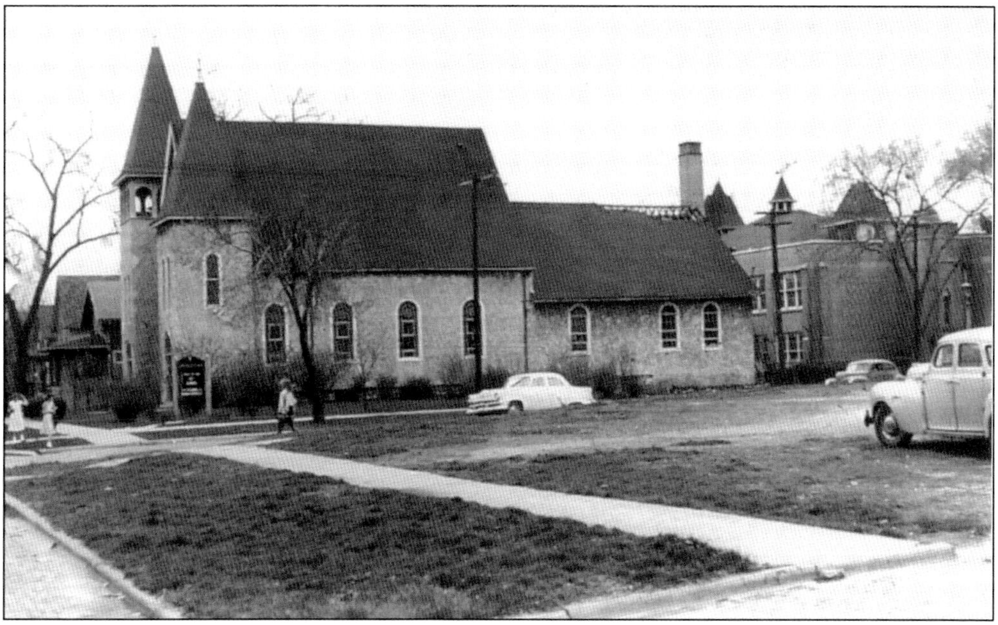

This 1950s photograph of St. Paul's is interesting on several levels. Grant School is visible on the far right, and it appears the roof of the church has fire damage. Also note the empty lot on the southwest corner of Dixon and Brown Streets. Records indicate the house currently at 135 Brown Street was built in the early 1920s, so it may have been relocated to this lot during the expressway construction. (Courtesy of St. Paul's Church.)

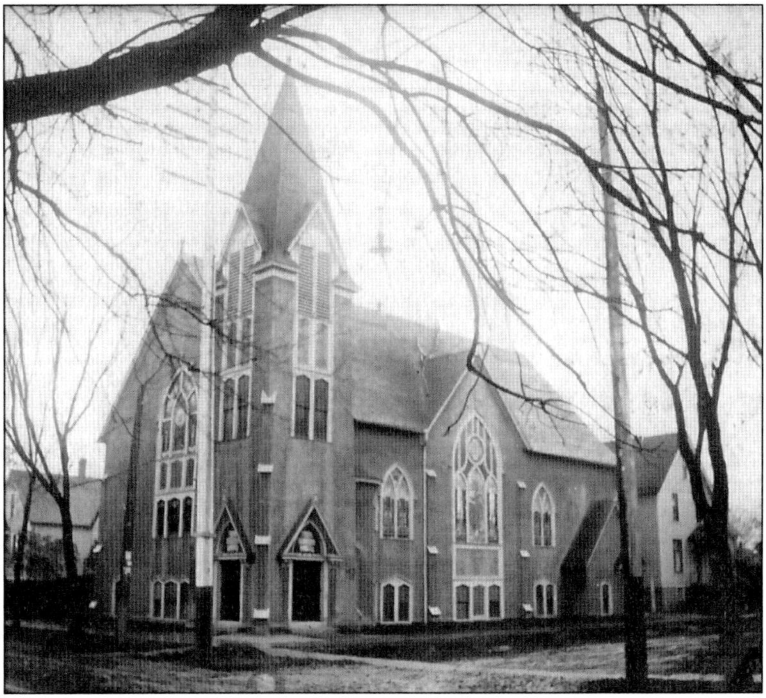

Since it was constructed in 1903, the Forest Park Baptist Church at Harlem Avenue and Dixon Street has changed very little on the outside. The interior, however, underwent a major remodel when the edifice was only 18 years old. The choir loft was lowered and the organ pipes were hidden, creating a more open and airy feeling. (Courtesy of Forest Park Baptist Church.)

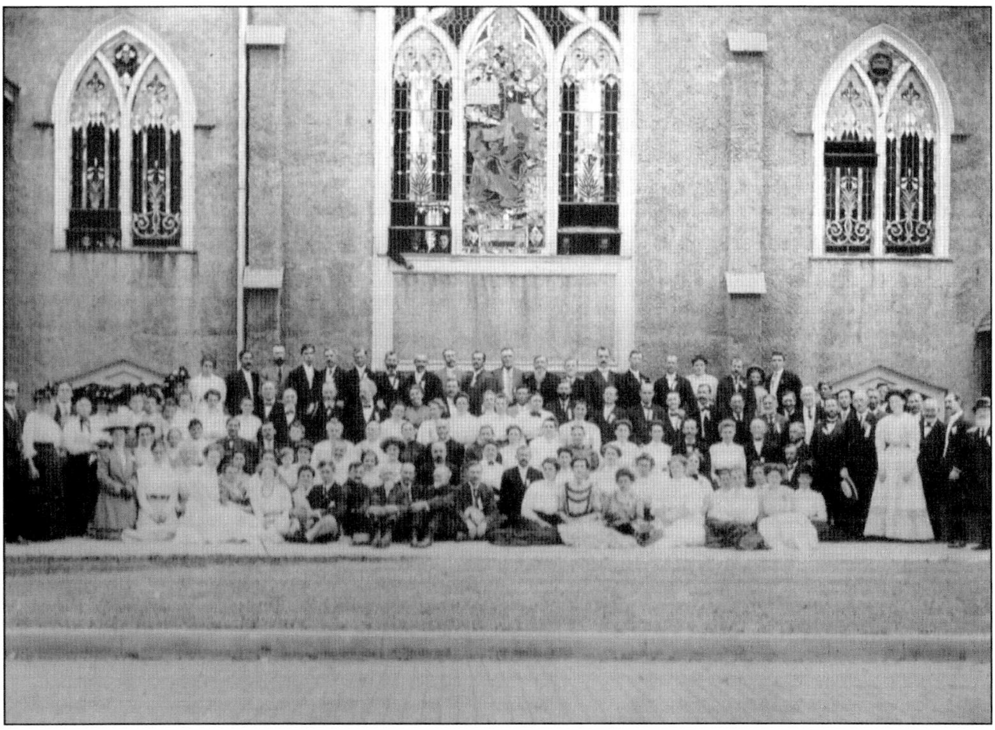

Little has changed in the nearly 100 years since this photograph of the "Central Conference" was taken at the German Baptist Church at Dixon Street and Harlem Avenue. Dixon Street, pictured in the foreground, is one of many streets that have remained brick. Note the people peeking out of the windows from inside the church. (Courtesy of Forest Park Baptist Church.)

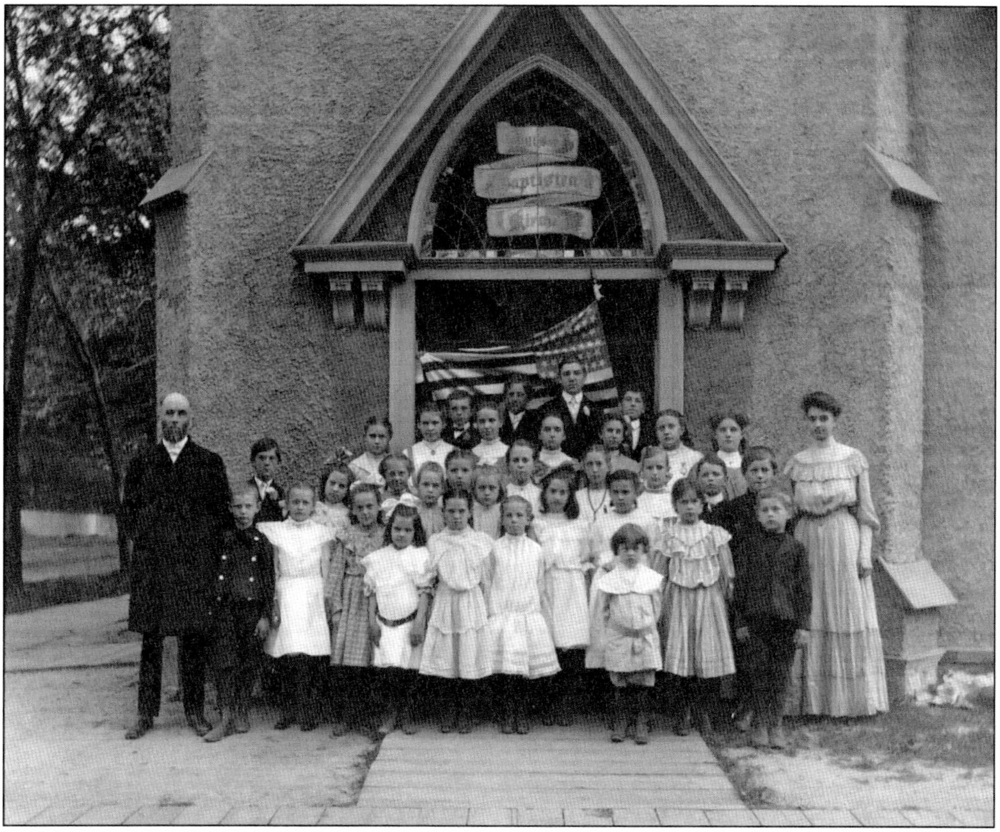

Both German and American heritage are celebrated in this photograph of a Sunday school class at the Baptist church on Harlem Avenue. The sign above the door is in German, yet a sense of patriotism is evident by the display of the American flag. Note the wooden sidewalks. (Courtesy of Forest Park Baptist Church.)

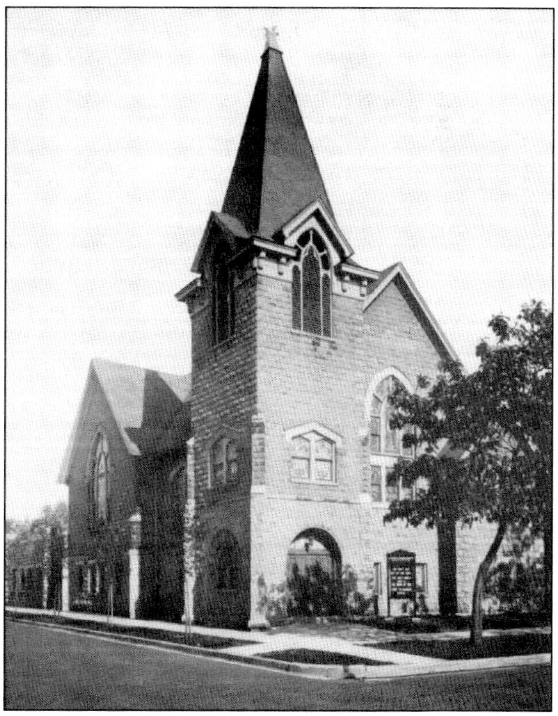

The cornerstone for St. Peter's Lutheran Church at Hannah Avenue and Adams Street was laid in 1899, but construction was soon halted for reasons unknown. The congregation briefly worshipped in a hall at the Forest Park State Bank. The portion of the church above the doorways was built after 1909. The delays resulted in the use of two types of stone, and the transition can still be seen today. (Courtesy of Historical Society of Forest Park.)

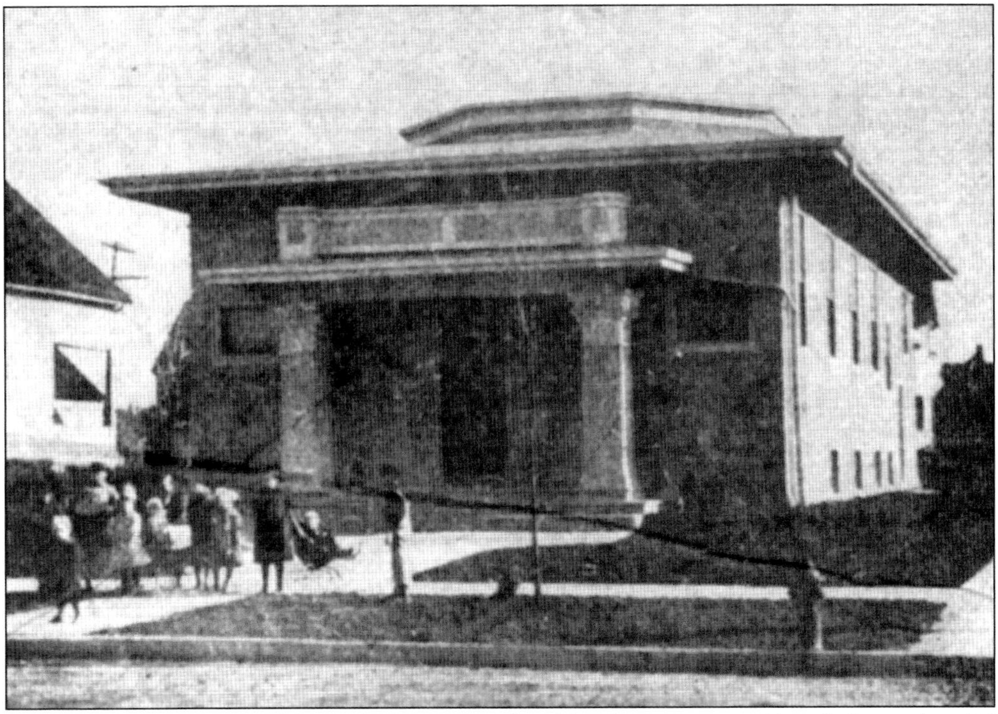

Often overlooked as one of the early churches is the old Calvary Mission Church, located at 446 Hannah Avenue. The building has housed many tenants over the years, including the Forest Park Club, the Minutemen, and currently the Fraternal Order of Eagles Aerie No. 1344. It also served as a parish house for St. Peter's and a preschool.

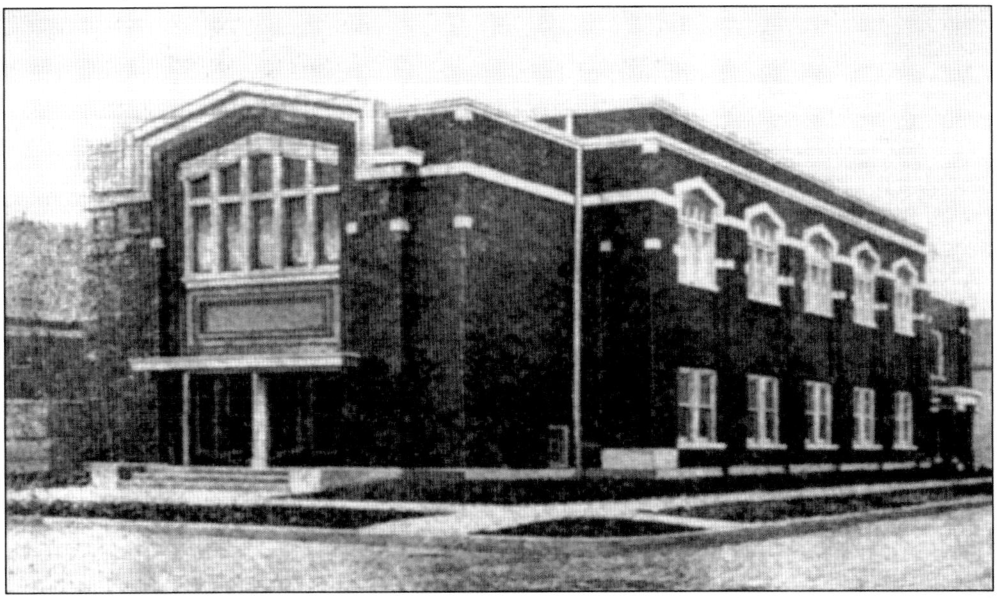

The Forest Park Methodist Church started as an offshoot of the Onward Mission at Marengo and Franklin Avenues. The church at Thomas and Adams Streets was dedicated in 1919. Later known as Wesley United Methodist, the church was the original home of the Circle Theatre group. A fire on June 7, 1988, destroyed the building. The lot is now home to a small playground.

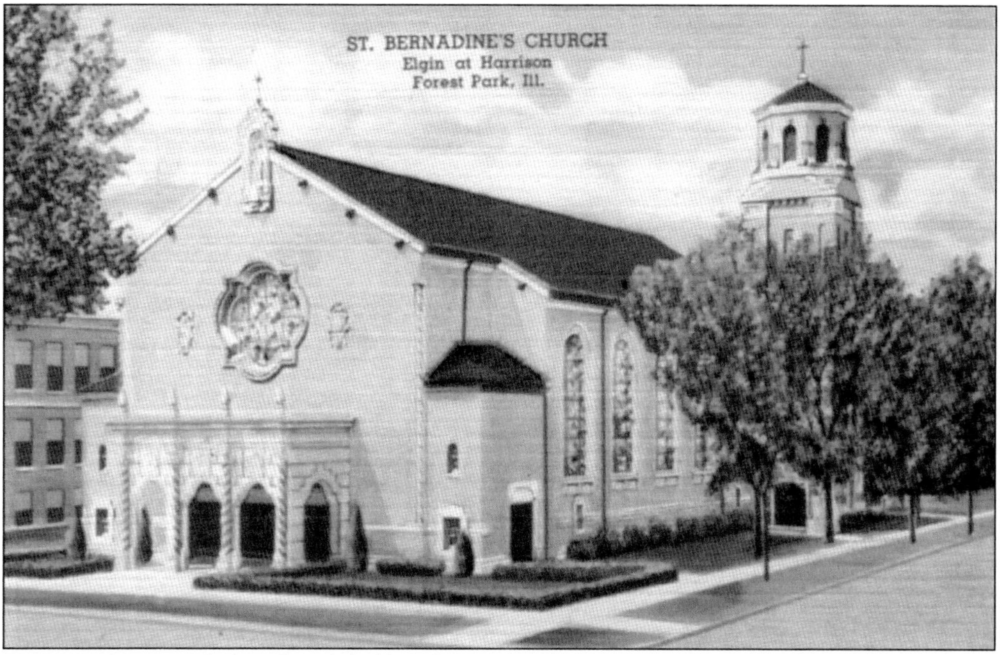

St. Bernadine's Catholic Church held its first service in a temporary structure on Christmas Eve 1911. The first permanent structure, dedicated in 1916, housed both the school and the church and is still in use. The current Spanish mission–styled church building shown in this postcard was dedicated in 1940.

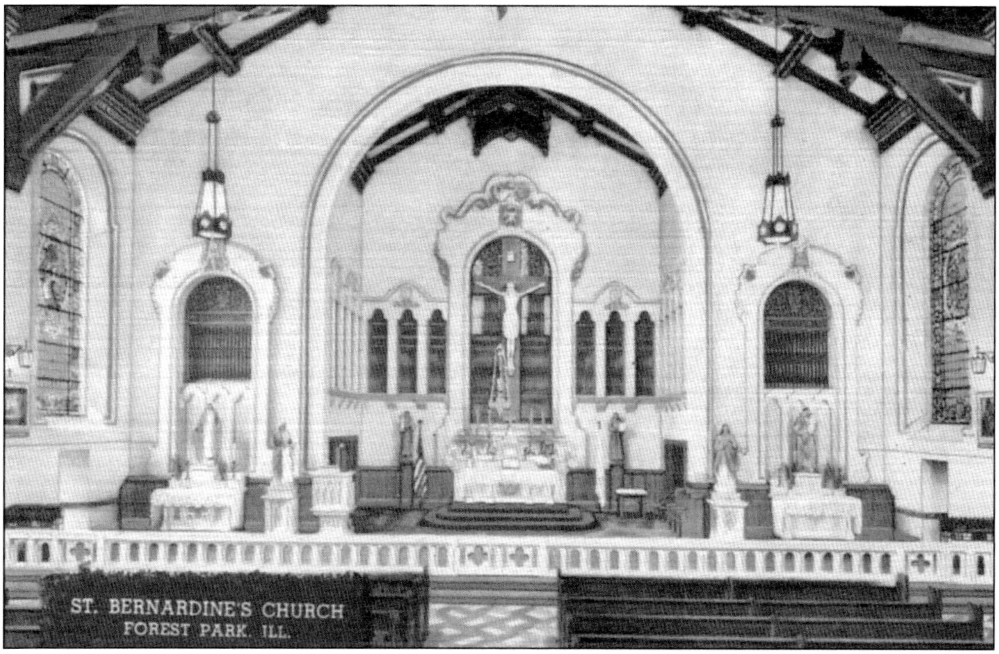

This colorized postcard of St. Bernadine's Catholic Church, located at Harrison Street and Elgin Avenue, dates to the pre-Vatican II era. Since that time, the Communion rail was removed, and several of the statues were taken down from the altar. As the sender of this postcard wrote, "It doesn't look quite like this, it's nicer!"

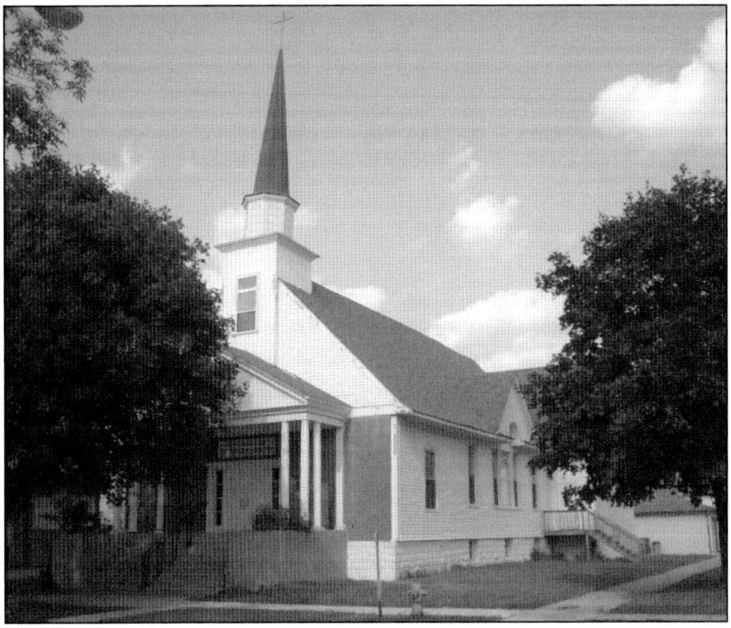

The Pioneer Chapel was the first church in the village built in the 20th century. It opened in 1900 at the northeast corner of Lexington Street and Ferdinand Avenue. In 1925, the church became known as First Presbyterian and remained so until 1968. It later became the Filipino Community United Presbyterian Church. The church became the Chicago Christian Center Church in 1999.

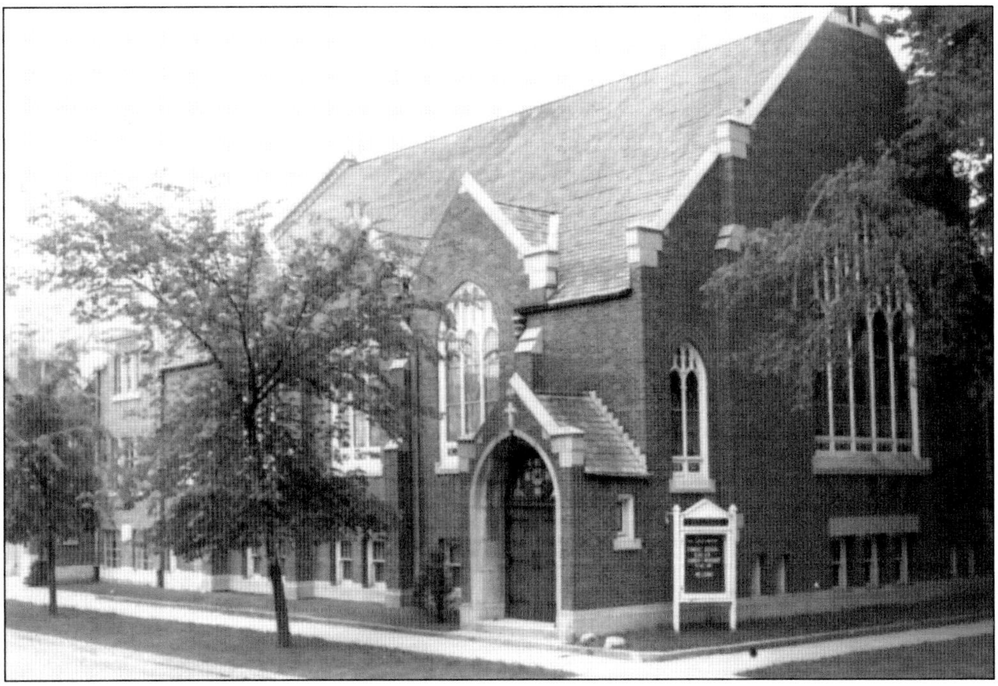

The First United Church of Christ, located on the southeast corner of Elgin Avenue and Harvard Street, began as the First Evangelical Reformed Church. Like many others, the church was once located in the city, with roots dating back to 1865. The current name was adopted in 1959 following the formation of the United Church of Christ. The current church was dedicated on November 11, 1928. (Courtesy of First United Church of Christ.)

Six

A New Era Begins

When Harlem changed its name to Forest Park on August 12, 1907, a new era was about to begin. The *Chicago Tribune* declared, "Harlem drops tainted name." The town had a reputation for gambling halls and beer gardens, but that certainly was not the reason for the new name.

The amusement park opened the following year, and people from all over came to enjoy themselves, with many deciding to relocate here. In 1910, Proviso High School was formed, the golf course expanded from nine holes to a full 18, and on Thanksgiving Day of that year, a huge fire consumed hundreds of stables at the old racetrack. The population of Forest Park in 1910 was just 6,780 people, but by 1917, the population had nearly doubled to 12,000. As speculators had predicted, a building boom had begun, and homes and businesses began to spring up all over town.

Beginning in 1911, the public began campaigning for a public park. E. A. Cummings owned most of the land between Des Plaines and Harlem Avenues and from Jackson Boulevard to Harrison Street, as well as both north and south of the railroad right-of-way. The first proposal was to use the land north of the tracks as a public park. Nearly 20 years later, the park district was established, and the land south of the tracks was purchased. The building of the park was a large Works Progress Administration (WPA) project, and the park continues today to serve the community for both recreation and special events.

In 1915, a new village hall was built. Finally, Forest Park had a municipal complex to be proud of, which also included a public library. The next several decades would see rapid growth and development of the community.

The year 1919 brought with it Prohibition, and Forest Park found itself dry for the first time. Nearly all of the saloons and taverns became soft drink parlors. In all, 39 taverns were forced to stop selling alcohol. Regardless of the law, liquor could still be had at many Forest Park locations. The 1933 repeal of the Volstead Act ended "The Noble Experiment," and Forest Park returned to normal—that is, until December 7, 1941.

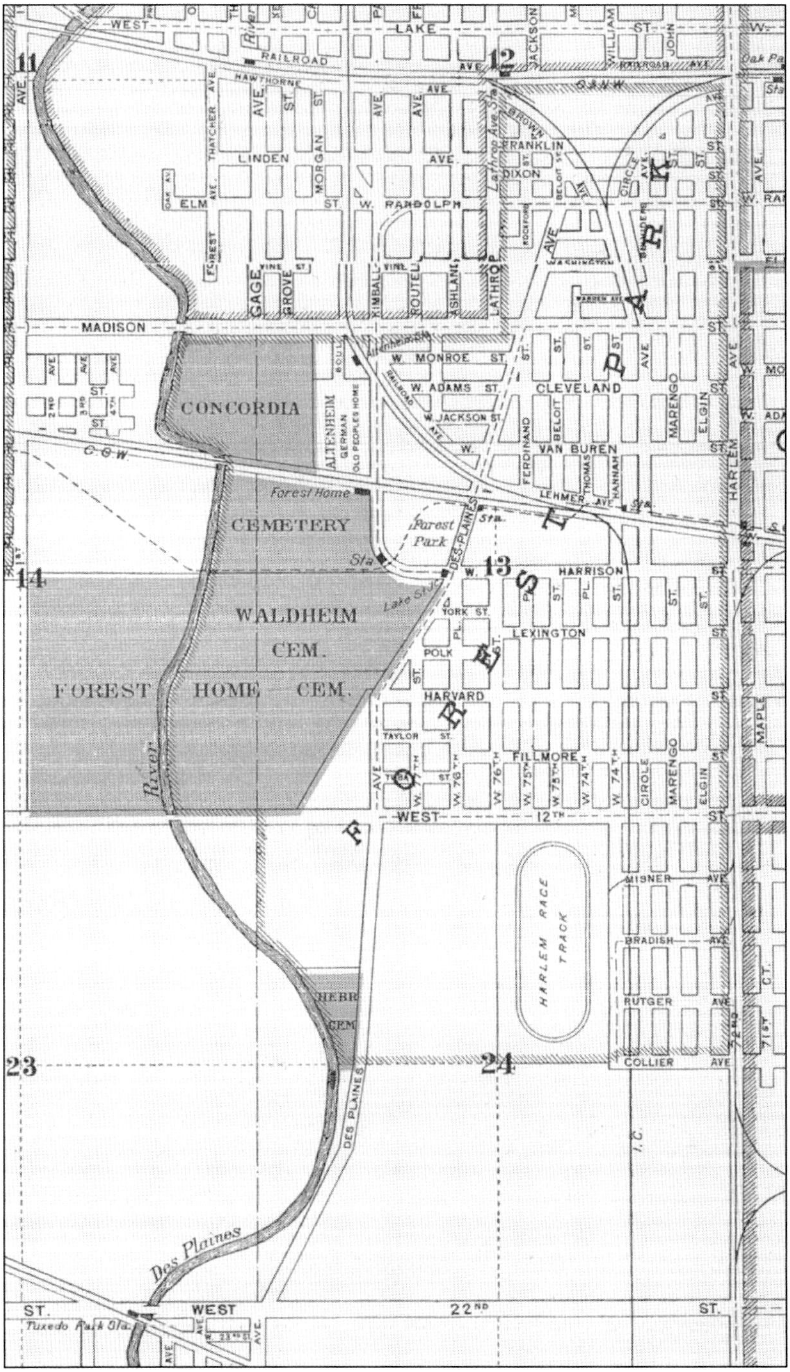

This is a map of Forest Park from 1910. The location of the amusement park is clearly visible. By this time, the names Elgin, Marengo, and Circle Avenues extended south of Roosevelt Road, although on this map it is still Twelfth Street. The street was not called Roosevelt Road until 1919, when it was renamed in honor of former president Theodore Roosevelt, who died on January 6, 1919. The old dummy rail line route is also more visible as well, running south from Randolph Street to Harrison Street. (Courtesy of University of Chicago Library.)

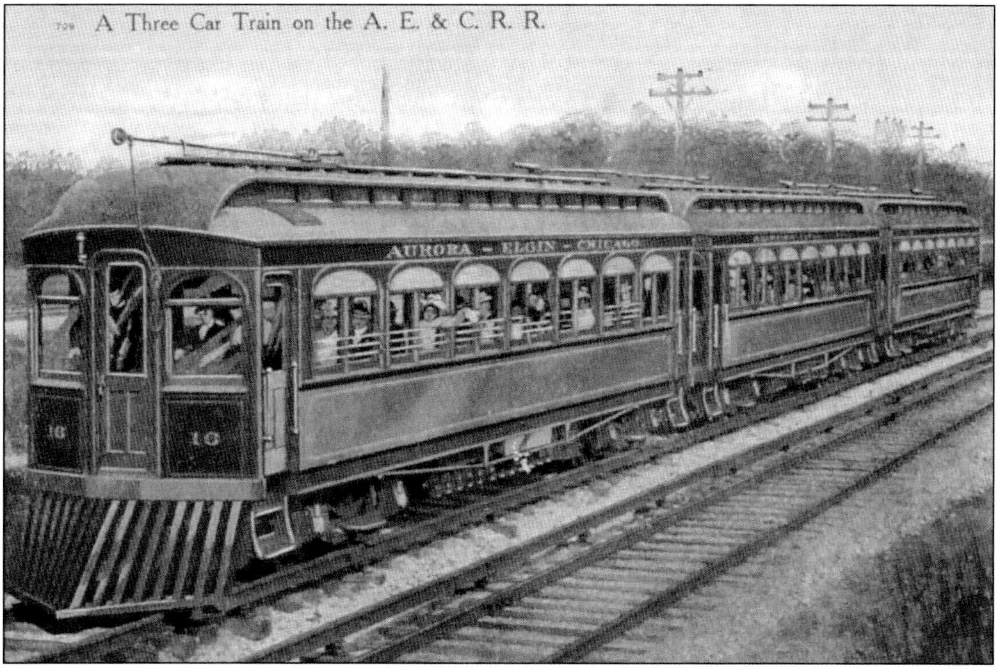

The Aurora, Elgin, and Chicago Railroad began operating in 1902 with service directly to Chicago, passing through Forest Park in trains such as the one shown in this 1908 postcard. It became the Chicago, Aurora, and Elgin, or CA&E, in 1922. In 1953, the CA&E shortened its route, terminating in Forest Park. Commuters were forced to transfer to the "L." The CA&E ended service abruptly and without notice just after noon on July 3, 1957, stranding 3,500 commuters.

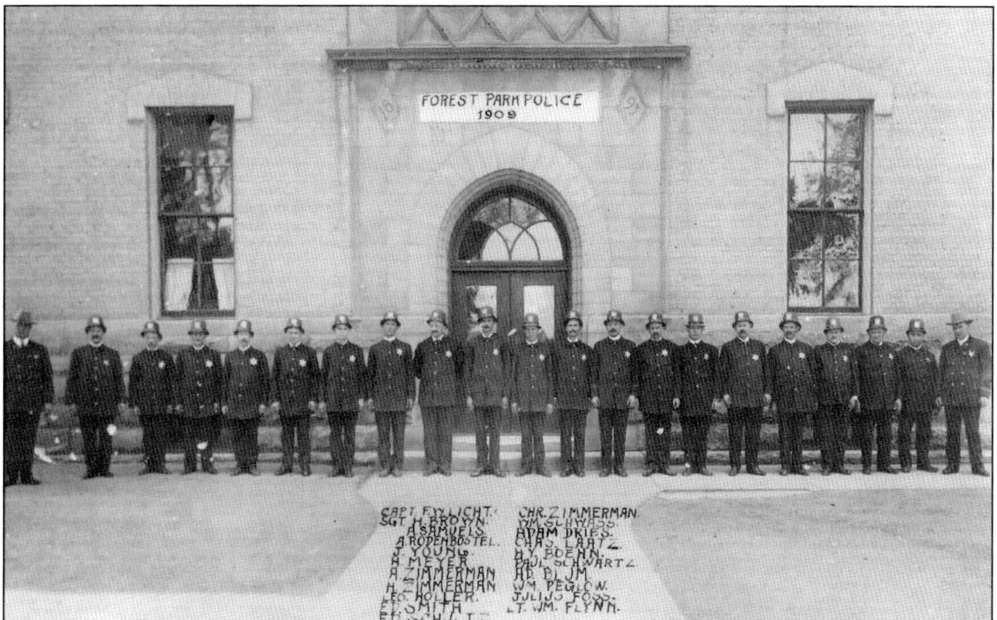

In 1909, Fred Licht (far left) became captain (chief) of the police department after serving one year as a patrolman. In those days, the police walked their beat. Often a thankless job, the average pay for an officer was $900 a year, which would be around $22,000 today. (Courtesy of Jeff Oswalt.)

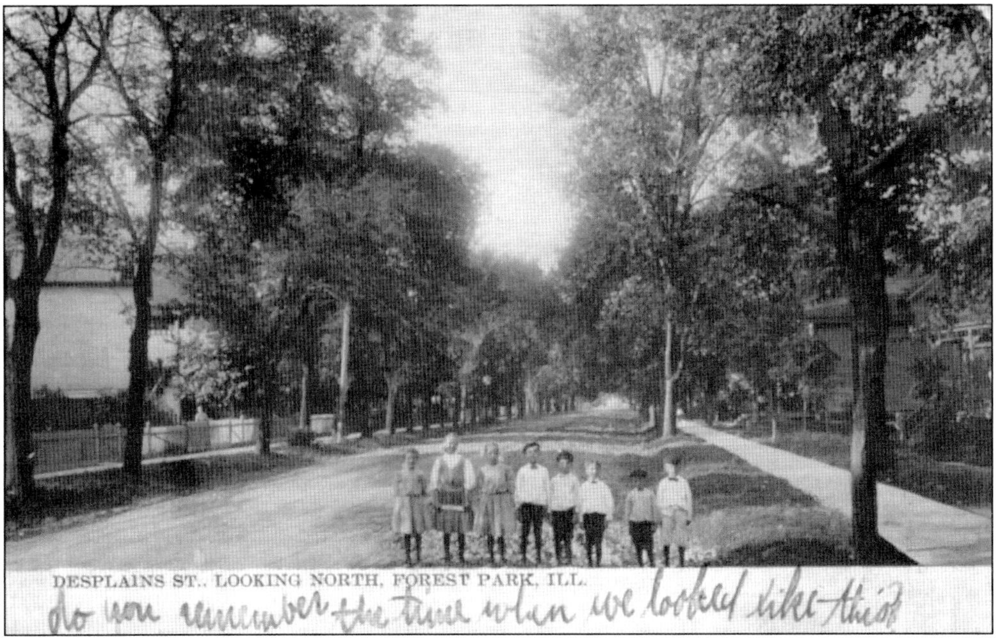

Des Plaines Avenue appears unpaved in this early-20th-century postcard. The view is most likely north of Randolph Street. A large number of homes on the 100 blocks of Rockford and Des Plaines Avenues date to the late 1800s. The roundhouse, built by the Chicago and Galena Union Railroad, was located nearby.

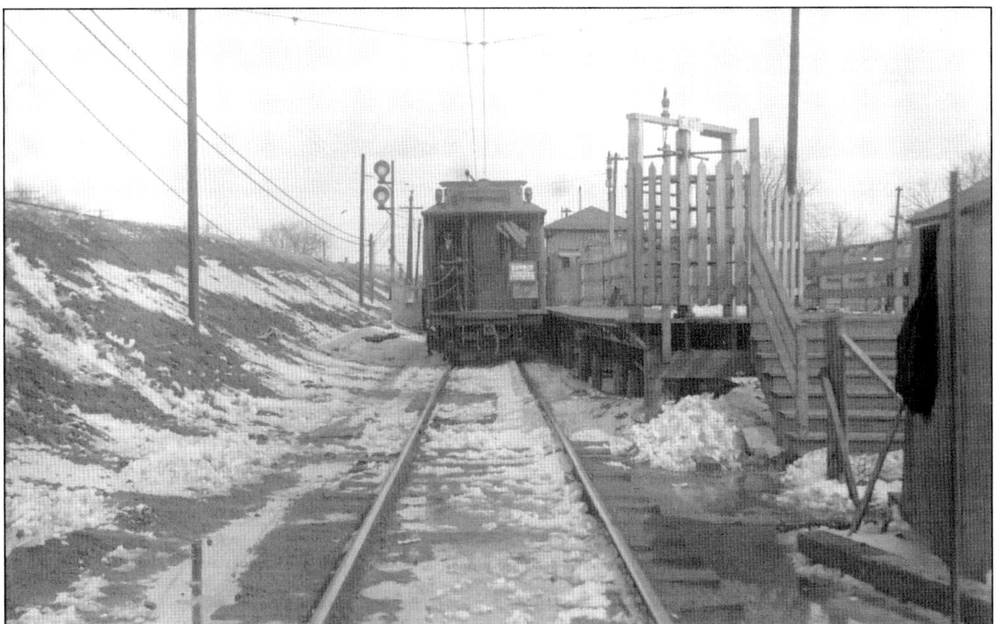

The Lake Street "L" began operating in 1893 but was not extended to Forest Park until 1910. This photograph shows the original station at Circle and Harlem Avenues, located a bit further west than it is today. It was originally built as a surface line, meaning that it crossed Harlem Avenue at street level. It was raised onto the Chicago and North Western embankment in 1962 to ease traffic congestion. The current station opened in 1964. (Courtesy of Walter R. Keevil.)

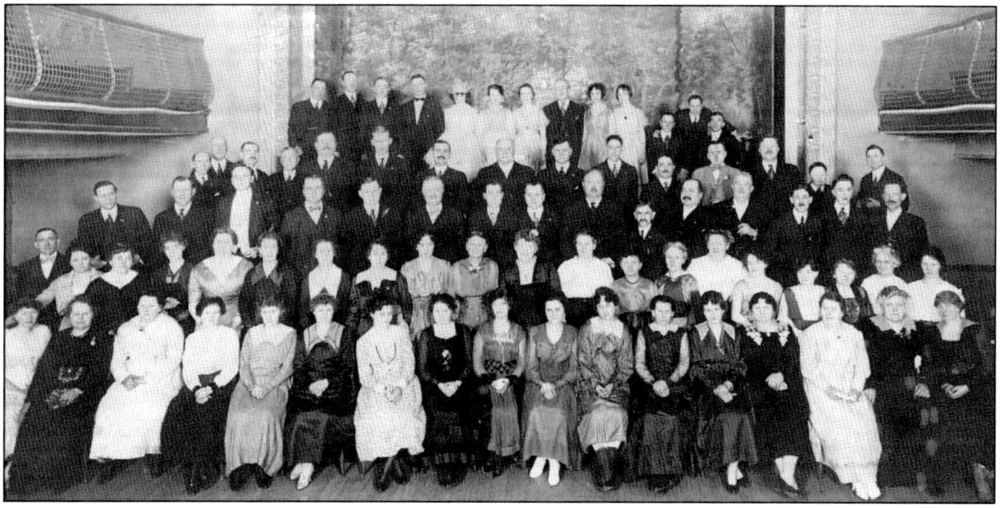

On March 12, 1918, the Forest Park Businessmen's Association held their fourth annual banquet at Gaden's Hall. Built by John Gaden in 1892 for $30,000, the large building located at the southeast corner of Madison Street and Des Plaines Avenue was home to the Forest Theatre beginning in 1920. The building was demolished in 1963. It was replaced by a gas station, and the location is now home to McDonald's. (Courtesy of the Mohr family.)

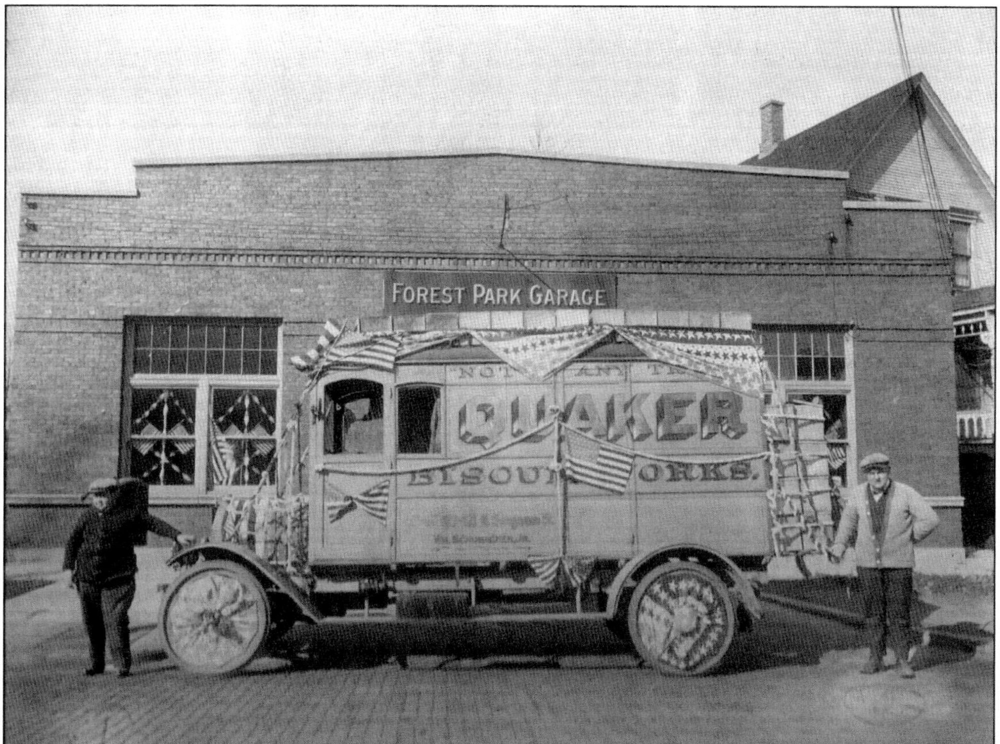

The entire country was awash in patriotism during World War I. William Schumacher and his son are posing with their delivery truck in front of the Forest Park Garage, which was located at 343 Des Plaines Avenue. The building was demolished, but the home behind it still stands. Most of the village streets were paved with bricks by 1911. (Courtesy of Tim Shanahan.)

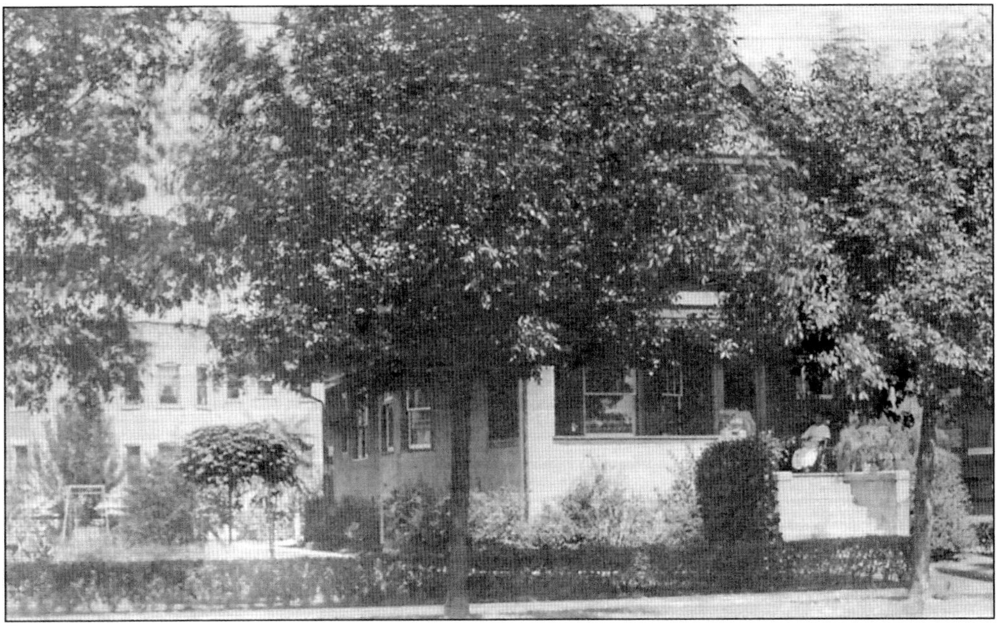

The Loeck home at 7239 Jackson Boulevard, shown here in 1916, was the scene of a progressive dinner held by the Oteyokwa Club on February 18, 1928. *Oteyokwa* is a Native American term meaning "friendly gathering." The club, which was popular in the 1920s, was a social organization that consisted of members from the surrounding communities who held parties at each other's homes throughout the year. (Courtesy of the Thomas A. Walsh Jr. family.)

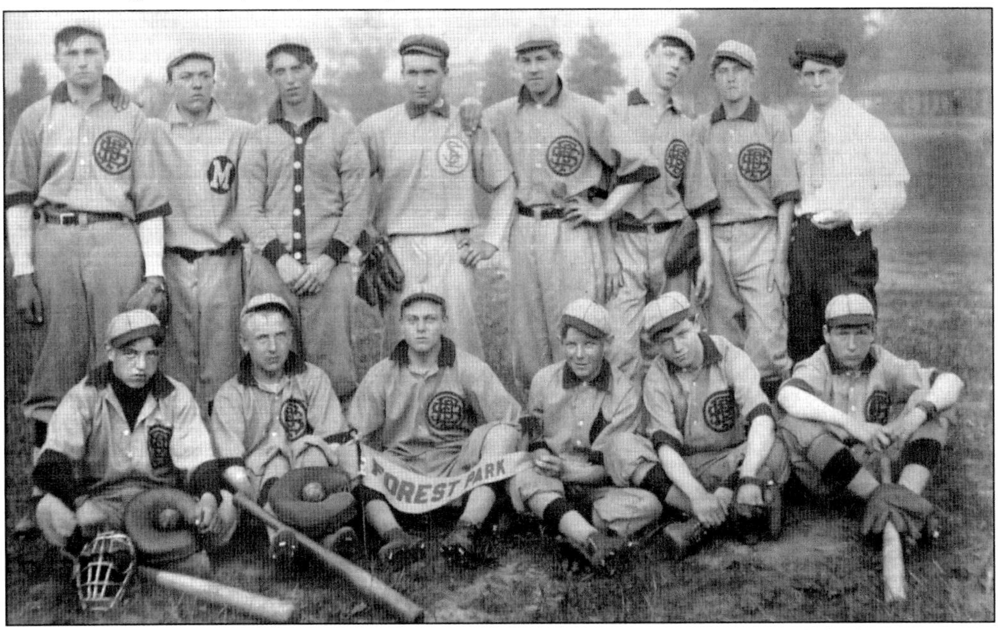

Baseball was widely popular in the early days of the 20th century. Forest Park had many teams that played in sandlots all over town. Games were held at the southeast corner of Hannah Avenue and Jackson Boulevard, as well as Marengo Avenue and Harrison Street, and later Harlem Avenue and Harrison Street. This unidentified photograph seems to show players from several teams, as they are sporting at least four different uniforms. (Courtesy of Tim Shanahan.)

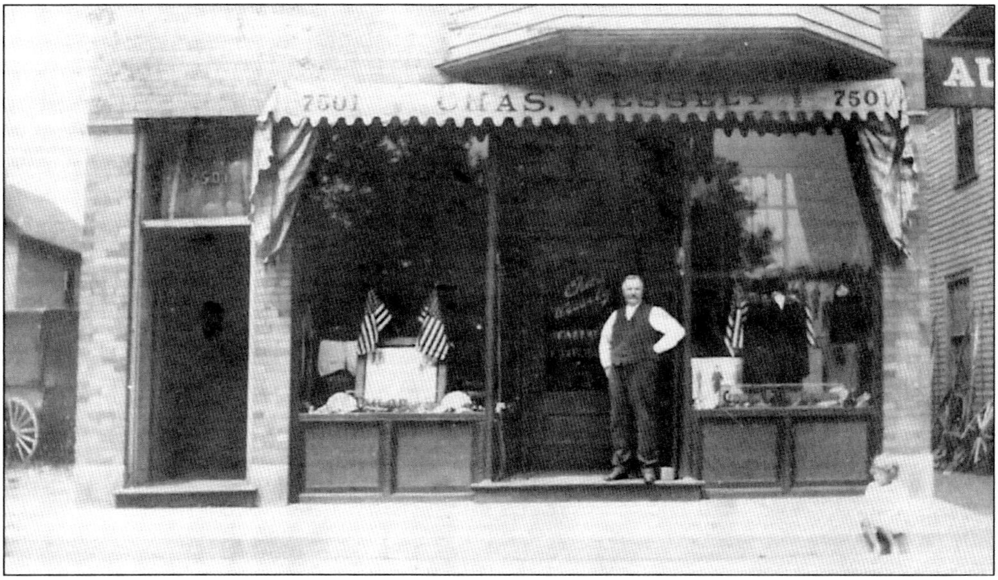

This postcard view was most likely snapped during World War I, evidenced by the patriotism of the window display. Charles Wessely stands in front of his tailor shop at 7501 Madison Street. The building was later home to Charles Hutter, also a tailor, as well as Ray's Service Shop (television repair), Dot's Discount Store, and currently the home of Krenek's Antiques. Note the wagon to the left of the building.

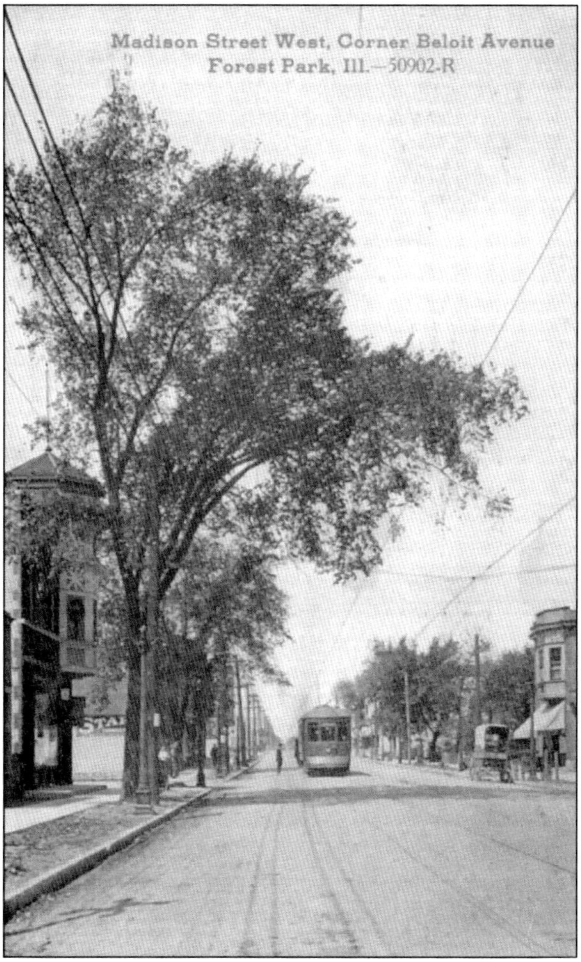

This postcard view shows a streetcar stopped at Madison Street and Beloit Avenue, near the drugstore operated by O. A. Fritz at 7446 Madison Street. Fritz sold the store to H. E. Semper, who occupied the location for many years. In 1948, Forest Park had seven pharmacies. The building at 7446 still stands and currently houses Old School Records.

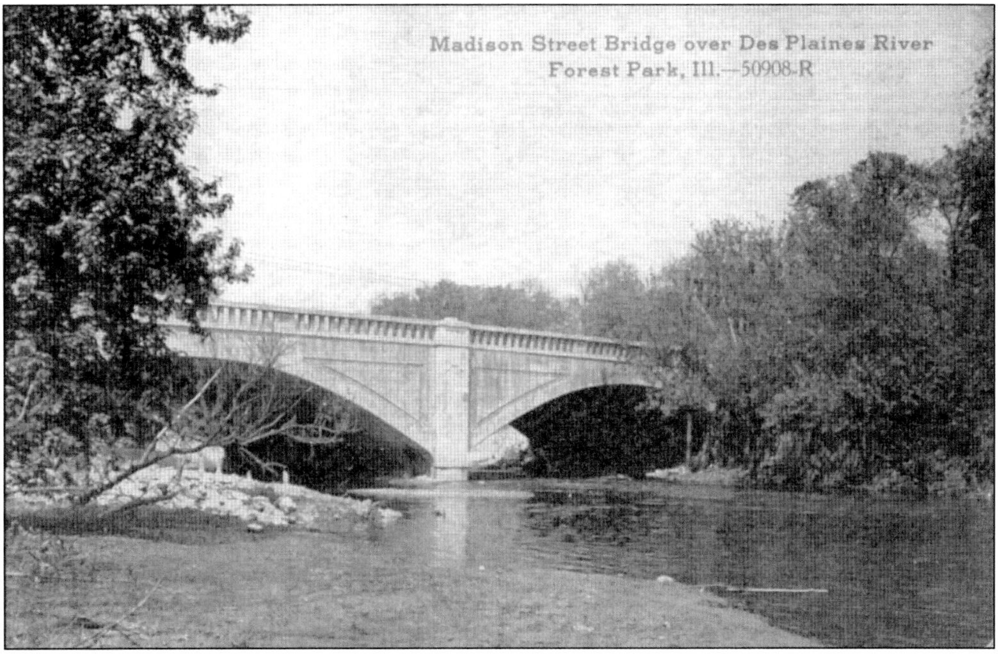

This 1918 postcard features the Madison Street Bridge over the Des Plaines River. The river was a favorite hangout for many local youngsters, which included Ernest Hemingway, who was known to raft on the river and search for Native American artifacts along the banks. This bridge served until 2002, when a new, taller bridge was built.

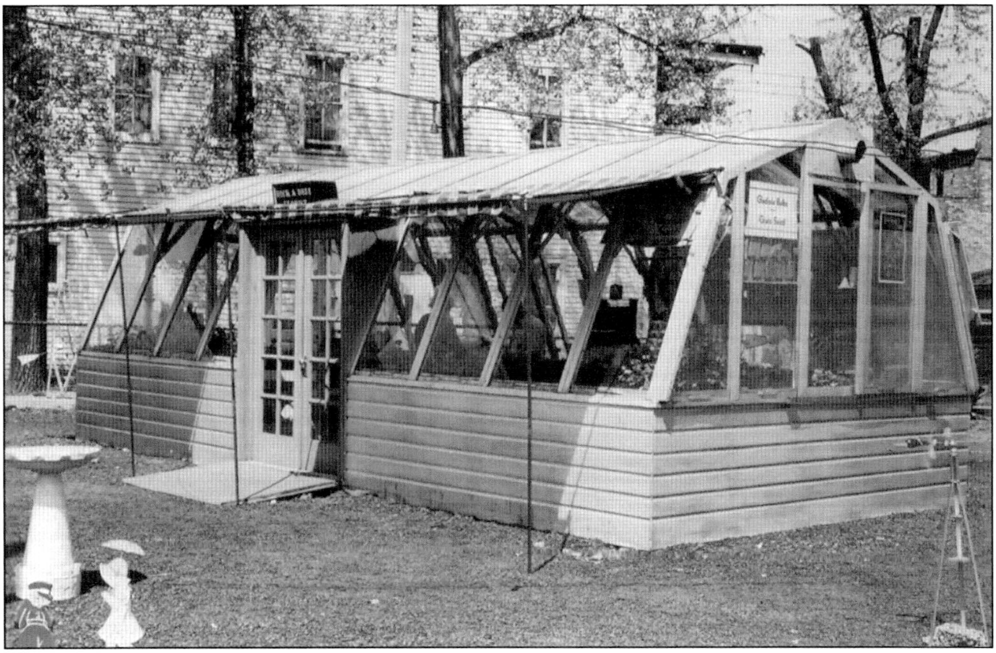

In the 1920s, Adele Quitsch and her four children, Gertrude, Earl, Myrtle, and Roy, began selling fresh flowers to mourners visiting the area's cemeteries. In the 1930s, Adele, along with her husband, Richard, built this small greenhouse at Harlem Avenue and Roosevelt Road and named it Dick and Dells. (Courtesy of Dixie Quitsch Paugh.)

Around 1927, Oldrich Herman stands in front of his store, located at 7246 Roosevelt Road. The faded name of Henry Boll can still be seen above the door. Boll ran the grocery for many years before selling it in 1919. The Peterson family operated a store in the building in the 1970s. The building was demolished in 1978 for a municipal parking lot. (Courtesy of Jeff Oswalt.)

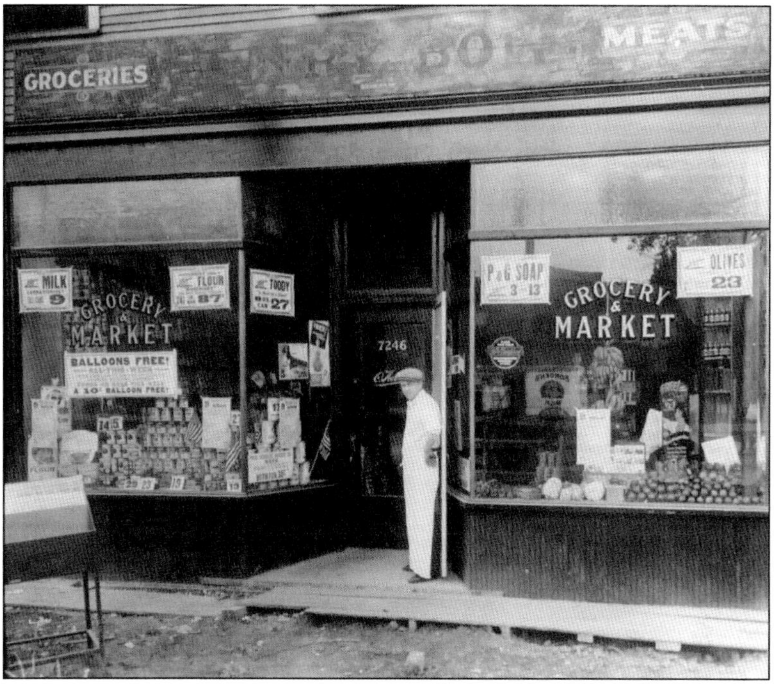

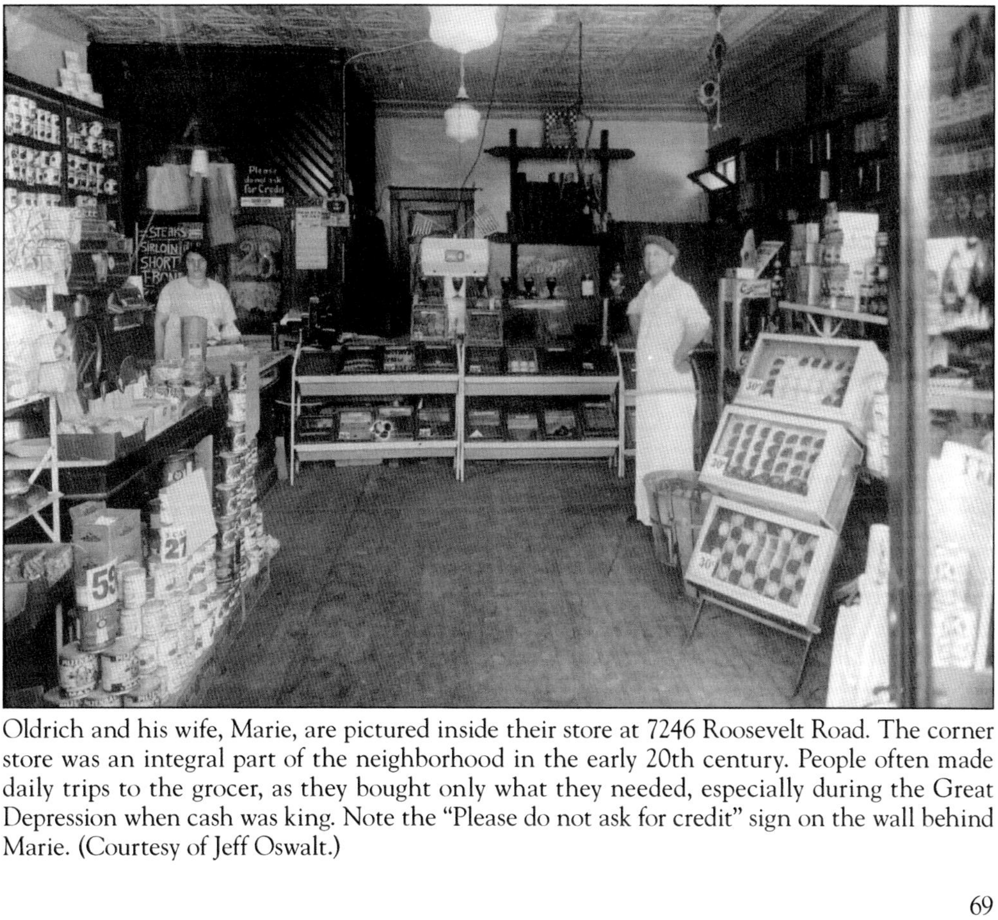

Oldrich and his wife, Marie, are pictured inside their store at 7246 Roosevelt Road. The corner store was an integral part of the neighborhood in the early 20th century. People often made daily trips to the grocer, as they bought only what they needed, especially during the Great Depression when cash was king. Note the "Please do not ask for credit" sign on the wall behind Marie. (Courtesy of Jeff Oswalt.)

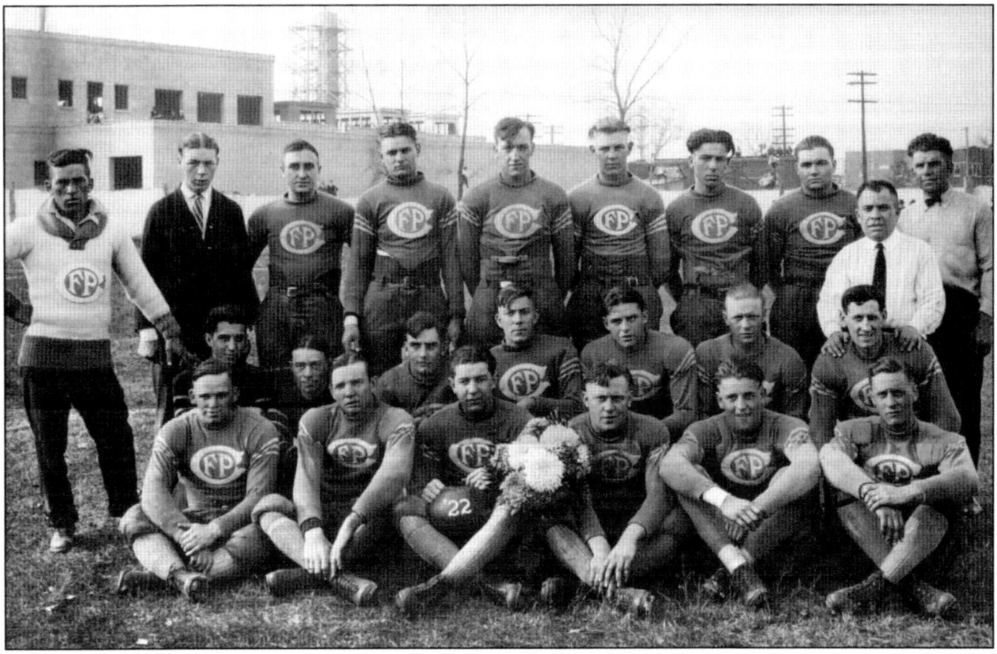

Football was a popular sport in 1922. Forest Park had a team in the Midwest League called the Forest Park Club. Herman Ziebell, a star player for Proviso, was among the team leaders. Games were played at Harrison Street and Harlem Avenue in front of large crowds. It is uncertain where this photograph was taken, but spectators can be seen on top of the buildings and in the trees. (Courtesy of the Mohr family.)

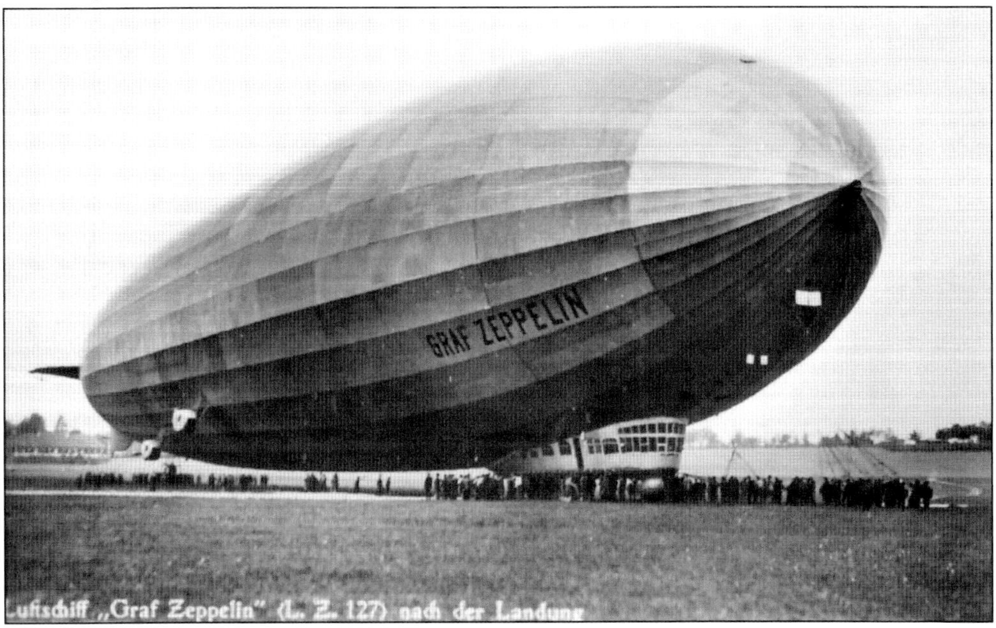

The German airship *Graf Zeppelin* passed over the south end of Forest Park on August 28, 1929, during its trip around the world. Thousands of people watched it float along its route at an altitude of between 1,200 and 2,500 feet. It traveled east from Broadview over the Checkerboard airfield, the Jewish cemeteries, and the golf course, just south of Roosevelt Road, on its way to the city.

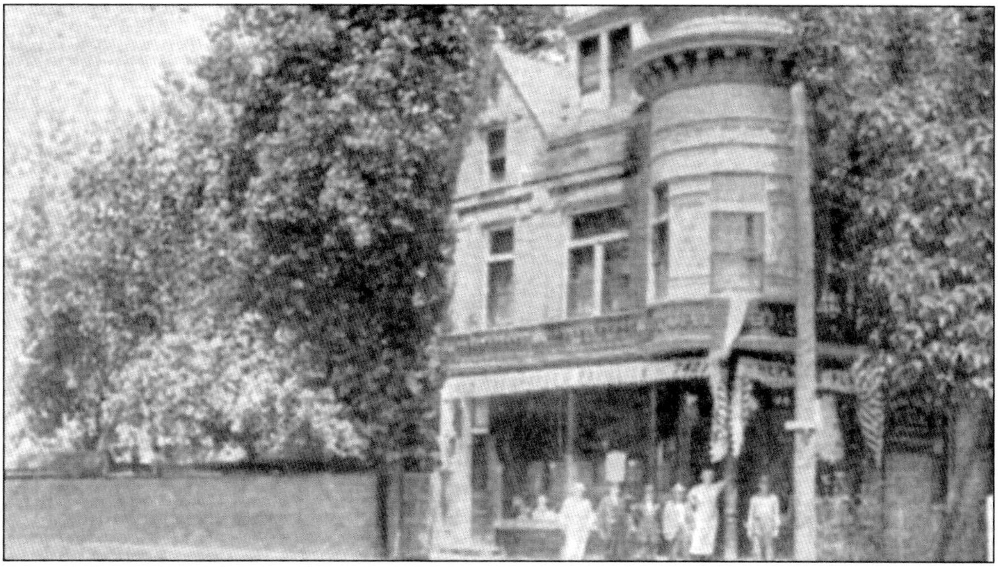

Roosevelt Road Gardens in the 1920s was located at 7427 Roosevelt Road. Advertised as being across from the Harlem Golf Club, the location was later home to the Lodge in the 1930s. A new structure at the location later housed the Torpedo Tap, which became the Armory Lounge in the 1950s and 1960s. It was also home to Nancy's Pizza and has been known as Andrea's for the past 30 years.

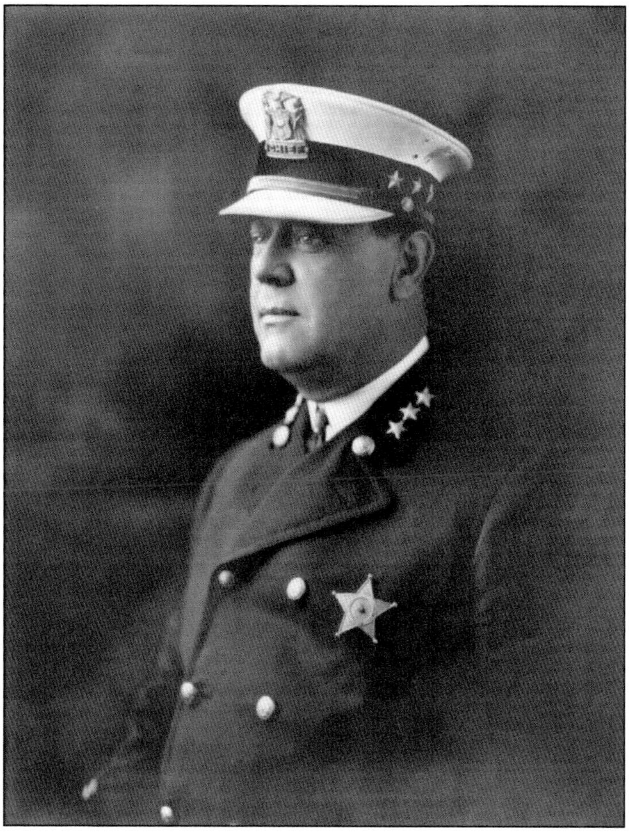

Seen here in his 1920s uniform, Police Chief Fred Licht would become the longest serving police chief in Forest Park history. Chief Licht joined the force in 1908 and had served over 30 years in the top position, retiring January 31, 1944. He and his wife, Mary, died in 1947 less than a week apart. (Courtesy of the Licht family.)

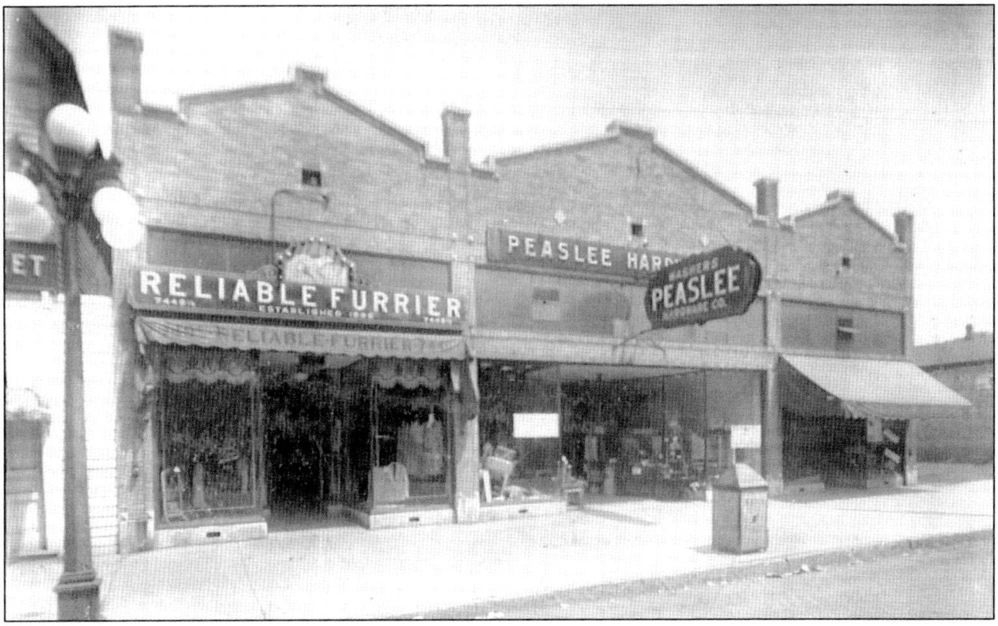

In 1926, Peaslee Hardware constructed a new building at 7449 Madison Street. The lot was purchased in 1925 for $45,000. They leased the left side to Reliable Furrier and the right side to the Streeter Shoe Company. Don Peaslee sold the business in 1987. The Schauer family, who had been in the hardware business for over 60 years, purchased the business in 1996. The business continues as Schauer's Hardware. (Courtesy of Wayne and Richard Schauer.)

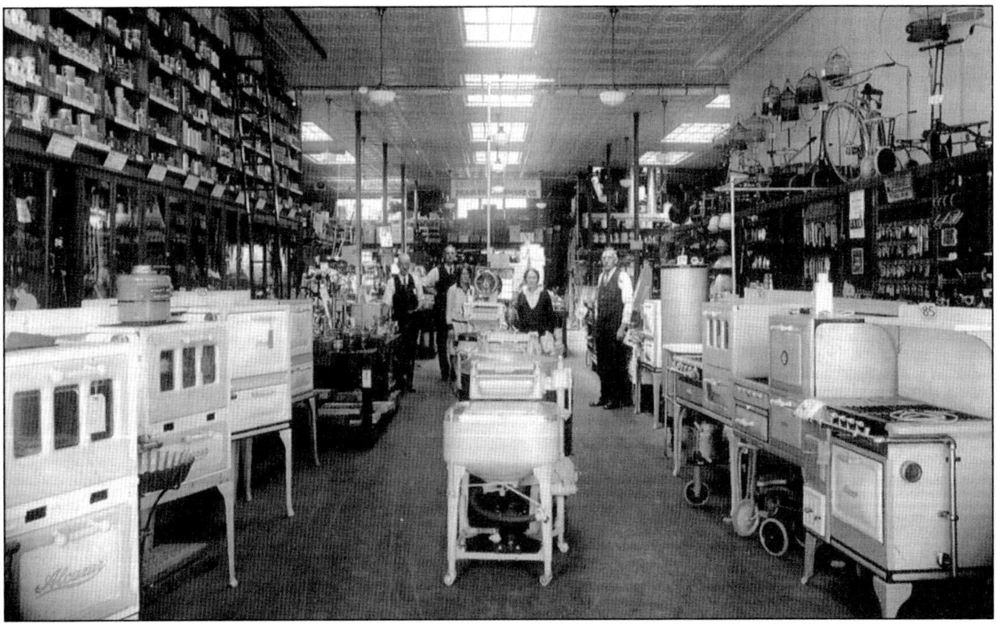

In 1926, one could buy a Alcazar range like the one seen on the left for $69.50 ($842 in 2009) or spend as little as 69¢ for a cast iron frying pan at Peaslee's Hardware Store. Herbert Peaslee (on right) is standing with some employees amidst the many household goods available at his store. They even offered a wide array of birdcages for the discerning pet lover. (Courtesy of Wayne and Richard Schauer.)

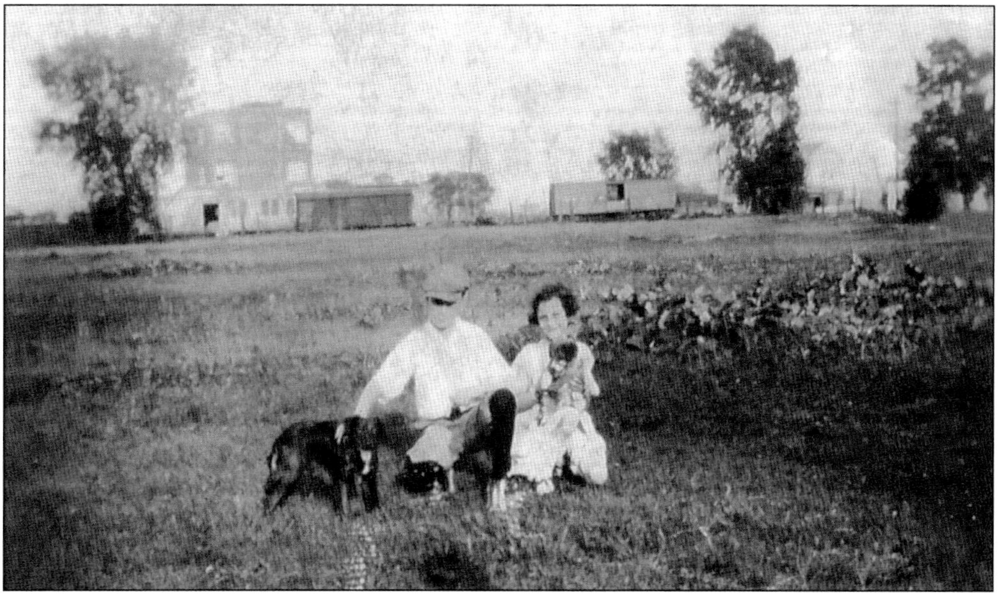

Many south side kids spent time looking for pieces of mica along the tracks behind 1525 Circle Avenue, the former home of the U.S. Mica Company. The building is seen in the background, as Elmer Licht and his sister, Loretta, pose with their dogs on the old golf course grounds in an undated photograph. (Courtesy of the Licht family.)

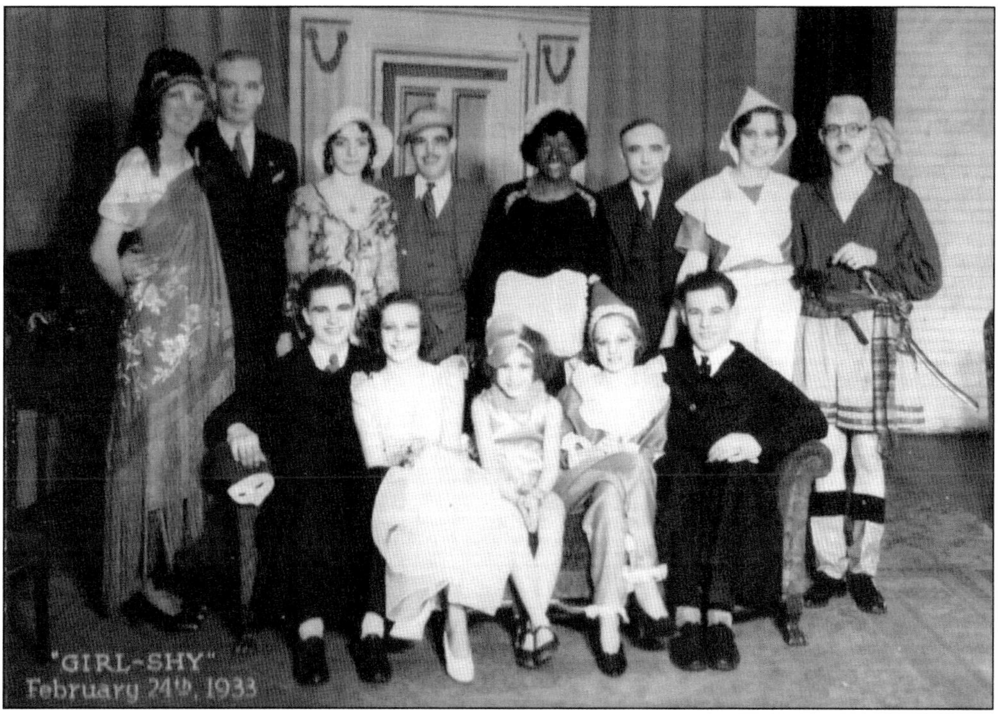

St. Peter's Church had an active drama club, which performed many plays over the years. This photograph was taken of the cast of *Girl Shy* in 1933. Among the actors were Loretta Licht, seated second from the left, and her brother, Elmer, standing second from the left. (Courtesy of the Licht family.)

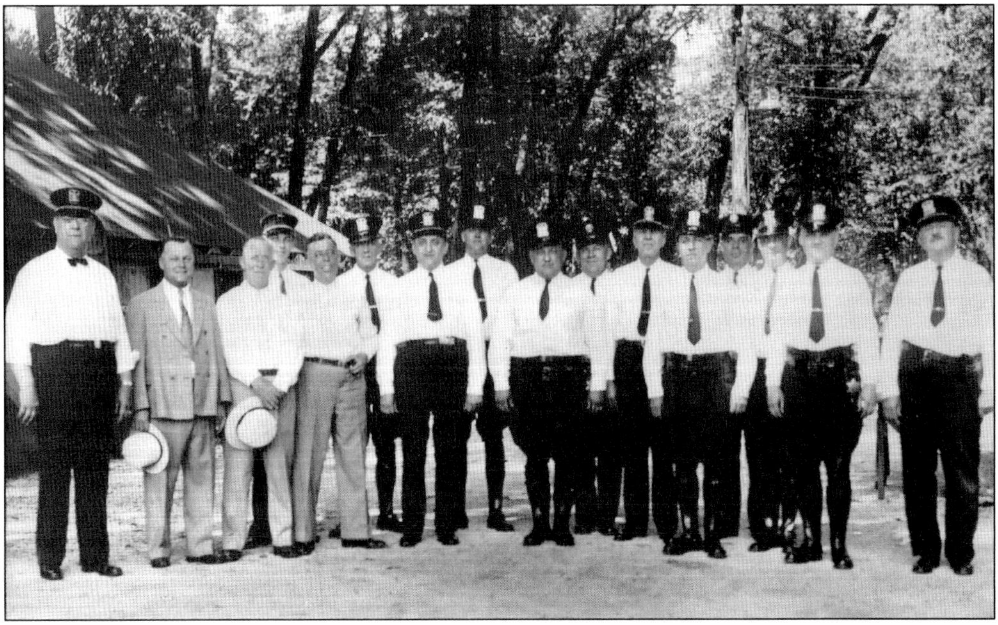

The picnic grove at Altenheim has hosted many picnics throughout the years. This June 23, 1934, photograph of the St. John's School picnic features a few local dignitaries. From left to right are Police Chief Fred Licht, Commissioner Louis Oswald, Mayor George Gold, Glen Cross, and Commissioner Otto Reich. Some of the officers seen here are Otto Henry Oldorff, Herman Ziebell, Harry Kroger, and Peter Mayer. (Courtesy of Jeff Oswalt.)

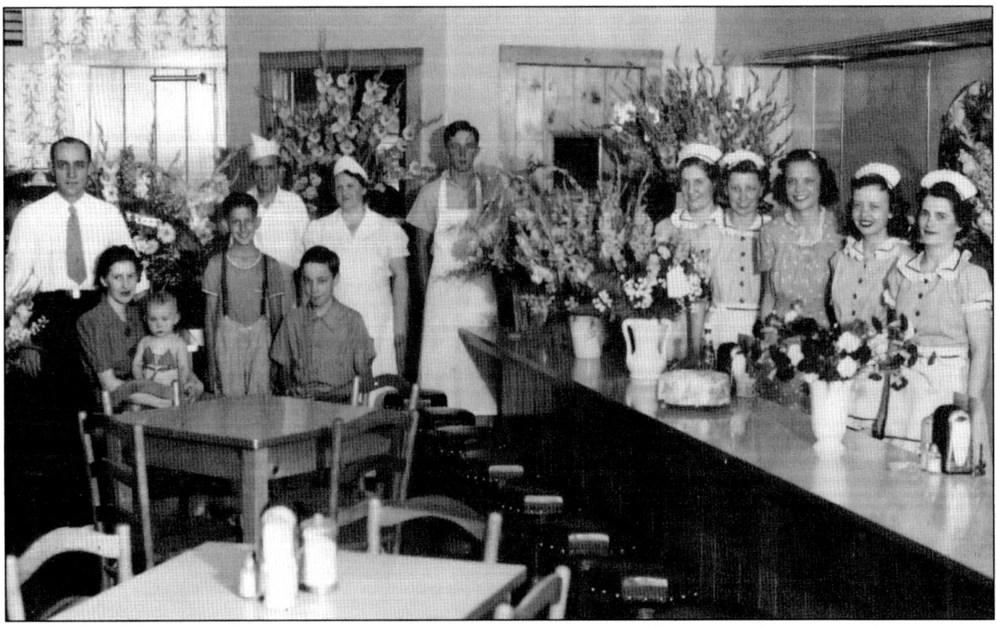

Homers Bale's restaurant started as a small sandwich shop named Wimpy's, but copyright concerns forced Homer to change the name. Homer is pictured at left around 1940 with his with his wife, Ann, who is holding baby Tony, Ann's brother Albert, and son Bill (right), along with the staff. Their daughter, Susan, born after this image was taken, would grow up to become a beloved teacher for 35 years at Betsy Ross. (Courtesy of Tony Bale.)

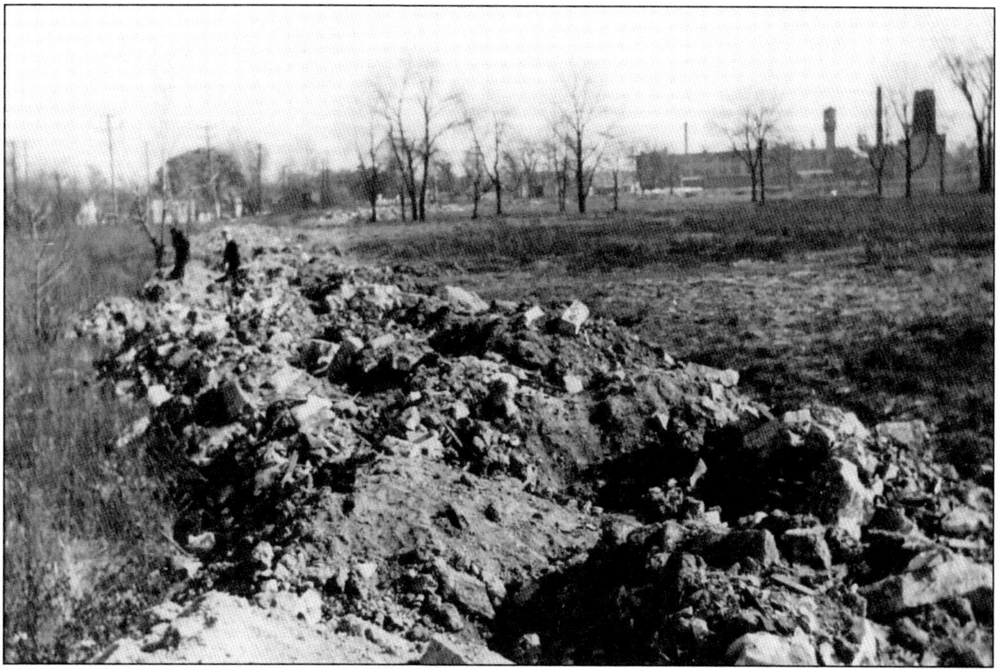

The land north of Harrison Street between Lathrop and Hannah Avenues was a desolate and foreboding landscape that was used by local children for ball games and for frog hunting. It was often referred to as "the swamp" prior to being purchased by the park district. The view in the above photograph is looking east from around Beloit Avenue. The Roos factory can be seen in the background. The land had once belonged to E. A. Cummings, who owned the land to the north and the south of the Great Western tracks, better known now as the Soo-Line tracks. (Courtesy of Park District of Forest Park.)

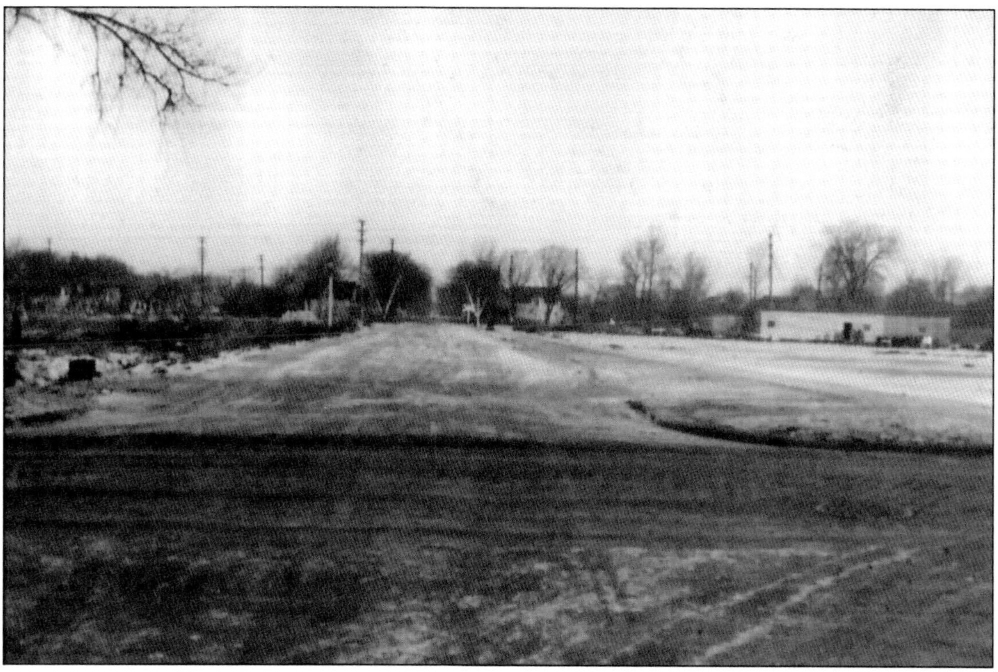

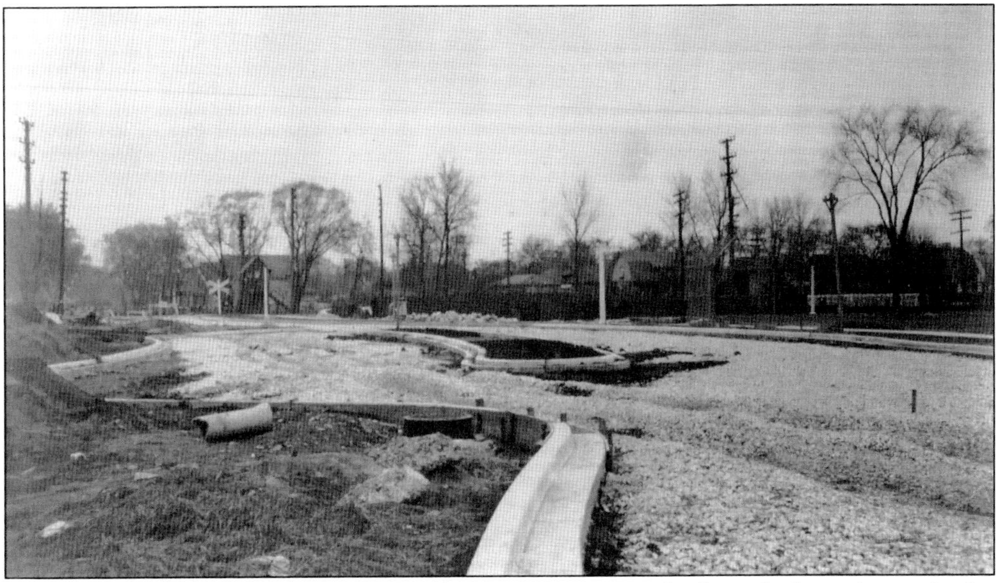

Before the expressway was constructed, Beloit Avenue ran straight through the park area. In the background, the crossing gates for the tracks used by the Chicago, Aurora, and Elgin (CA&E); Garfield Park metropolitan "L" line; and freight trains are visible. The curving islands were created to slow traffic passing through the park. (Courtesy of Park District of Forest Park.)

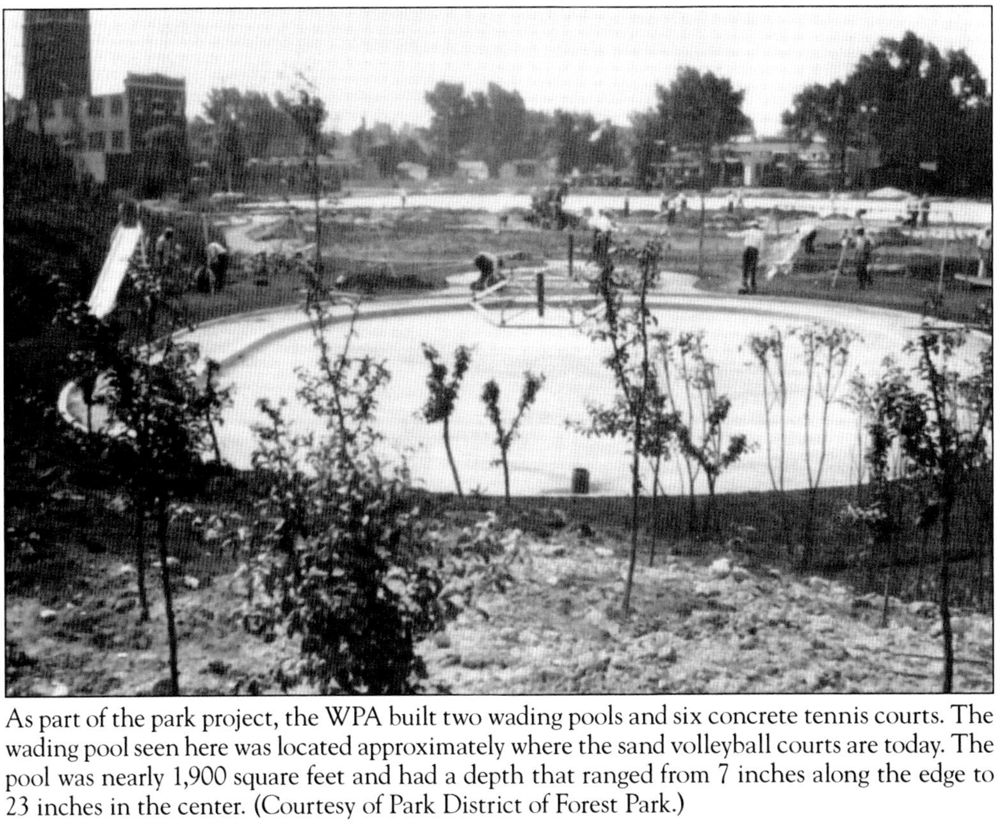

As part of the park project, the WPA built two wading pools and six concrete tennis courts. The wading pool seen here was located approximately where the sand volleyball courts are today. The pool was nearly 1,900 square feet and had a depth that ranged from 7 inches along the edge to 23 inches in the center. (Courtesy of Park District of Forest Park.)

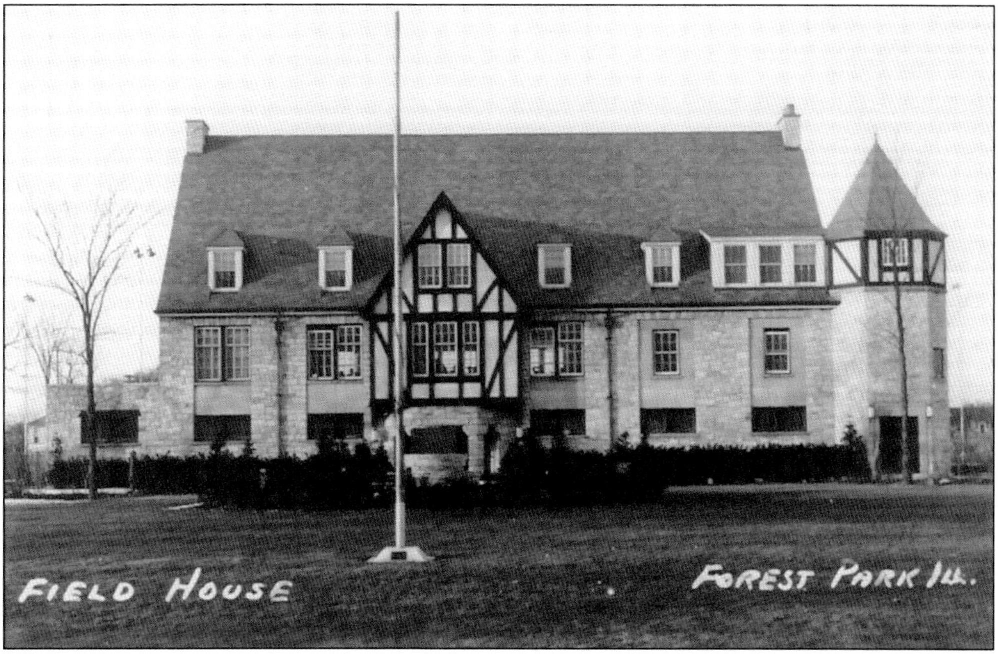

The Tudor-style Park District Administration Building, designed by local architect Carl J. Kastrup, was opened in May 1938. It received extensive remodeling in 1967 and again in 2008, which was when a new handicap-accessible entrance was added to the east side of the building. The photograph for this postcard was taken before the stonework around the windows was completed.

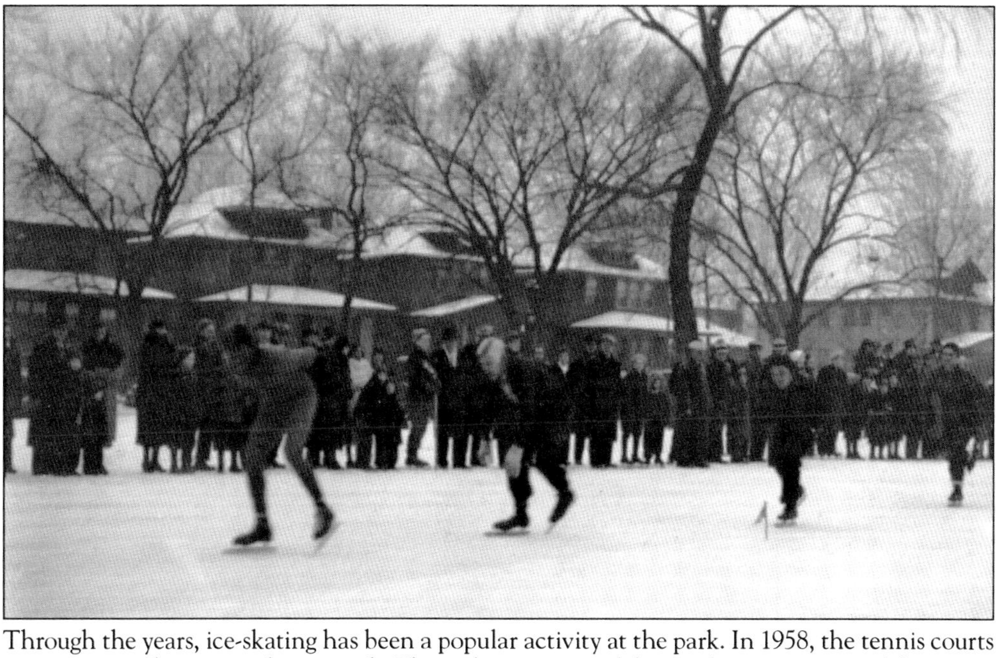

Through the years, ice-skating has been a popular activity at the park. In 1958, the tennis courts were converted to an ice-skating rink. The rink was removed during the renovations of the 1960s. The warming house was used for many years as a preschool and is still standing. Here is a group of skaters racing on what are now the baseball fields along Harrison Street near Lathrop Avenue. (Courtesy of Park District of Forest Park.)

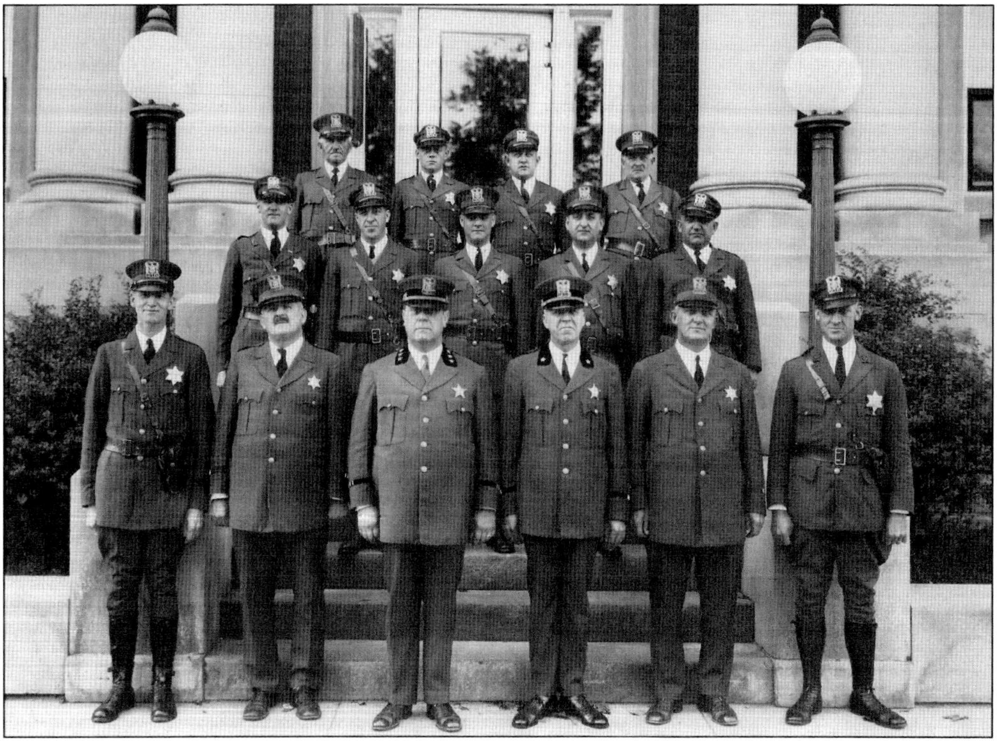

The Forest Park police force poses on the steps of the village hall around the 1930s. The department seems to have shrunk in size compared to earlier photographs. Perhaps fewer officers were needed after the closing of the amusement park. The department apparently had at least two motorcycle officers, judging by the boots worn by the men at either end of the first row. (Courtesy of Tim Shanahan.)

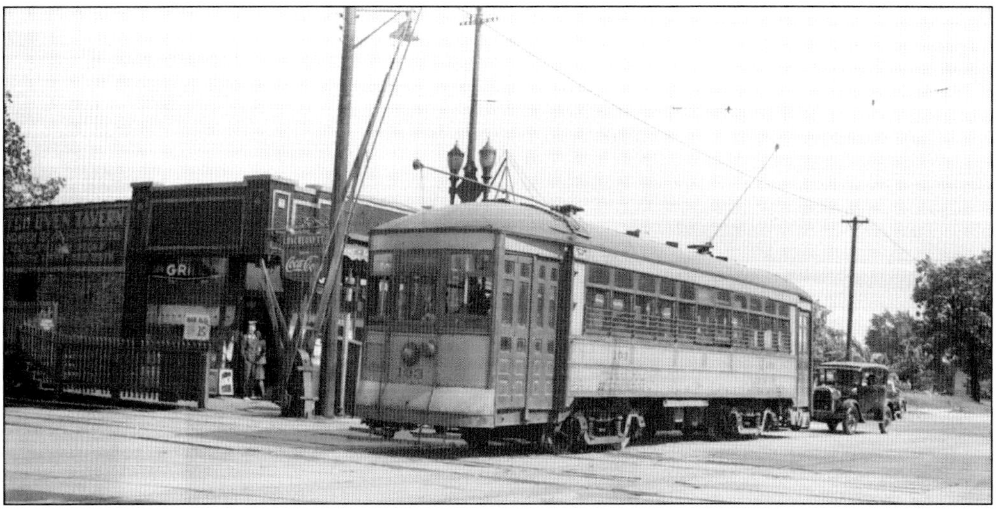

This photograph shows a streetcar heading north along Des Plaines Avenue, at the crossing of the CA&E and "L" tracks. In this photograph from June 1940, the Dutch Oven Tavern can be seen in the background. The building was constructed by the Theodosakis family in 1913. In those days, half of a fried spring chicken and fries totaled only 35¢. (Photograph by Fielding Kunecke; courtesy of Walter R. Keevil.)

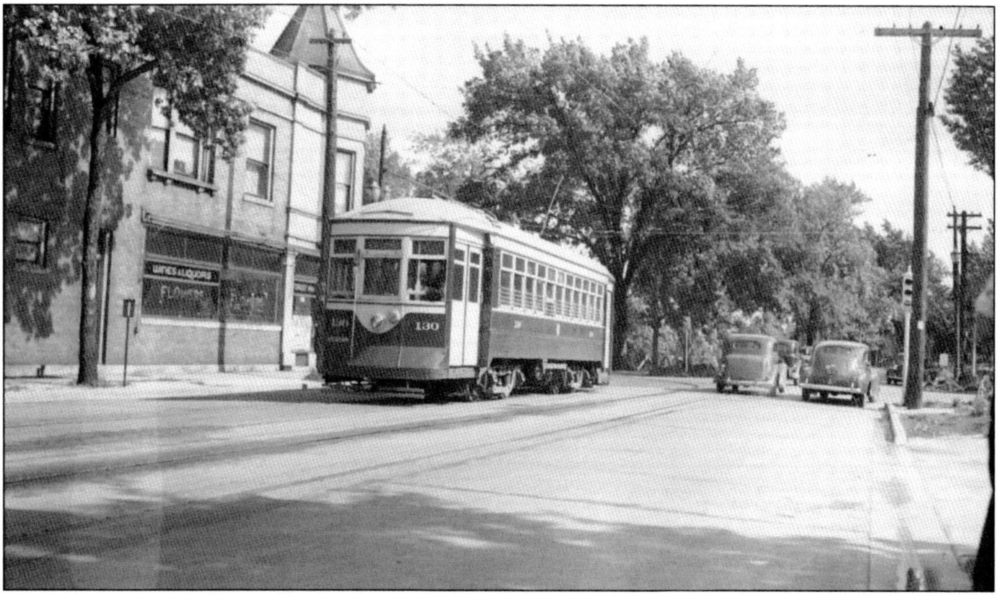

This photograph from June 1940 shows a streetcar just after making the turn from Roosevelt Road to northbound Des Plaines Avenue. The Forest Inn at 7749 Roosevelt Road was a high-class restaurant in the 1920s and boasted about its "highest paid cooks." It even featured an orchestra for entertainment at dinnertime. The corner is now home to a 7-Eleven. (Photograph by Fielding Kunecke; courtesy of Walter R. Keevil.)

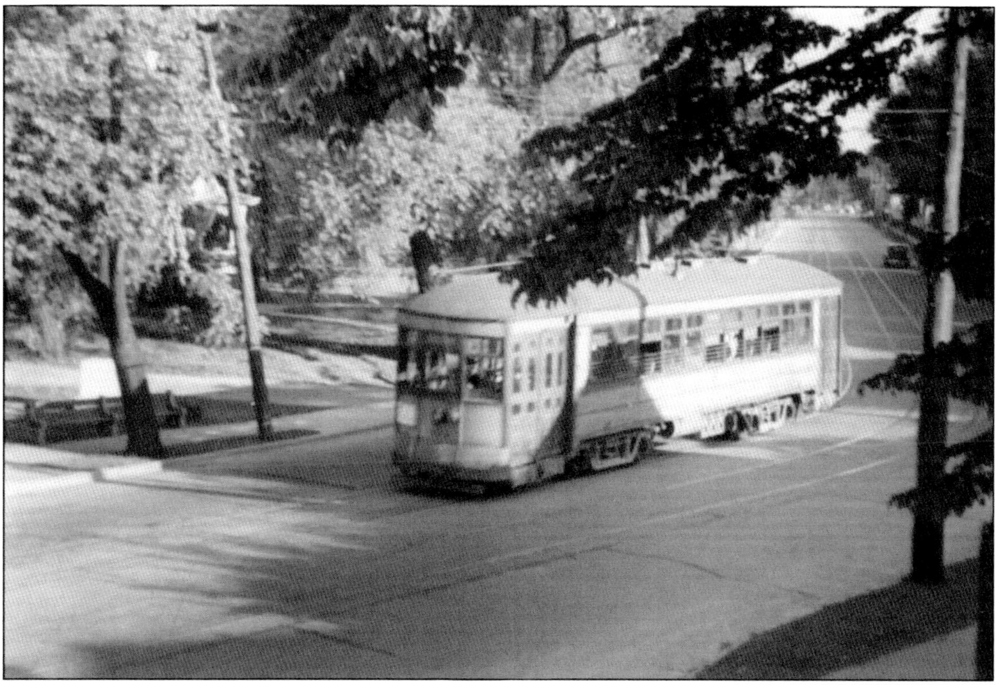

This photograph showing a streetcar navigating the infamous curve in Des Plaines Avenue was taken from the entrance to Forest Home Cemetery. The Kistenbroker mansion is barely visible behind the tree and the telephone pole on the left. The curve is reputed to follow an early Native American trail. (Courtesy of the Kistenbroker family.)

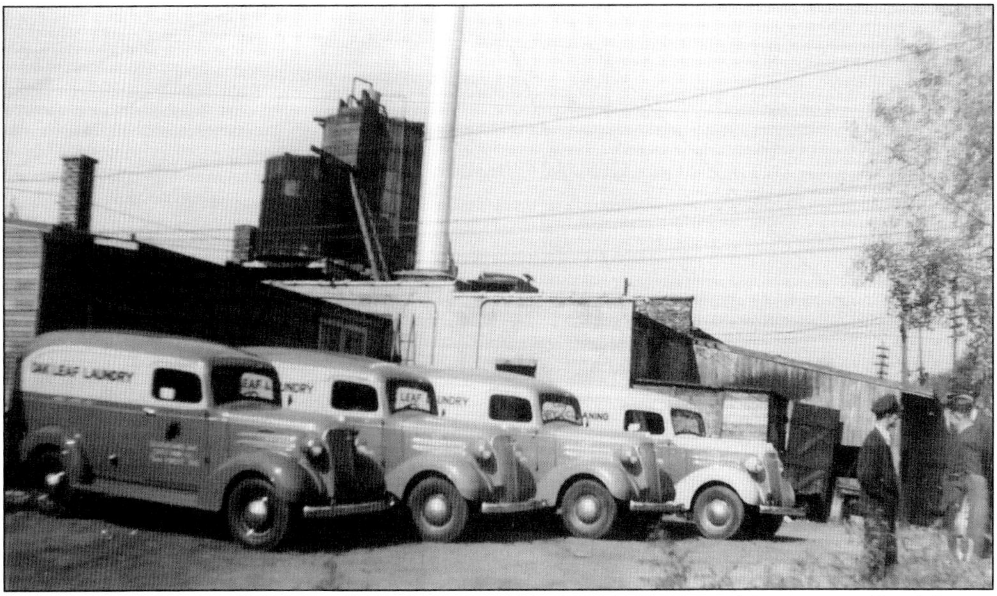

The Oak Leaf Cleaners had just about run out of room at their original location on Des Plaines Avenue, when this photograph was taken behind the shop. In 1938, they moved into a new home at Harrison Street and Hannah Avenue. The Theodosakis Building on the 700 block of Des Plaines Avenue would be demolished in 1957 to make room for the expressway. (Courtesy of the Reda family.)

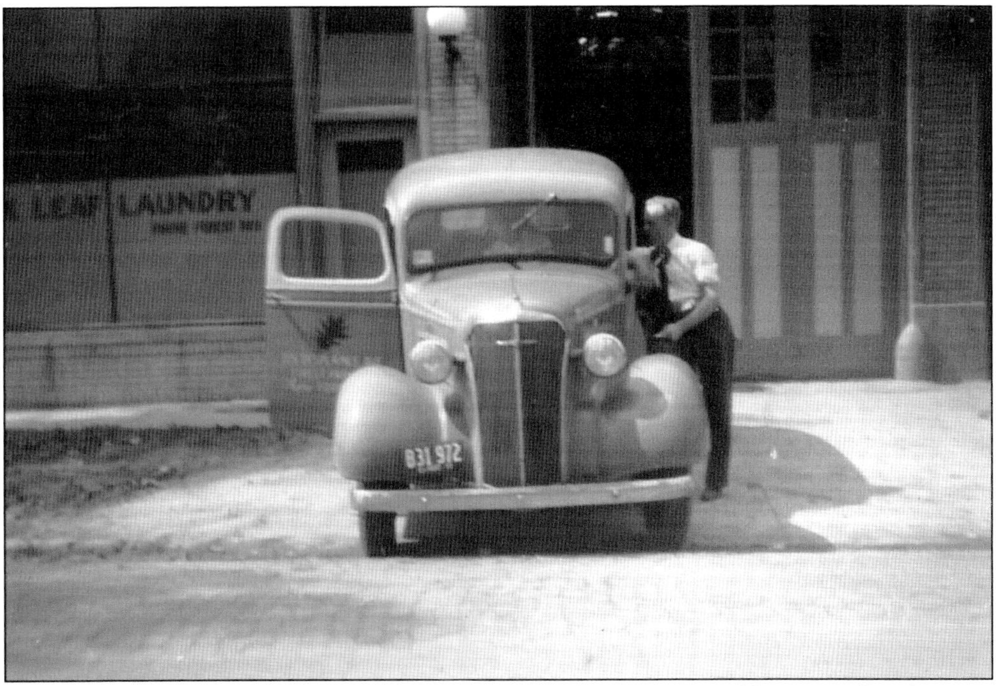

In this photograph, the laundry truck still displays a Des Plaines Avenue address even though owner Al Reda had moved the Oak Leaf Cleaners to 805 Hannah Avenue in 1938. Reda would later move the business to a new building he constructed in 1952 on Harrison Street. The 805 Hannah Avenue building is currently home to H and R Auto Repair. (Courtesy of the Reda family.)

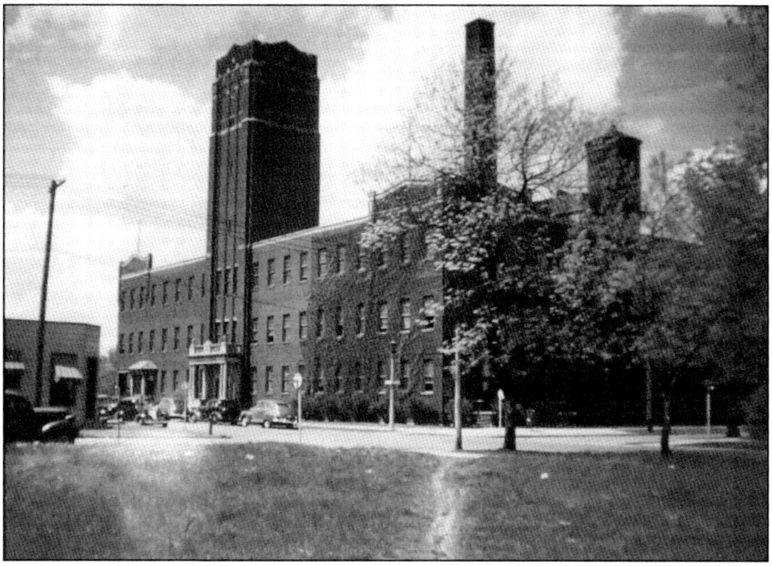

The Ed Roos Building at 7329 Harrison opened in 1918 and is seen here during its peak in the 1930s. The Roos family sold the company in 1951, and it ceased operating in 1953. The Fisher Pen Company called the building home during the 1960s. (Courtesy of Gail Roos and Edward Roos IV.)

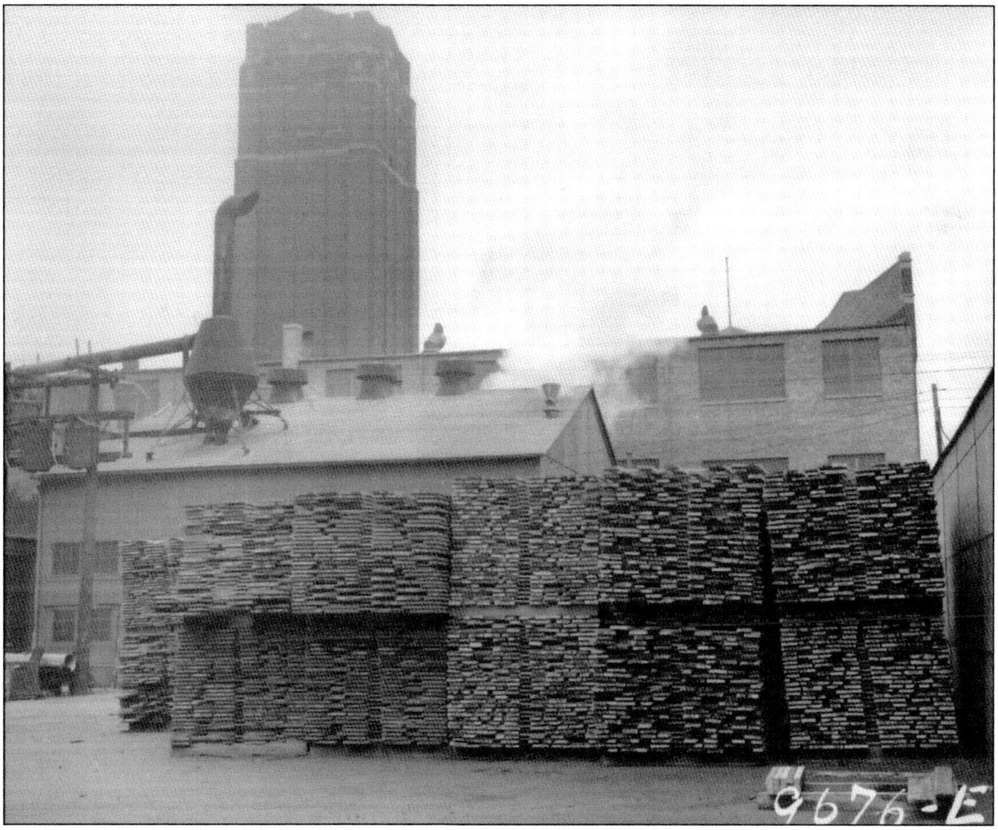

This photograph shows the backside of the Roos factory. During the peak years, the company would use three million feet of cedar per year. The proximity of the factory to the railroad tracks allowed for easy shipping and receiving. The landmark tower, added during the 1929 building additions, was not merely a decorative feature but actually hid the water tanks that were needed for the sprinkler system. (Courtesy of Gail Roos and Edward Roos IV.)

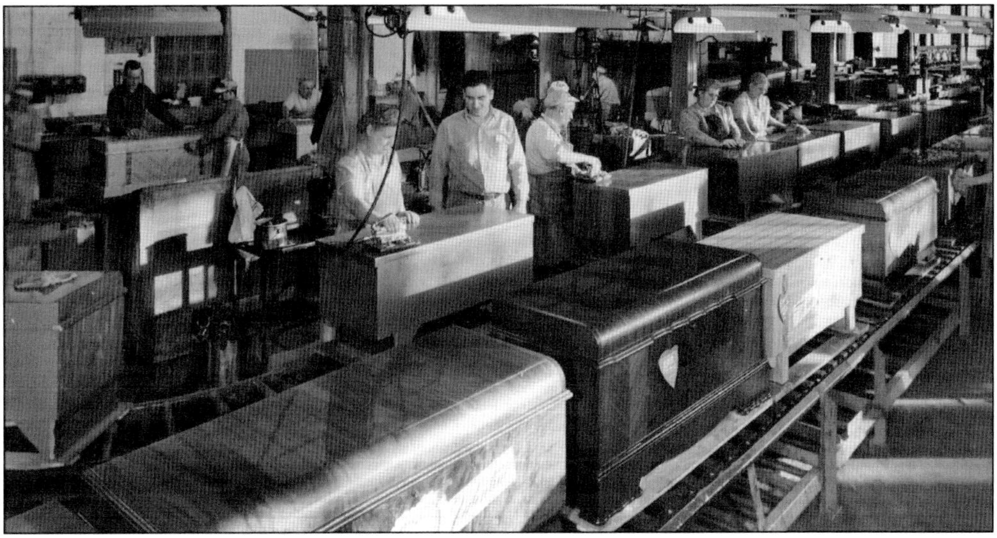

The Roos company employed between 250 to 400 employees, of whom 20 to 30 percent were women. The plant was capable of producing up to 200 chests per day of various styles. Production ceased in 1953, but the chests live on in homes throughout the country. (Courtesy of Gail Roos and Edward Roos IV.)

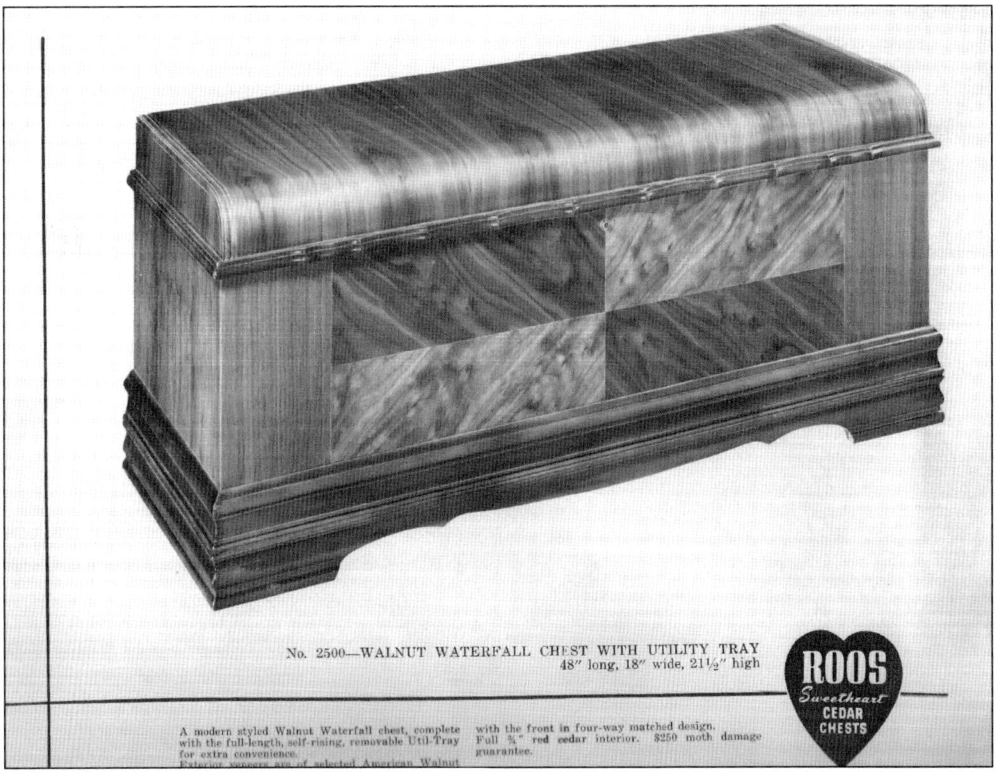

The fine craftsmanship, attention to detail, and the patented "Sealtite lid" are part of what set the Roos cedar chests apart from the crowd. This 1930s catalogue page shows the very popular waterfall design. It was so named because the graceful curve of the lid and the grain of the wood gave the appearance of flowing water. (Courtesy of Gail Roos and Edward Roos IV.)

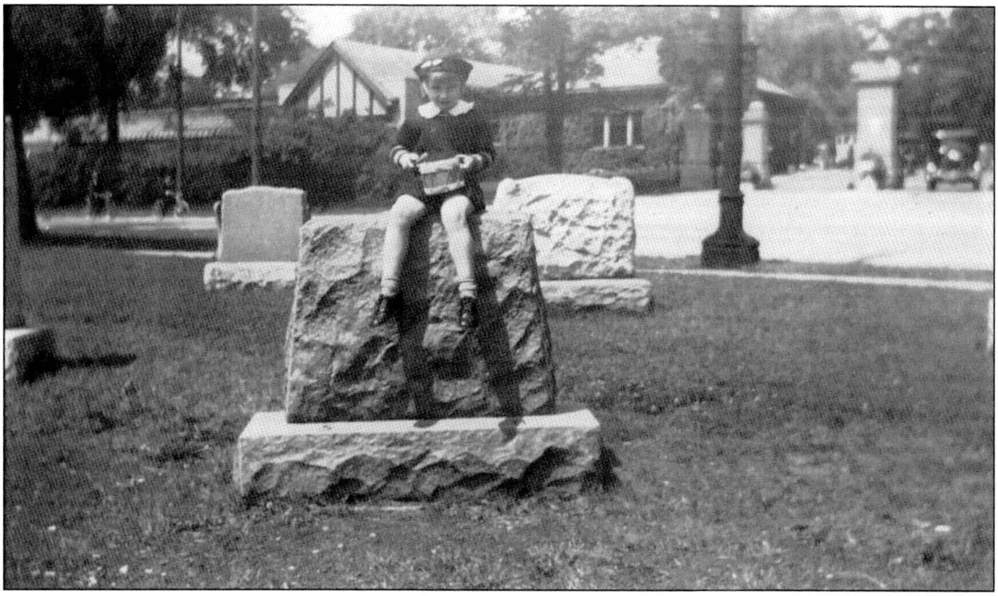

Although this appears to be a photograph of a little girl playing in a graveyard, Joan Kistenbroker is actually sitting atop a tombstone at the family's monument company. The business was located directly across the street from the Forest Home Cemetery entrance at 1004 Des Plaines Avenue. (Courtesy of the Kistenbroker family.)

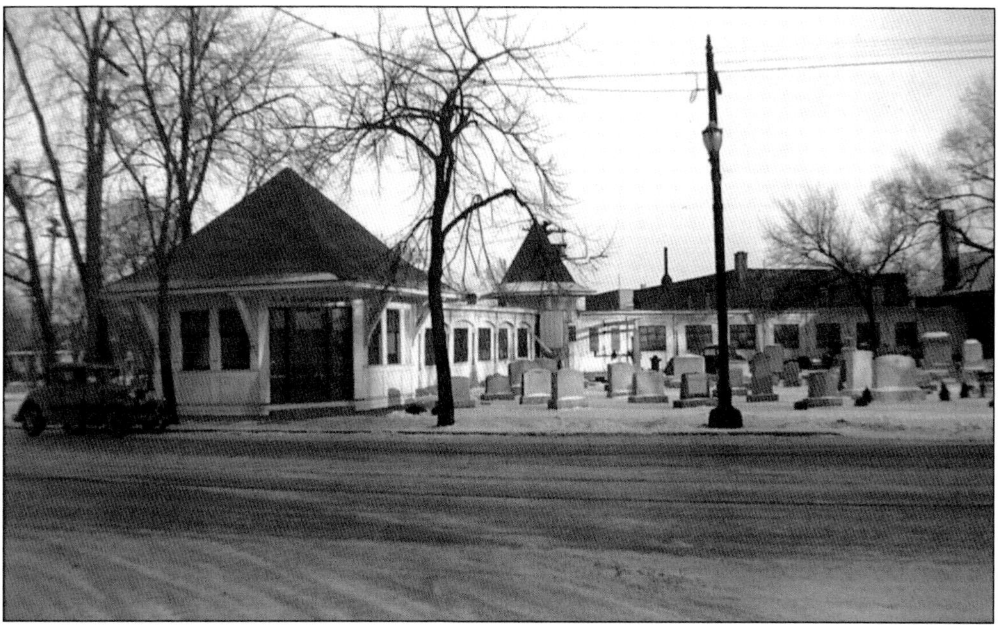

The Kistenbroker Monument Company at 1004 Des Plaines Avenue, which opened in 1881, was one of many monument companies in Forest Park. The Kistenbroker Monument Company, along with Troost, Otto Reich, S. Berliner, Soroka, and others, provided some of the truly artistic and fascinating monuments that populate the cemeteries. S. Berliner was the last to close its doors when they merged with the Peter Troost Monument Company, located in Hillside, in 1990. (Courtesy of the Kistenbroker family.)

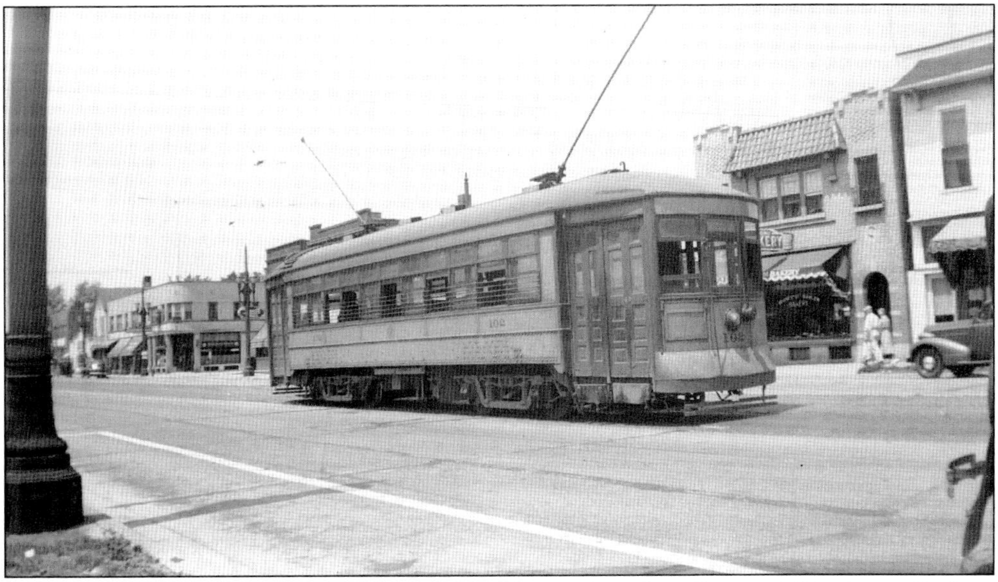

This July 6, 1940, photograph shows streetcar No. 102 traveling along Roosevelt Road, near Harlem, as it passes the Roosevelt Road and Harlem Bakery at 7209 Roosevelt Road. The bakery would later be the longtime home of Dewey's Sandwich Shop and is the current home of the Final Cut hair salon. (Photograph by Fielding Kunecke; courtesy of Walter R. Keevil.)

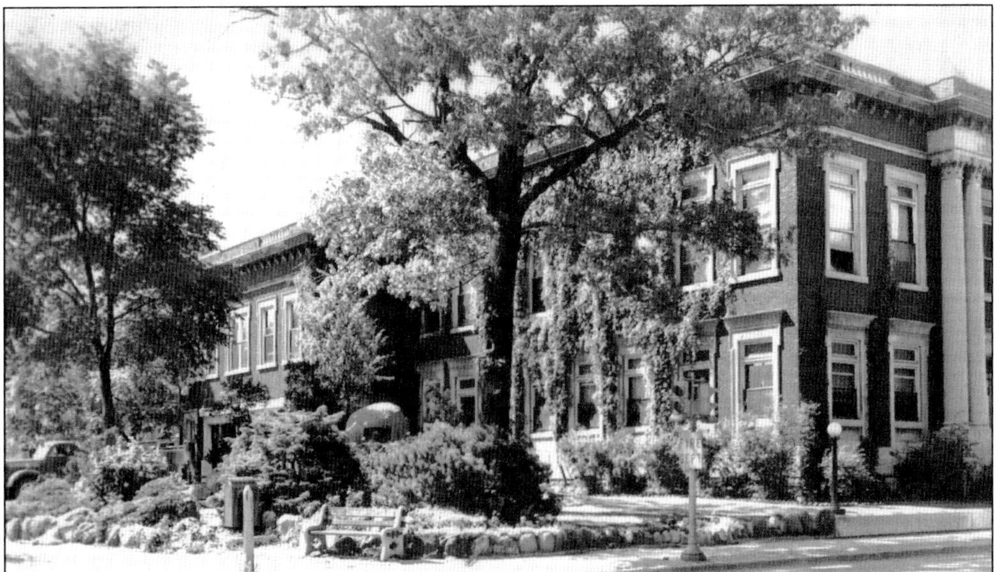

A stately oak flanks the ivy-covered walls of the village hall in the late 1930s or early 1940s. The village had a sleepy, small-town charm during those days. Note the streetcar tracks running down Des Plaines Avenue. The large boulder near the oak is a war memorial nestled in a serenely landscaped setting designed by Svend Lollesgard. (Courtesy of Jeff Oswalt.)

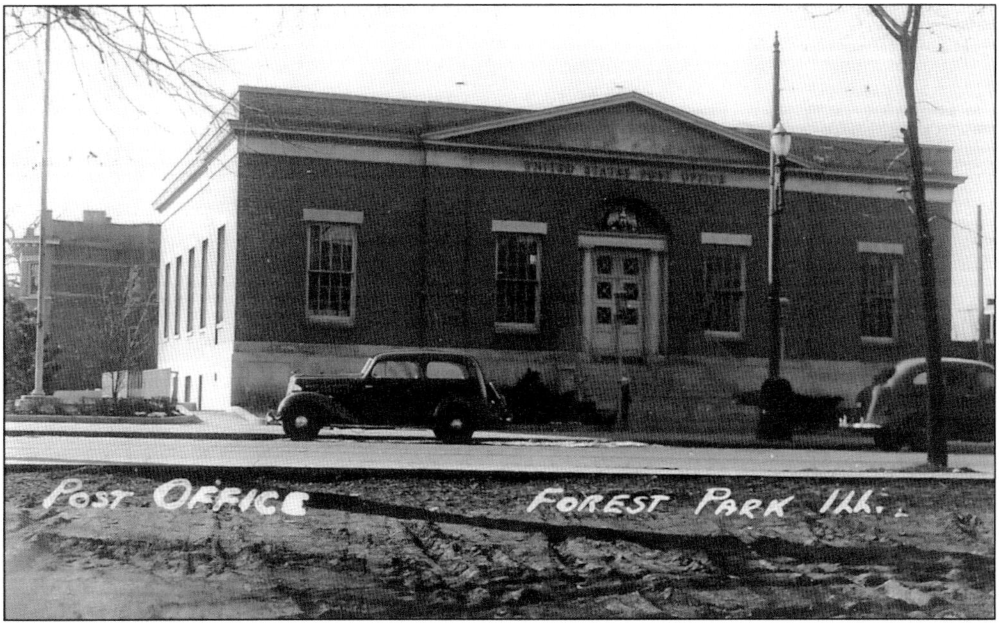

The post office at 417 Des Plaines Avenue, shown in this 1940s-era postcard, opened in 1938, replacing a much smaller post office located at 314 Circle Avenue. Forest Park did not get its own post office until 1922, although it was the main reason for changing the name from Harlem. The first was housed in the old Wolf brothers building on Madison Street. The building on Circle Avenue was constructed in 1927 and is still standing. (Courtesy of Tom Krenek.)

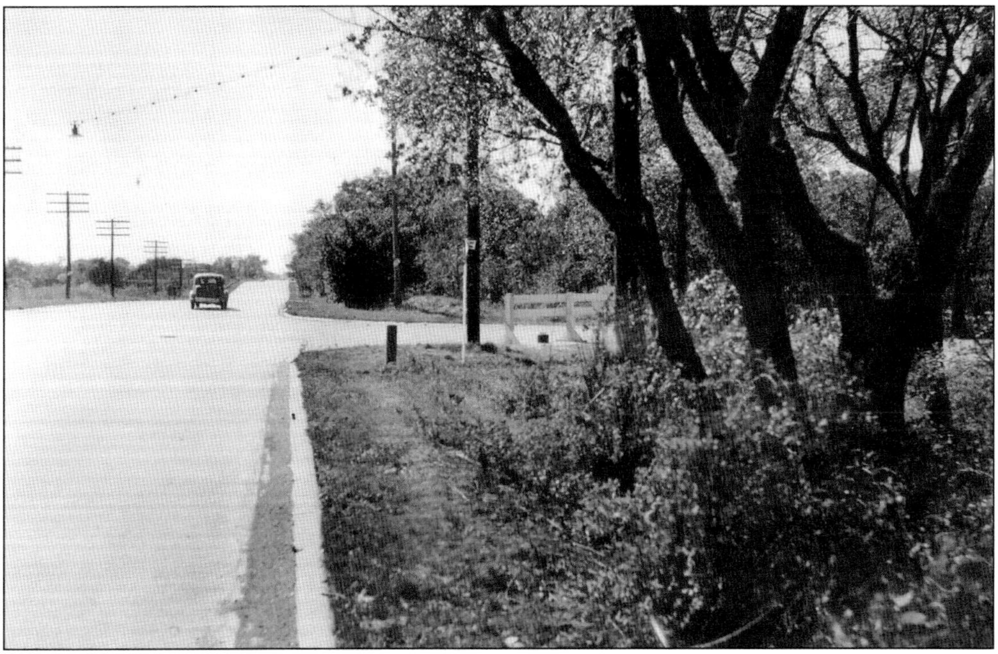

The corner of Cermak Road (Twenty-second Street) and Des Plaines Avenue looked rather desolate in this 1940s photograph. A substantial increase in traffic is not the only change. In 2006, Woodlawn Cemetery opened the 1,200-square foot Woodlawn Funeral Home and Memorial Park on the Northeast Corner. (Courtesy of Woodlawn Cemetery.)

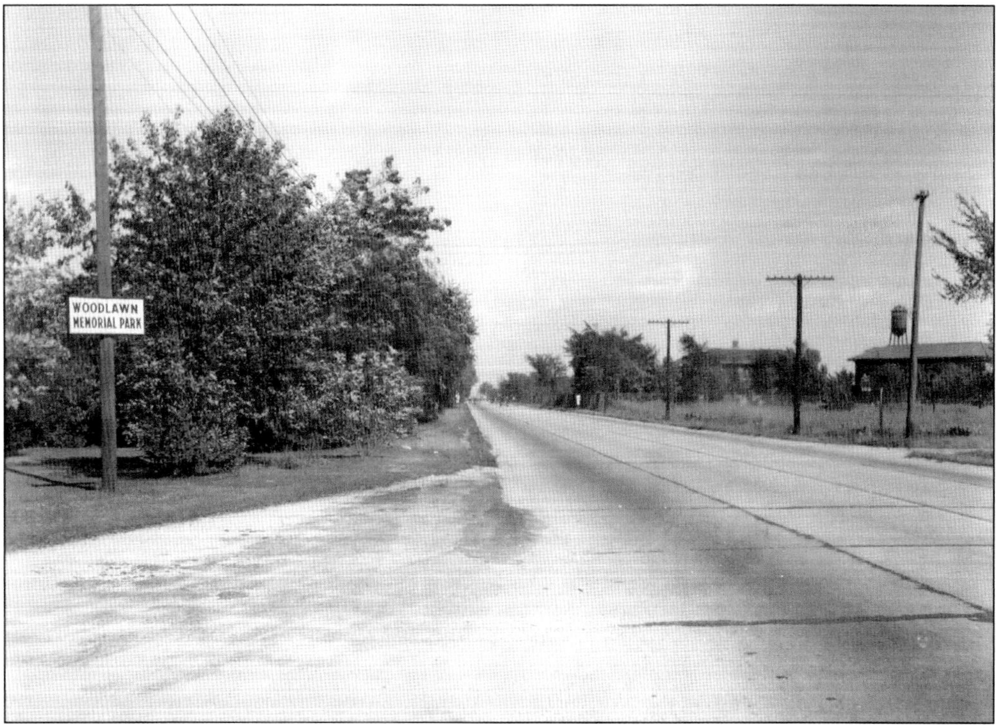

An undated photograph from the 1940s shows the view looking east on Twenty-second Street from the Woodlawn entrance. On the south side of the street can be seen the buildings that once housed the Cook County School for Boys until 1931; it later became a tuberculosis sanitarium. (Courtesy of Woodlawn Cemetery.)

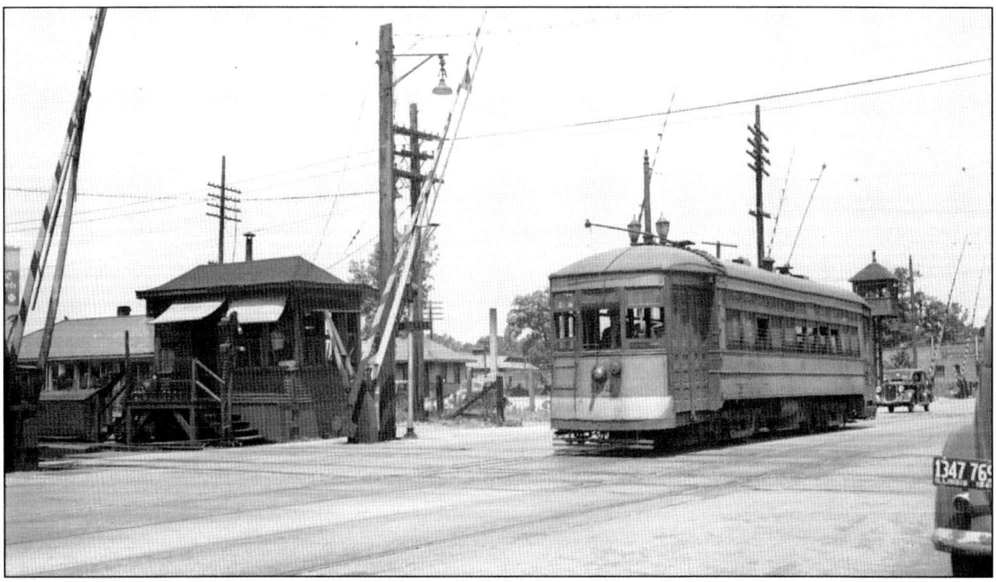

Before the expressway was built, Des Plaines Avenue was flat. One can imagine the traffic delays with so many crossings. The CA&E, "L", Great Western, and the Soo-Line all crossed Des Plaines Avenue, as seen in this photograph looking northwest from the 700 block. (Photograph by Frank Krejcik; courtesy of Walter R. Keevil.)

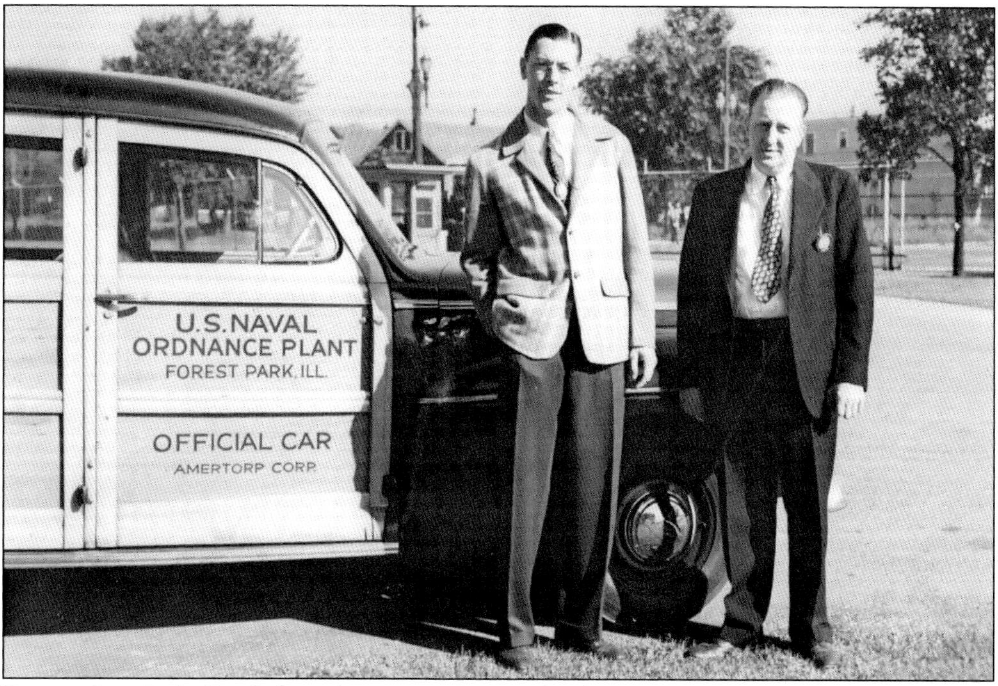

Two unidentified officials from Amertorp, the naval ordnance plant, pose alongside the official car in front of the office, with Roosevelt Road in the background. The plant opened on October 28, 1942, as a subsidiary of American National Can Company. An aircraft engine plant had originally been targeted for the site, but the deal collapsed when the landowners could not agree on a price. (Courtesy of Village of Forest Park.)

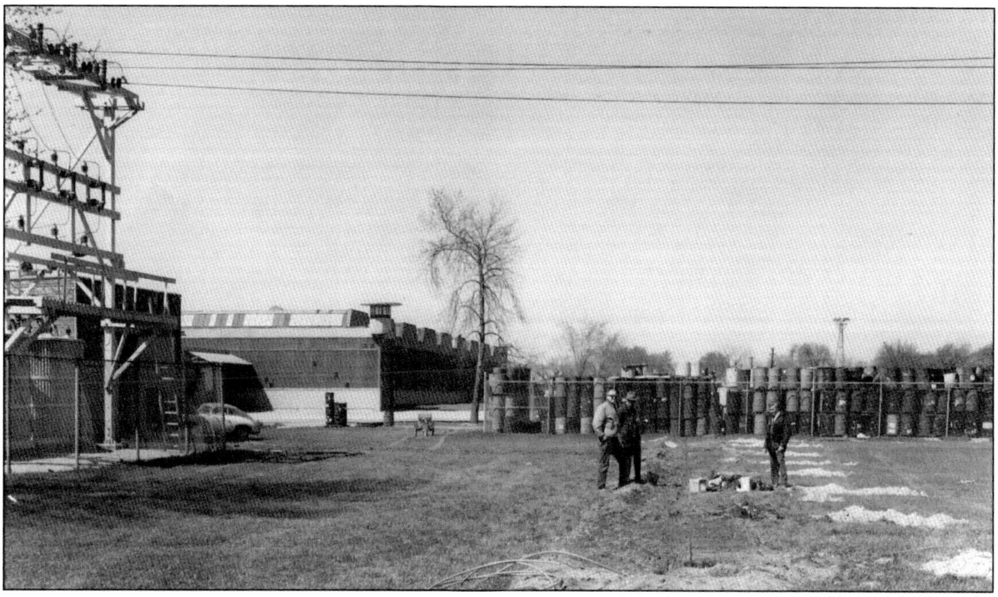

The tall tree in the center of the photograph is one of the sole survivors from the days of the old golf course. The main factory building, designed by noted architect Albert Kahn, had guard towers located at each corner of the building. The towers were removed when the structure was converted into the Forest Park Mall in the early 1980s. (Courtesy of Village of Forest Park.)

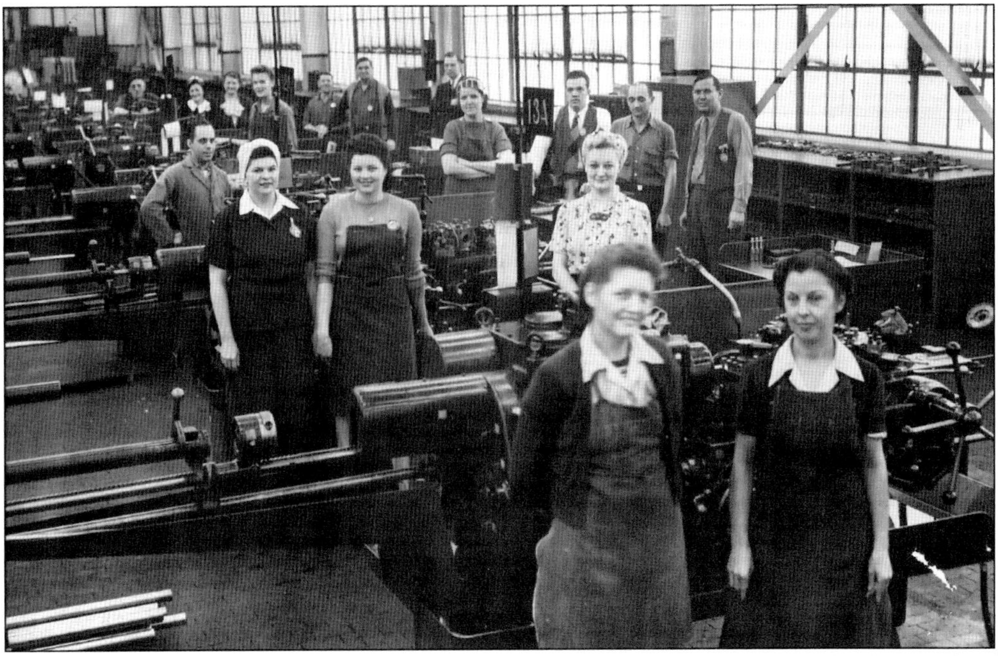

"Rosie the Riveter" was a popular song during World War II that paid tribute to the thousands of women who worked in the factories during the war. The Amertorp factory employed hundreds of "Rosies," as one-third of the workers were women. They worked eight-hour shifts, and Christmas Day was the only day the plant was closed. (Courtesy of Village of Forest Park.)

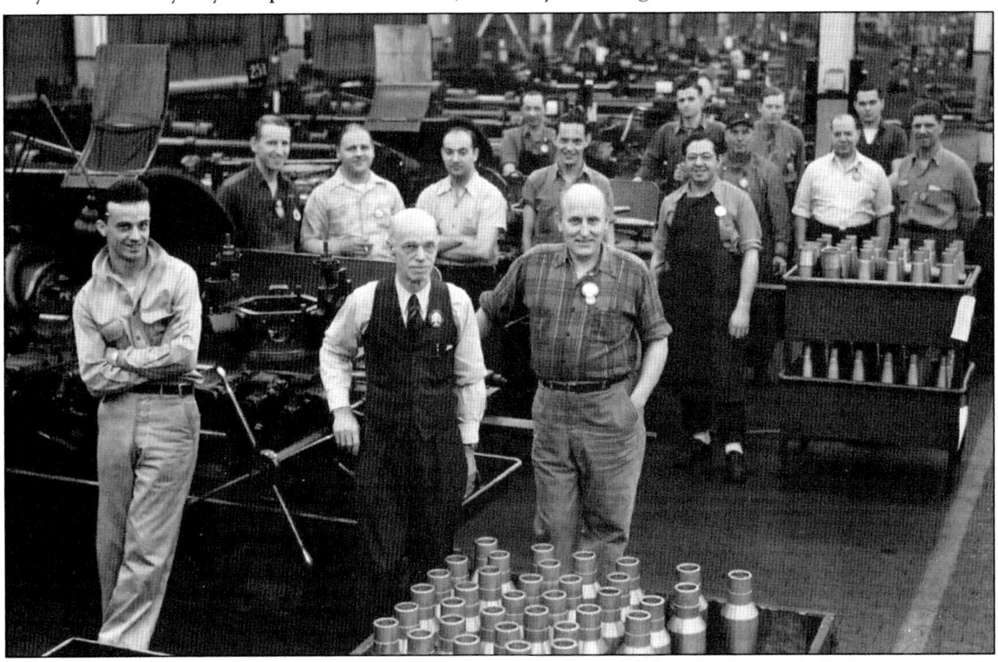

The Amertorp plant offered a decent paying job to many of the locals. An unskilled worker could earn 75¢ per hour (approximately $10 per hour in 2009), while a skilled craftsman could earn double that amount. Many of the workers were older or otherwise deemed unable to serve in the armed forces. (Courtesy of Village of Forest Park.)

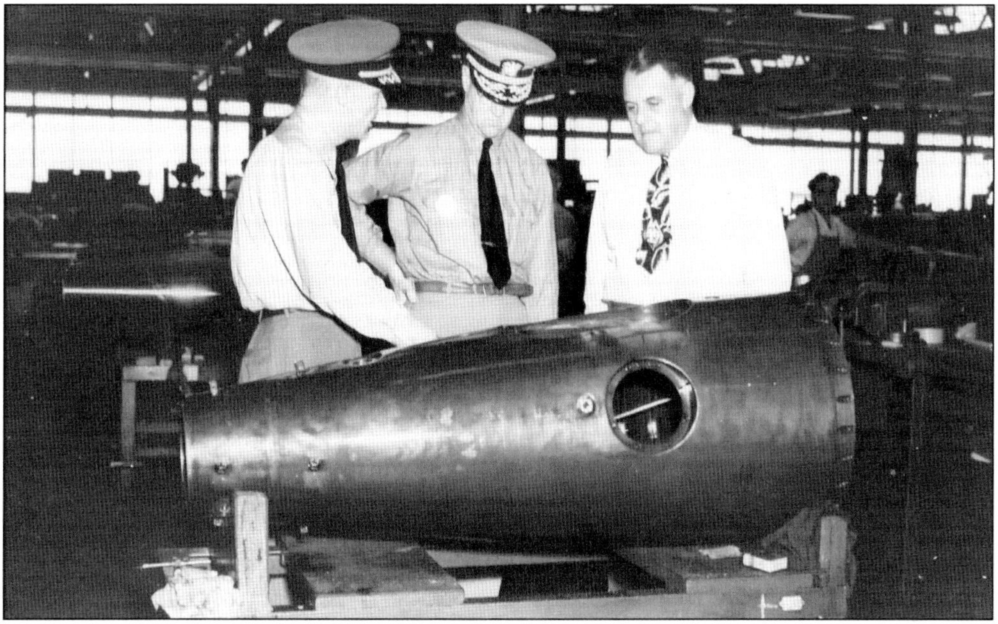

Two naval officers and a civilian examine the rear section of a torpedo. The plant manufactured over 8,000 torpedoes during World War II and 17,523 in total. Each torpedo contained over 5,000 individual parts. Production continued throughout the Korean and Vietnam Wars and included over 146,000 rockets and 5,762,000 artillery fuses. The last torpedo was manufactured in 1971. (Courtesy of Village of Forest Park.)

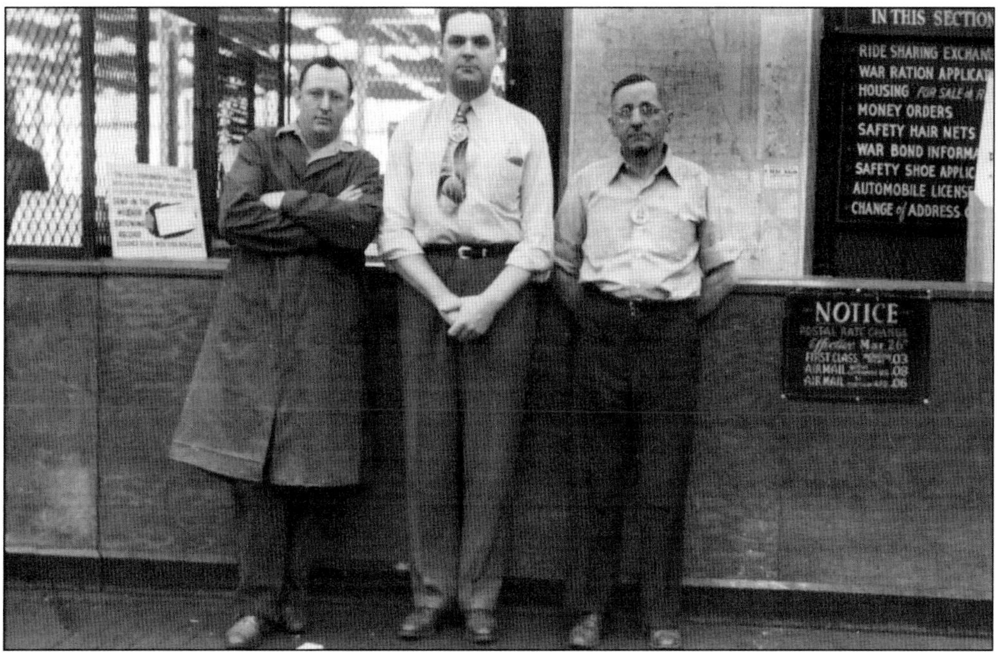

The torpedo plant employed some 6,000 people and was a virtual city unto itself. A cafeteria and a service bureau were needed because production continued around the clock, which made it difficult for employees to get to a bank or run errands. The service bureau was a post office, currency exchange factory store, and offered many other services. (Courtesy of Village of Forest Park.)

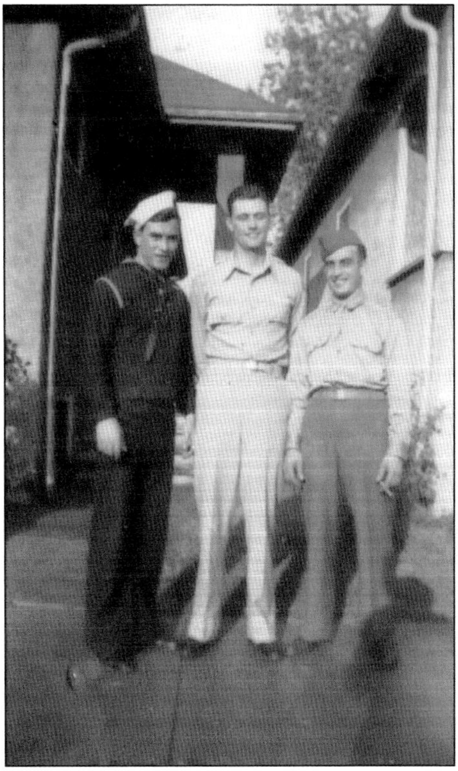

Pictured in this photograph from May 1943 are James Sansone (left), Roy Mohr (center), and James's brother, Tony "Squeek" Sansone (right). Roy Mohr would not return from the war. James Sansone went on to serve as a three-time commissioner until his sudden death in office in 1982. (Courtesy of the Mohr family.)

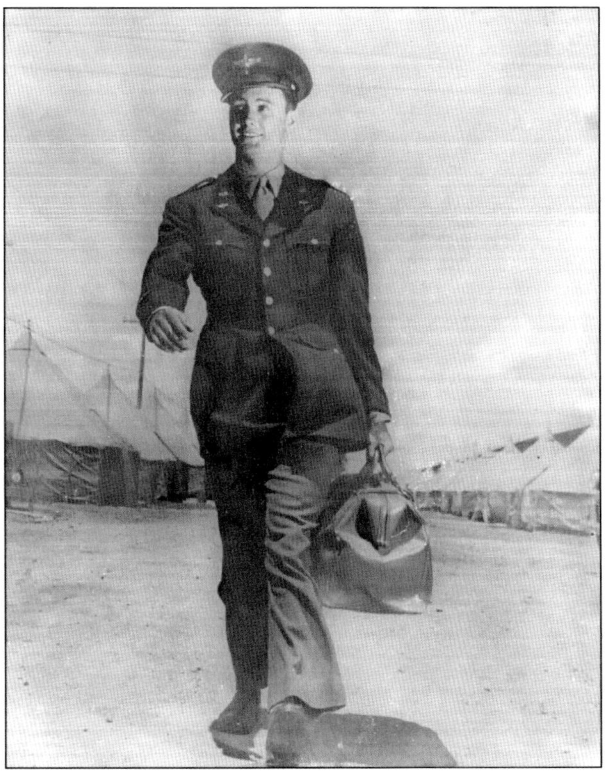

Roy Mohr Jr., the grandson of H. J. Mohr, was a decorated B-17 bomber pilot during World War II. He went missing after his plane *Shack-Up* was shot down over France on the return flight of his 13th mission on September 6, 1943. Six of the 10 men on board would survive. Lieutenant Mohr was one of 190 former Proviso East students who would lose their lives serving their country. (Courtesy of the Mohr family.)

Seven

THE POSTWAR YEARS

On August 15, 1945, the Japanese surrendered, thus marking the end of World War II. The GIs who came home were ready to get married, buy homes, and start families. The baby boom was about to begin.

The postwar boom of the 1950s and the rise in automobile ownership increased the need for the interstate expressway system. The Congress Expressway, later named the Eisenhower and now known as the 290, had its origins back in the 1940s. The cemeteries posed the biggest challenge to construction. A proposal had been made for an overpass, but in the end about 2,300 bodies were moved, as well as several homes. Concerns for public safety during the construction resulted in a temporary firehouse that was located at 1313 Circle Avenue.

In 1956, the village celebrated the first centennial of the settlement of the area. One headline claimed that 100,000 people viewed the parade, which started on Roosevelt Road, traveled up Circle Avenue to Madison Street, down Des Plaines Avenue, and ended at the park.

The baby boom brought about a need to enlarge and modernize the schools. School district No. 91 would embark upon a large-scale revitalization plan. Garfield would be completely rebuilt, Grant White's original building would meet the wrecking ball, and every school received some improvements.

In the early 1960s, Ferrara Pan Candy Company moved to Harrison Street and would become Forest Park's most famous export. The 1960s also saw the arrival of the high-rise. Many older homes would be demolished to make room for the large multiunit housing complexes.

In the mid-1970s, a new village hall would replace the elegant old structure that long served the village. The torpedo factory would close and ultimately become a mall. The changes kept coming, yet through it all, the heart of the small town remained.

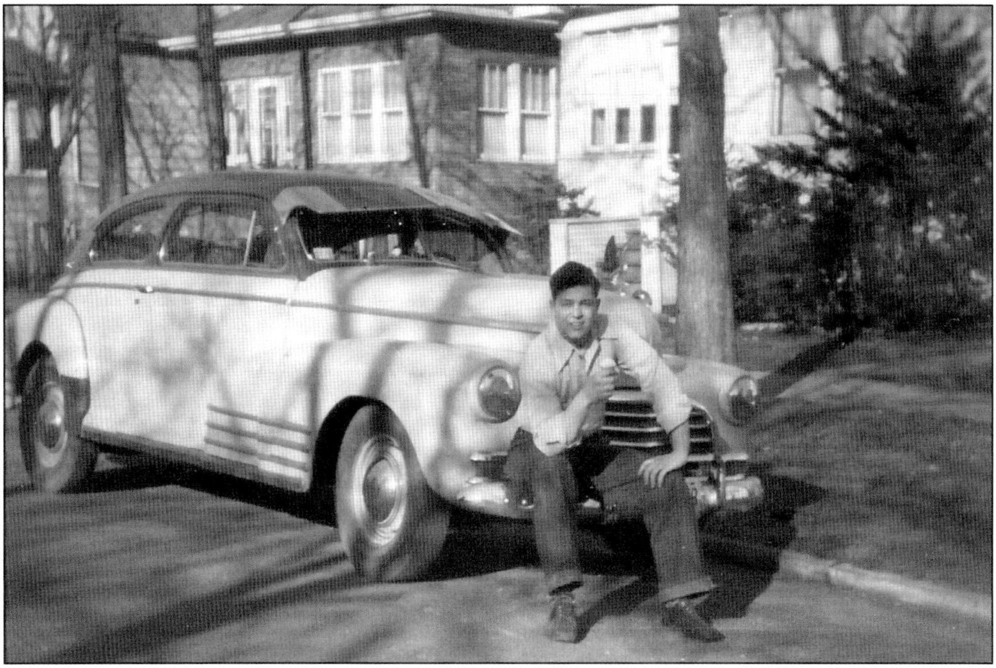

The 1946 Chevy Fleetline is a favorite today among streetrod and low-rider enthusiasts, but in 1948, it was seen as a "square" family car by postwar teenagers. Here is one such teen, Jim Papa, enjoying an ice-cream cone on the bumper of his car, across the street from his family home at 1319 Elgin Avenue. (Courtesy of Jim Papa.)

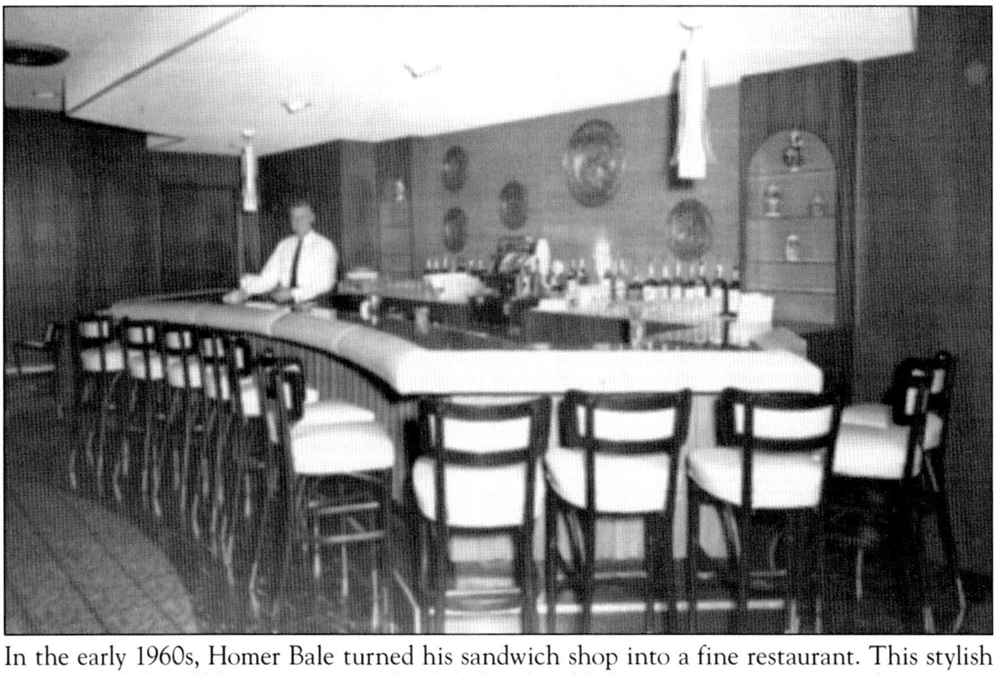

In the early 1960s, Homer Bale turned his sandwich shop into a fine restaurant. This stylish bar replaced the old lunch counter. The Bale family sold the restaurant in 1978. A fire on May 1, 1987, destroyed the building. The location is now a parking lot for the Forest Park National Bank. (Courtesy of Tony Bale.)

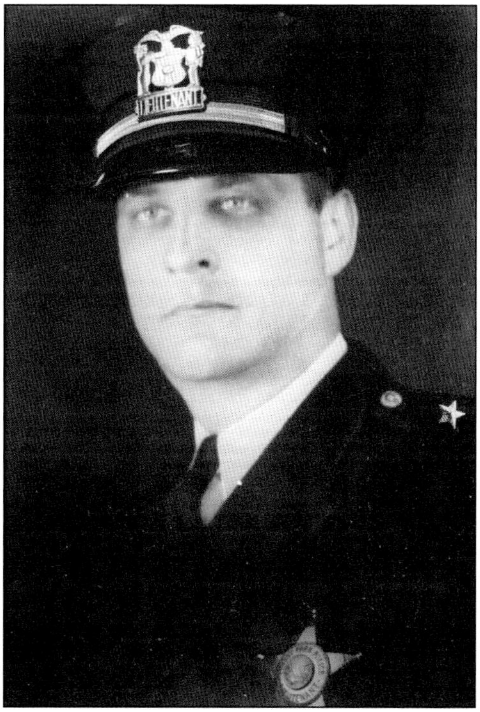

Three badges hang in the village hall to honor the police officers who gave their lives for the village. Officer Edward Pflaume was killed in a shoot-out on December, 13 1925. Lt. Herman Ziebell, shown in the photograph at age 46, was killed on September 30, 1946, while investigating a possible burglary. Ironically, 22-year-old Michael T. Caulfield was killed exactly 36 years to the date on September 30, 1982, during a shooting at the police station. (Courtesy of Herman Ziebell.)

Forest Park was notorious for using police on motorcycles to catch speeding motorists along Roosevelt Road. Motorcycle officer Edwin Ziebell is seen looking west across Circle Avenue at Roosevelt Road in the late 1940s. Ziebell joined the Forest Park police a year after his father, Lt. Herman Ziebell, was killed in the line of duty. Edwin Ziebell would eventually reach the rank of chief. (Courtesy of Herman Ziebell.)

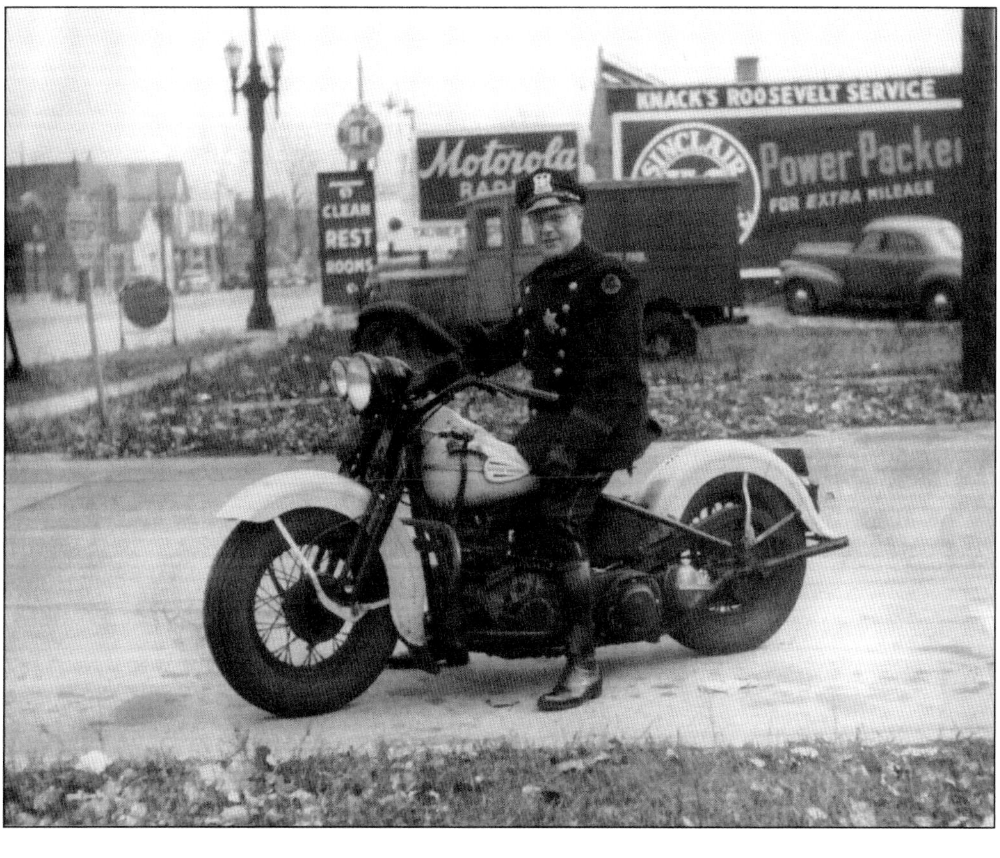

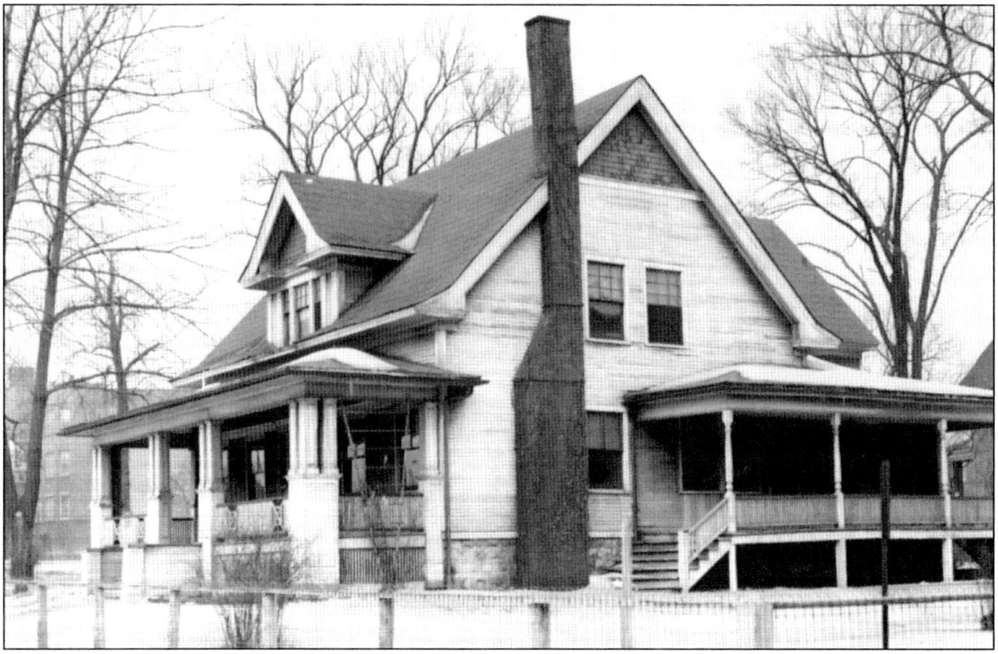

In 1946, the library board purchased the Polly Haase Thomas home, located at Jackson Boulevard and Des Plaines Avenue. Polly was the daughter of pioneer Ferdinand Haase. The library board had originally purchased the old post office at 314 Circle Avenue for use as a library, but this location was larger and better situated to serve the community. (Courtesy of Village of Forest Park.)

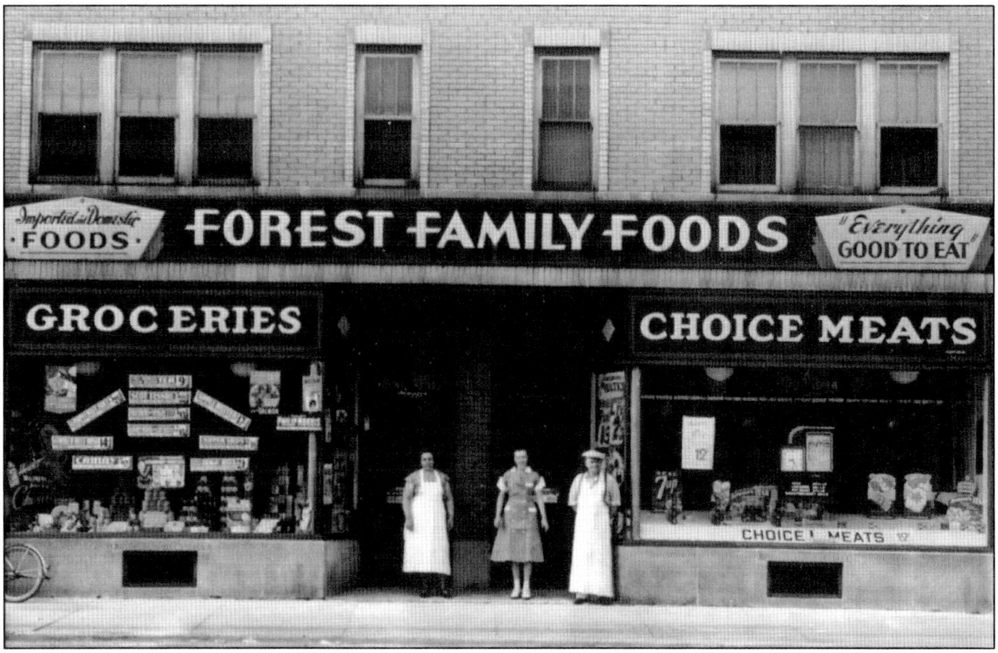

Oldrich Herman stands in front of his store at 7236 Roosevelt Road with his wife, Marie, and their daughter Betty. During the 1940s and 1950s, grocery stores continued to grow in size, as did the variety of products they carried. Though no longer an active store, the building is still standing. (Courtesy of Jeff Oswalt.)

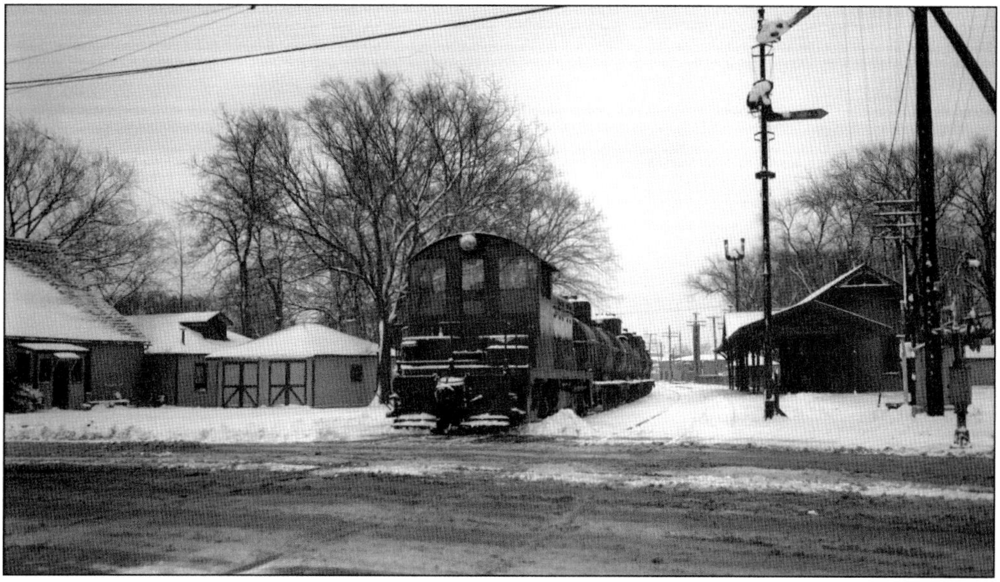

Soo-Line train No. 217 crossed Madison Street on December 29, 1946, as seen in this photograph taken from the River Forest side of the street. The former Altenheim depot can be seen on the right side of the photograph. Soo-Line dropped passenger service from Forest Park in the mid-1960s. The depot was used for storage for time before being demolished. (Courtesy of Walter R. Keevil.)

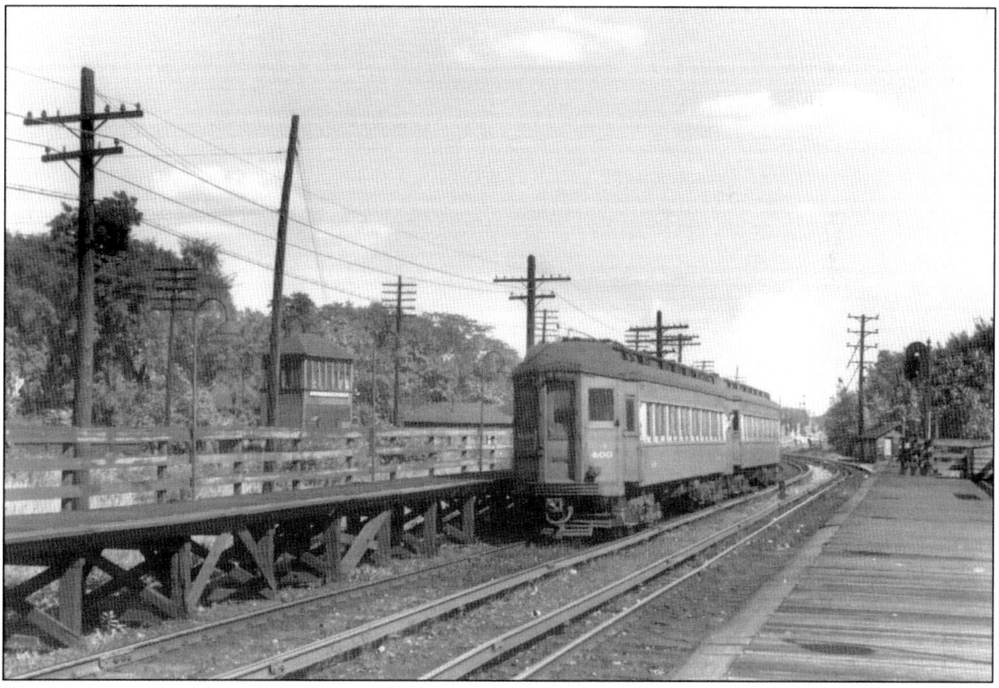

This photograph, taken sometime in the late 1940s or early 1950s, shows the train station platform located on the east side of Des Plaines Avenue. In 1953, the station was moved to the west side of Des Plaines Avenue. This occurred around the time that the CA&E stopped running all the way into the city, forcing riders to switch to Chicago Transit Authority trains at Forest Park. (Courtesy of Walter R. Keevil.)

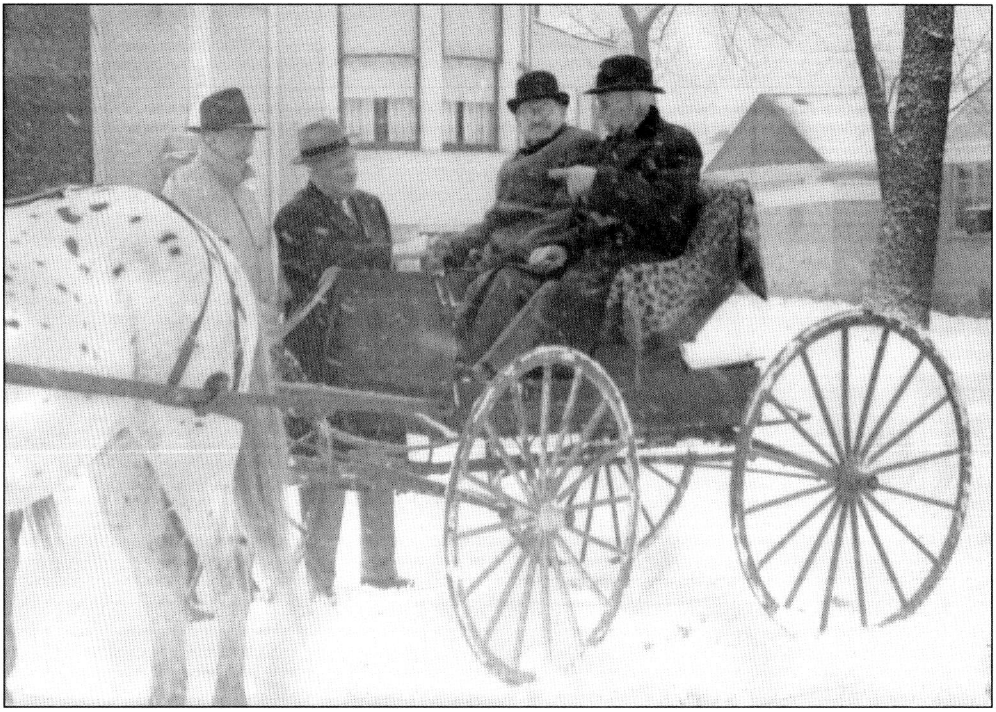

A visitor to Forest Park in 1956 would have seen many curious sights. This photograph shows, from left to right, Dr Henry H. Desens and Howard Sammon (president of the chamber of commerce) speaking with prominent businessmen Gottlieb Schwab and H. J. Mohr. Schwab had a beer hall, located at the southwest corner of Madison Street and Elgin Avenue, and Mohr served as both president of Harlem and mayor of Forest Park. The photograph was taken in front of the Kistenbroker mansion on Des Plaines Avenue. (Courtesy of Tim Shanahan.)

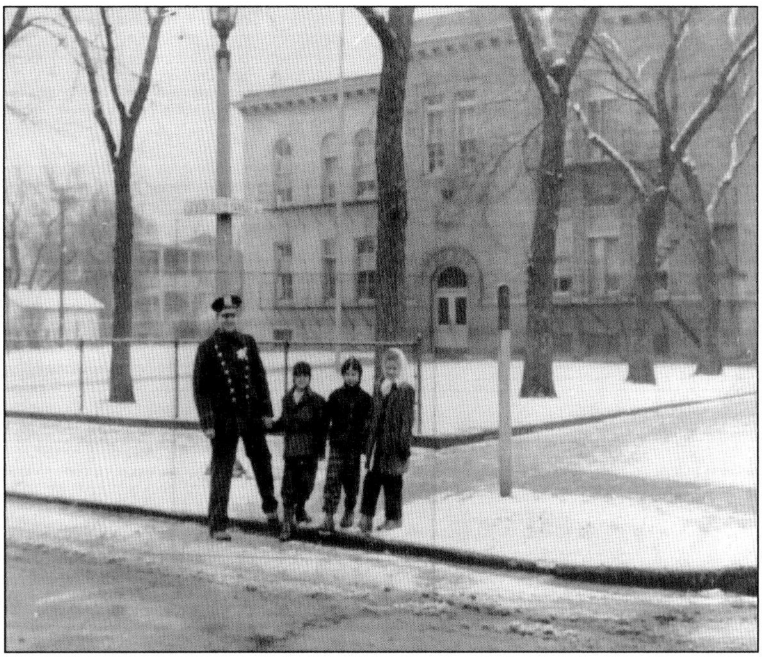

Forest Park police officers have long maintained a reputation as tough, no-nonsense protectors of the village. Here is a softer side of the law, as officer Bob Zimmerman helps some children cross Jackson Boulevard at Hannah Avenue. The old Farley School, which was renamed after President Garfield, can be seen in the background. (Courtesy of Jeff Oswalt.)

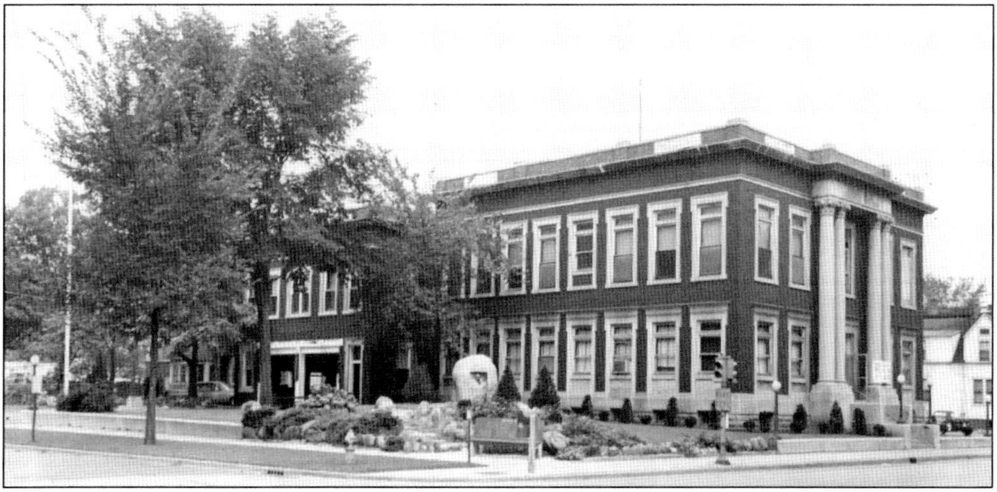

This photograph of the village hall and fire station can be dated to the 1950s, as the firehouse had not yet been enlarged. The 10-ton, red granite boulder in front of the building was dedicated in 1924 as a war memorial. It was later moved to the old library at Jackson Boulevard and Des Plaines Avenue, and is now located at the small park at Thomas and Adams Streets. (Courtesy of Tim Shanahan.)

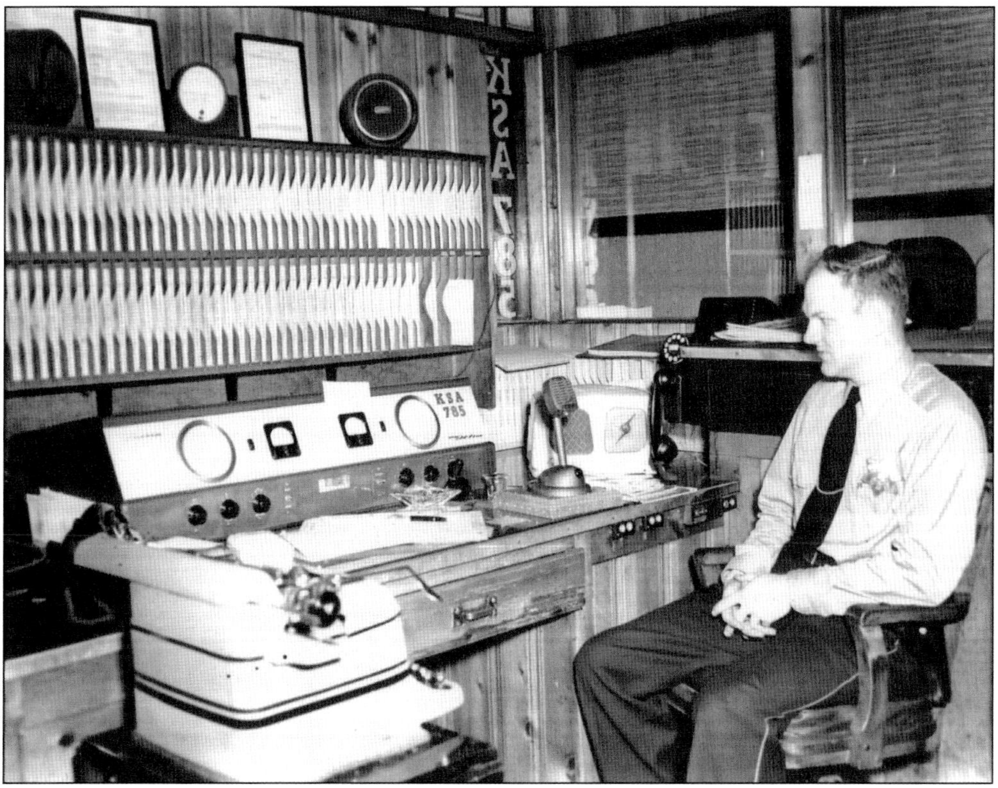

The radio dispatcher has long held a key position within the police department. While communicating with both the officers and the public, they must remain calm and levelheaded during stressful situations. Officer Victor Bengard is seen manning the radio in the police station in the 1950s. (Courtesy of Village of Forest Park.)

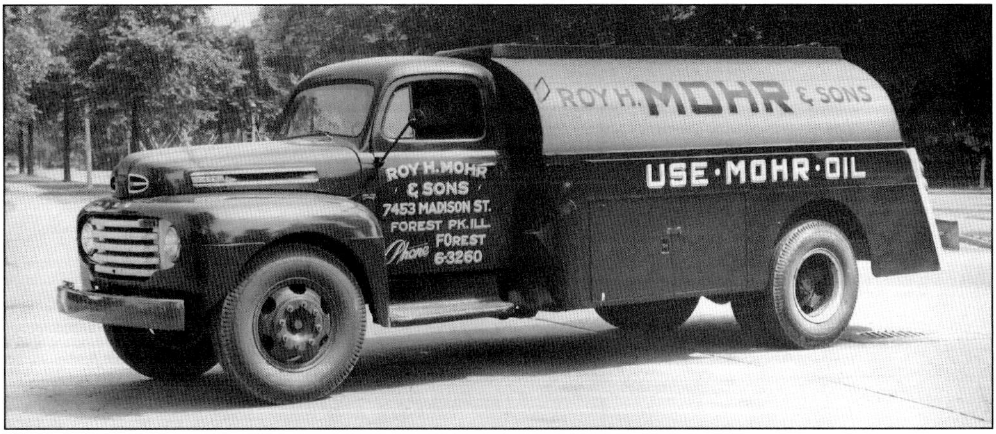

Mohr Oil Company was founded in 1950 by Roy H. Mohr, son of H. J. Mohr and father of Sen./Mayor Howard Mohr. The company started with one truck, seen above, at 7453 Madison Street and later moved to 7340 Harrison Street in 1959. The business is still family owned and operated at that location. (Courtesy of Mike Mohr.)

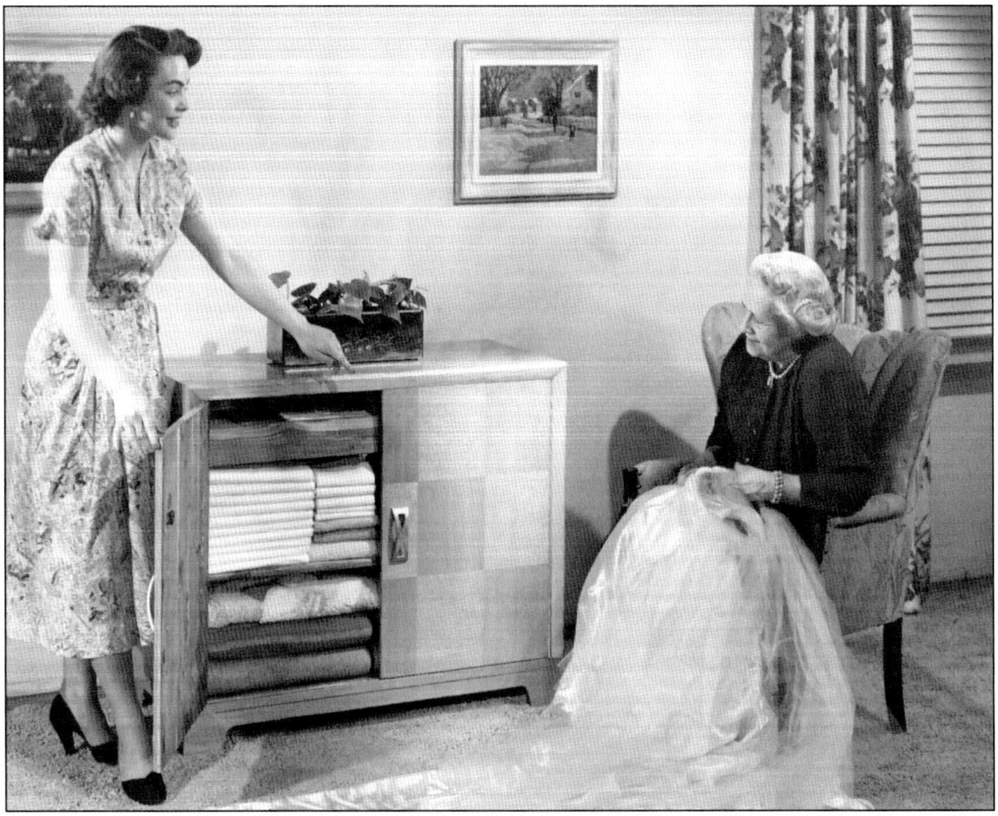

The 1950s ushered in an era of clean lines and modern style in furniture design. Attempting to stay current, the Roos Company unveiled a new line of chests. This advertisement shows a "modern" hope chest. The "Cedarette" was a cabinet-style chest with adjustable shelves. It boasted 50 percent more storage, while wasting 25 percent less space than a conventional cedar chest. However, chest sales continued to decline, and the company closed shortly after a change in ownership. (Courtesy of Gail Roos and Edward Roos IV.)

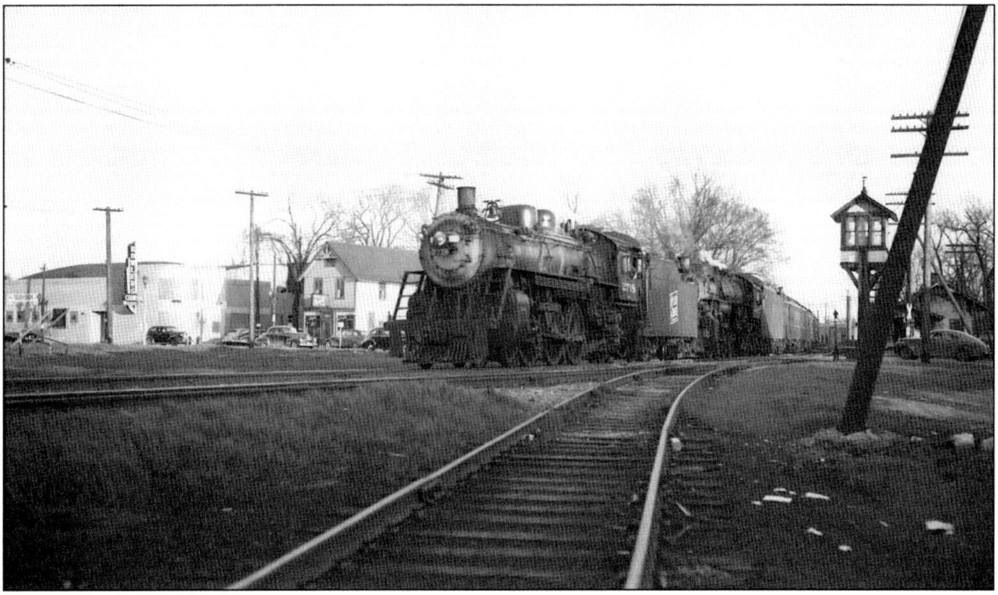

As the Soo-Line *Laker* crosses Madison Street on May 5, 1950, the Bowlers Club is seen at the far left. The next building on the right is Albrath's Tavern at 7802 Madison Street. Later generations would know Albrath's as Harry's Penny Bar, Scarlet O' Hara's, Xzotics Jungle Club, and lastly as the Bermuda Triangle. Dating back to the 1890s, the building was torn down and replaced by the Super Wash in 1995. (Photograph by Fielding Kunecke; courtesy of Walter R. Keevil.)

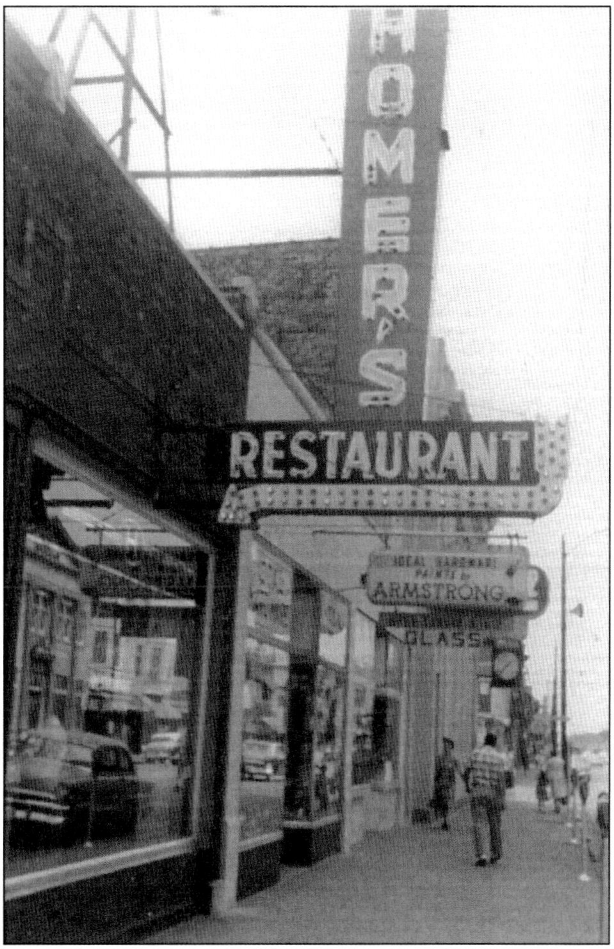

During the 1950s, Madison Street was home to two hardware stores, Peaslee's and Ideal. This 1950s photograph shows Ideal Hardware sandwiched between the Forest Park National Bank and Homer's Restaurant. Peaslee's actually started in the building at 7342 Madison Street in 1918 as a branch of Nicholas Hardware. In 1919, Herbert Peaslee and sons bought the business outright. (Courtesy of Tony Bale.)

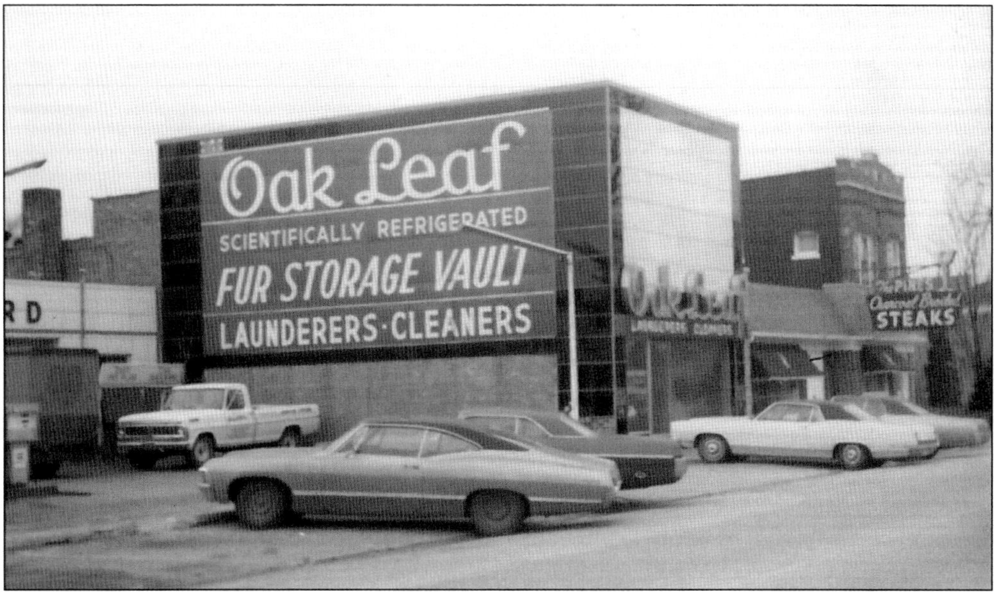

In the 1950s, Al Reda decided to add a dry cleaning to his laundry business. In 1952, he constructed a brand-new building at 7408 Harrison Street. The new building featured a state-of-the-art fur storage vault that could hold 4,000 coats. Over 500 people attended the grand opening on March 22, 1952. The Oak Leaf Building became a lounge in 1983. (Courtesy of the Reda family.)

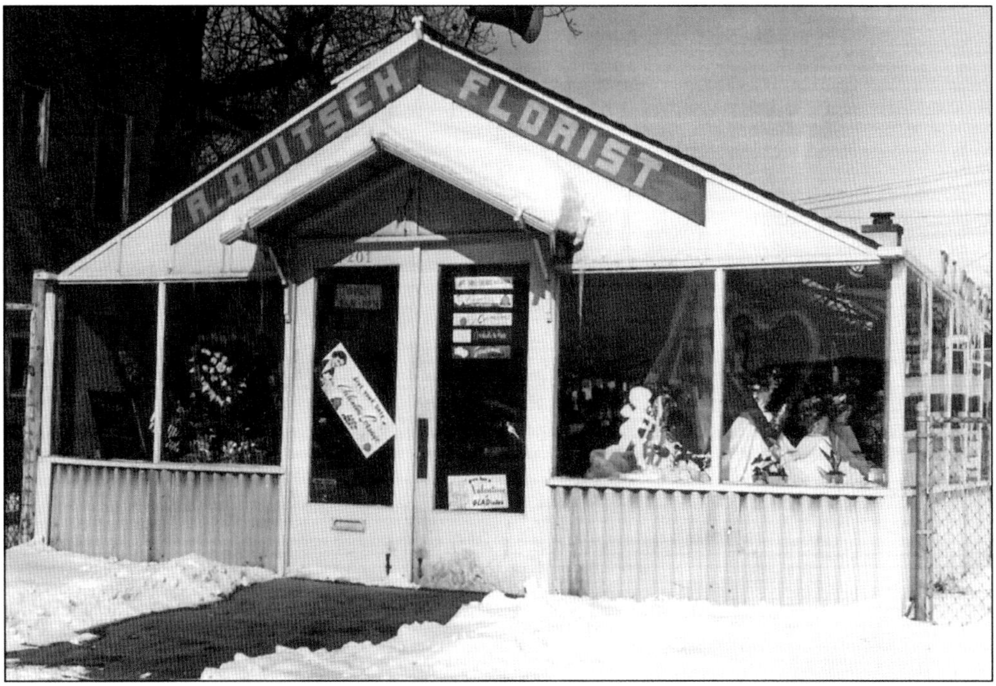

In the 1950s, Roy Quitsch, a World War II veteran, went to floral design school and joined the family business (see page 68). They built a larger greenhouse and renamed the business R. Quitsch Florist. In 1985, they built a new store at 7207 Roosevelt Road. In 2000, after the deaths of both Roy and his wife, Avalee, Dixie Quitsch Paugh became the owner and moved the business to 7405 Madison Street. (Courtesy of Dixie Quitsch Paugh.)

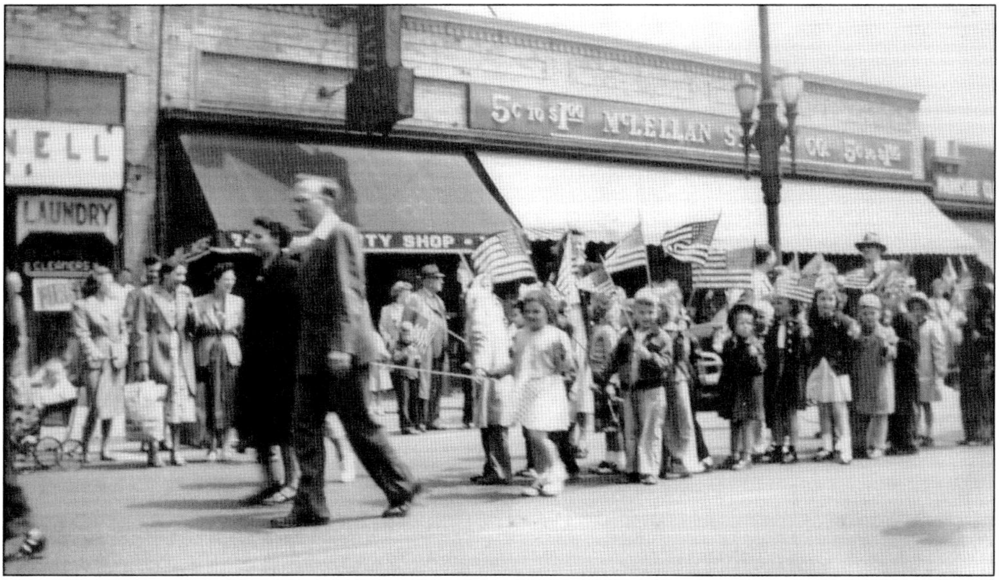

The dollar stores of today are reminiscent of the five and dimes of yesteryear. In this 1950s photograph, a group of children from St John's parades past McLellan's variety store on their way to a school picnic at the Altenheim grove. In 1958, the building at 7443 Madison Street became a Ben Franklin Store, and today the location is home to Schauer's Hallmark. (Courtesy of Harold Stover.)

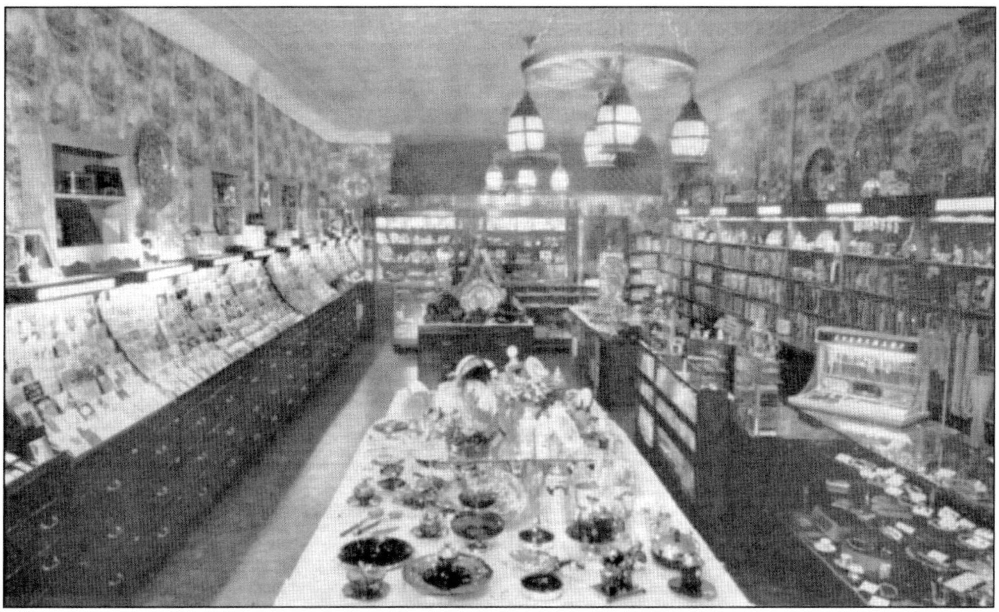

Roy Olsen and his wife, LaVada (Tommye), ran the book and gift shop, Tomaroy, at 7223 Madison Street. The shop later moved to 7210 Madison Street, its home for 36 years. This postcard view shows the wide assortment of cards and gifts one could purchase. They also repaired lighters and pens in the days before cheap disposables came into use.

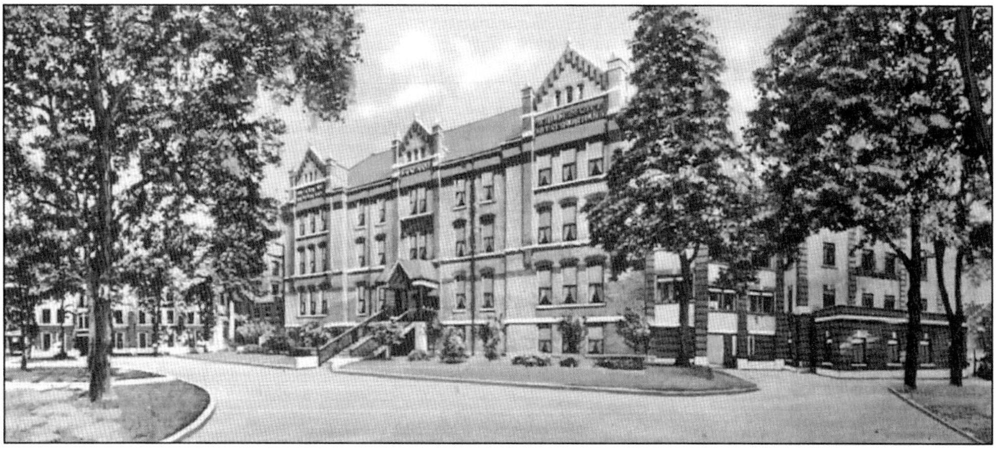

The caption on this postcard would be considered politically incorrect today as it read "Altenheim, German Old People's Home." The German writing on the left side of the building says, "German home in new land," the date of 1885 in the middle, and "Shelter it under your strong hands, Lord" on the right side. The picnic grounds are still used for many community events and picnics.

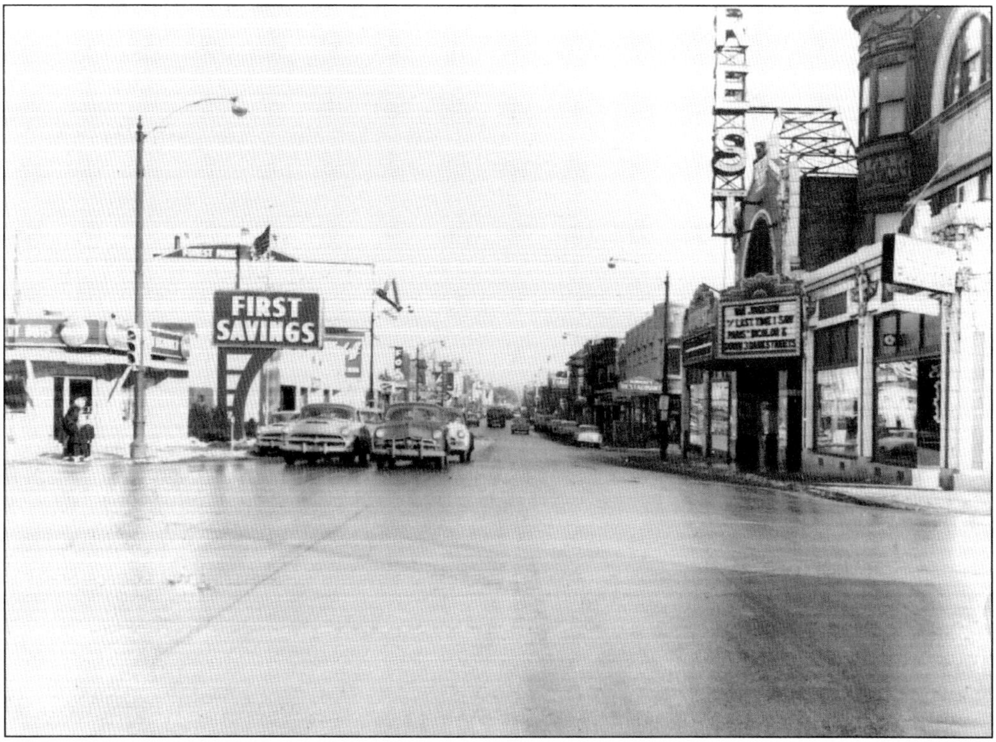

Here is a view of Madison Street, looking east from Des Plaines Avenue in 1954. The Forest Theatre was showing *The Last Time I Saw Paris*, starring Van Johnson and Elizabeth Taylor. The Forest Theatre was located in the building that was once known as Gaden's Hall. (Courtesy of Jeff Oswalt.)

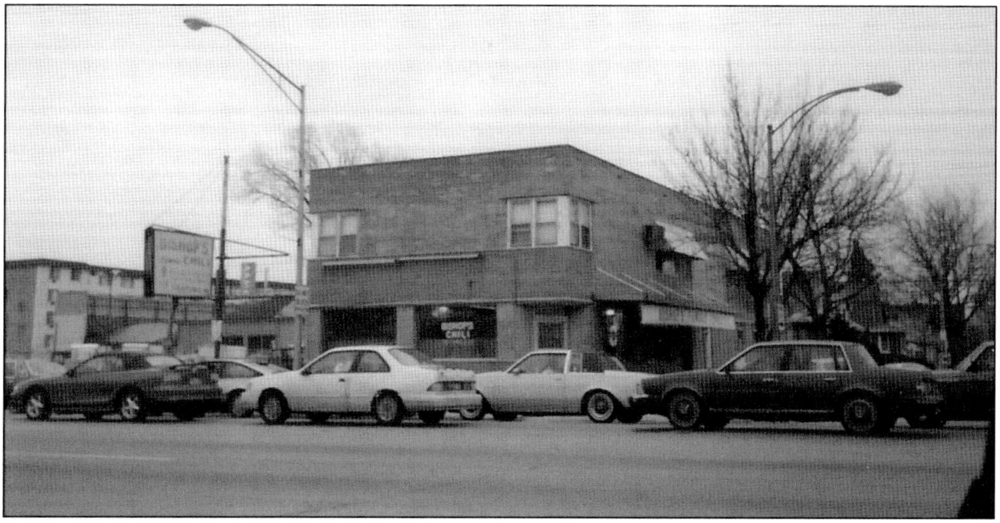

Bishop's Famous Chili was a staple on the southeast corner of Roosevelt Road and Elgin Avenue for over 30 years. The business was started in 1926 at Eighteenth and Damon Streets in Chicago. They opened at 7220 Roosevelt Road in 1960 and remained, until Walgreen's bought the property in the mid-1990s and leveled the building.

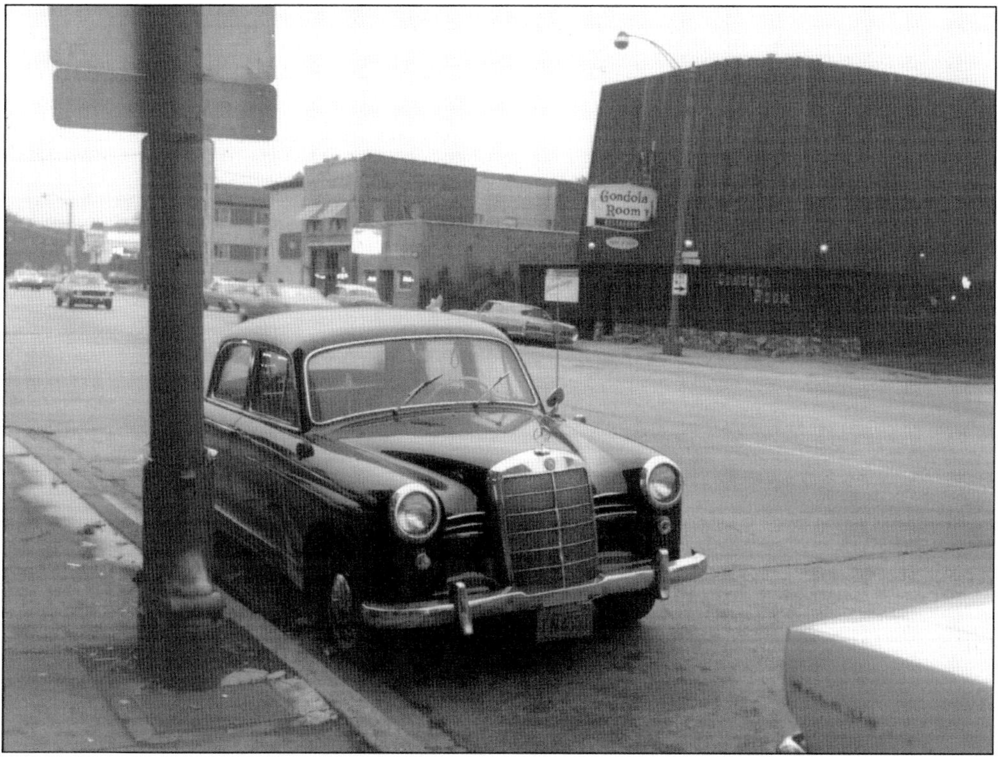

Originally built in the 1920s for Brazda's Grocery, 7301 Roosevelt Road served as the home of the Gondola Room, an Italian restaurant, which is pictured in the late 1960s. It has served the gay community since the mid-1970s, when it became known as the Hideaway II. Recently, the owners removed the vertical wood siding from the upper portion of the building, revealing the original brick facade. (Courtesy of Jeff Oswalt.)

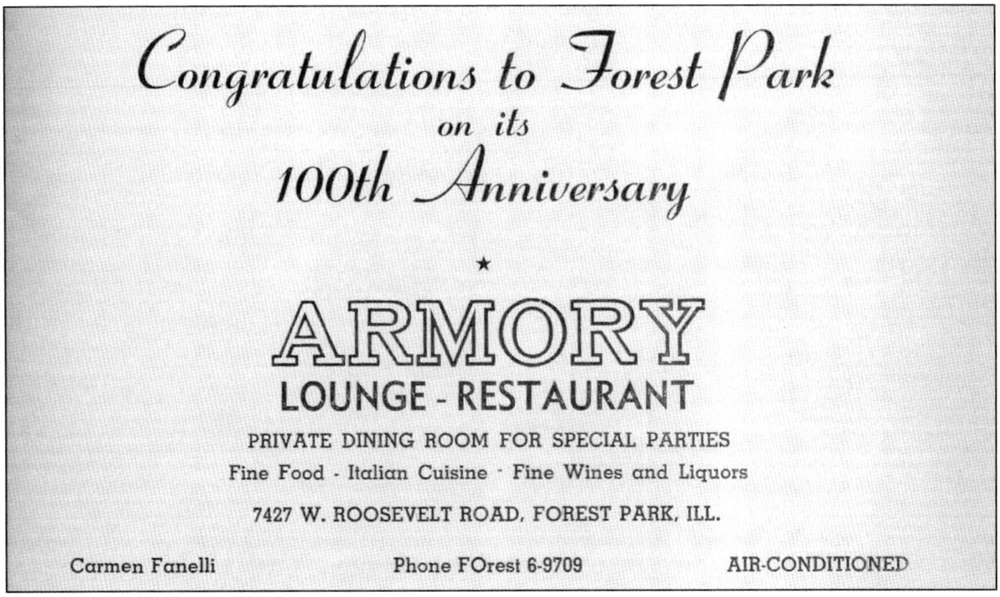

This advertisement is for the Armory Lounge. The Armory was wiretapped in the 1960s by the FBI because reputed mob boss Sam Giancanna kept an "office" in the back room of the restaurant. Frank Sinatra and Dean Martin had their picture taken during a visit to the Roosevelt Road establishment in 1958.

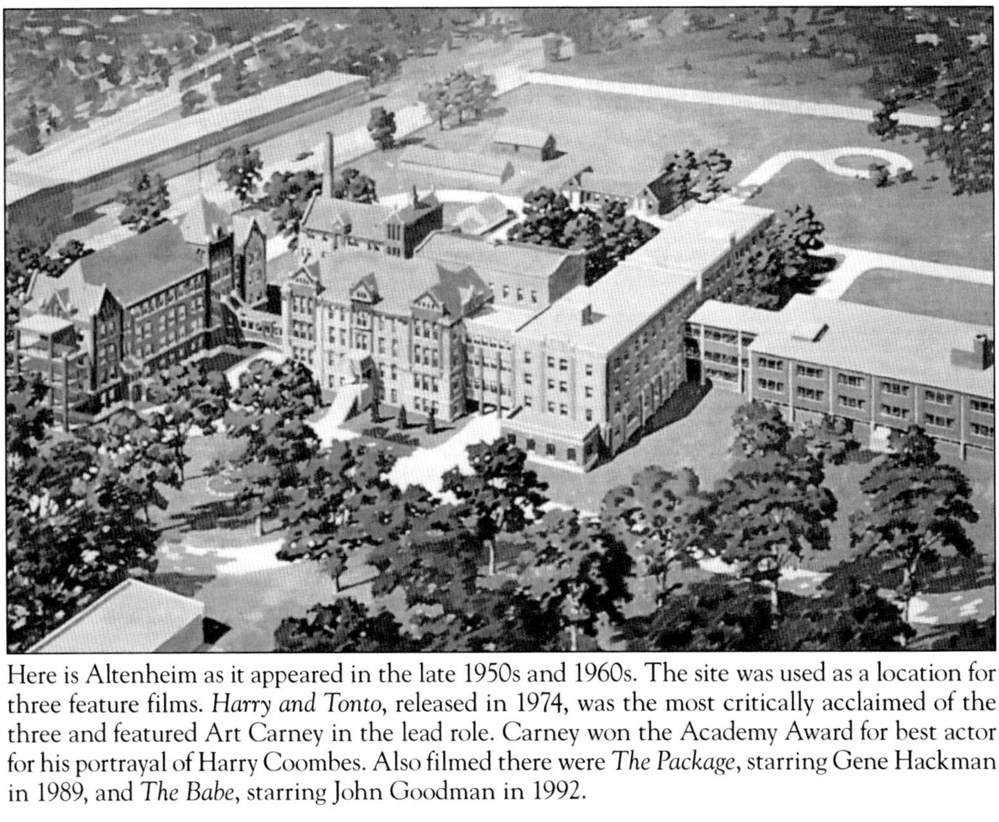

Here is Altenheim as it appeared in the late 1950s and 1960s. The site was used as a location for three feature films. *Harry and Tonto*, released in 1974, was the most critically acclaimed of the three and featured Art Carney in the lead role. Carney won the Academy Award for best actor for his portrayal of Harry Coombes. Also filmed there were *The Package*, starring Gene Hackman in 1989, and *The Babe*, starring John Goodman in 1992.

Few who have lived in Forest Park over the last 50 years will forget the wonderful smell of cinnamon wafting over the village whenever Ferrara Pan Candy Company, located at 7301 Harrison Street, was making a batch of its world famous Red Hots or Atomic FireBalls. The business came here in 1960 and took over the old Borden plant and Imperial Methods building. (Courtesy of Ferrara Pan Candy Company.)

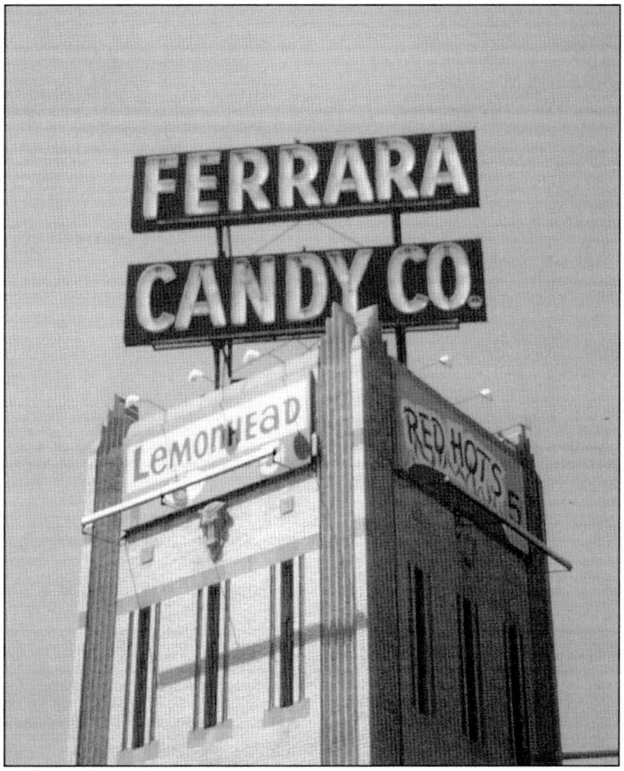

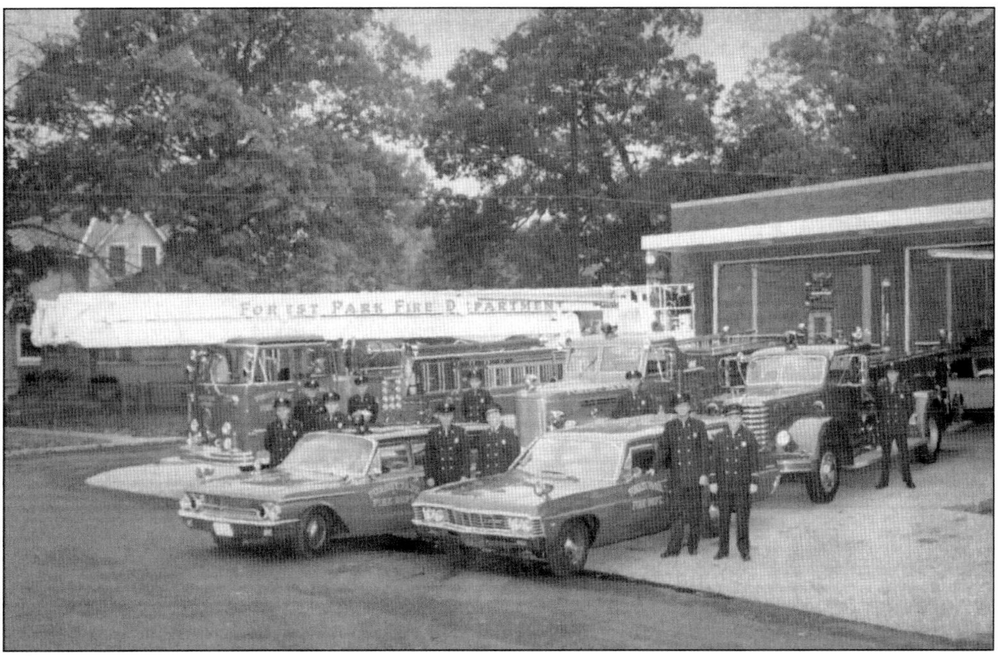

In 1962, the fire department purchased its first snorkel fire truck. The truck was controversial at first but proved to be a necessity with the arrival of the high-rise apartment buildings. The snorkel, with its 85-foot boom, was too long to fit into the firehouse, so the firefighters constructed an addition to the building themselves. (Courtesy of Village of Forest Park.)

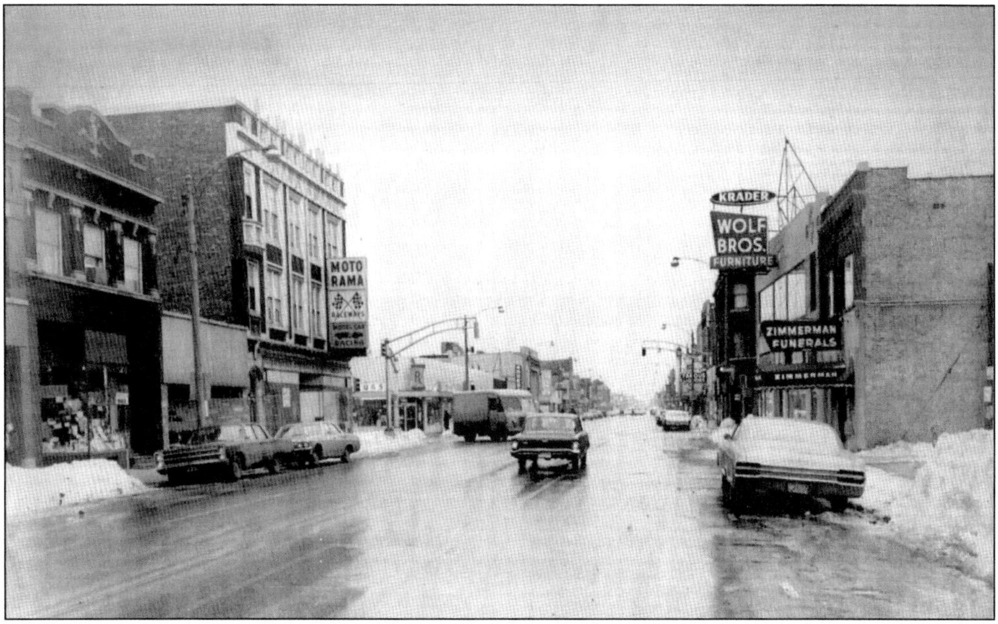

The view of westbound Madison Street, from Marengo Avenue, has not changed much since this late-1960s photograph was taken. The building at the northwest corner of Circle Avenue and Madison Street is gone, as is the siding on the drugstore. Moto Rama at 7320 Madison Street held model-car races on 30 lanes of miniature roadways. That building was the scene of a fire that took the life of fire captain Frank Schnurstein on March 28, 1969. (Courtesy of Village of Forest Park.)

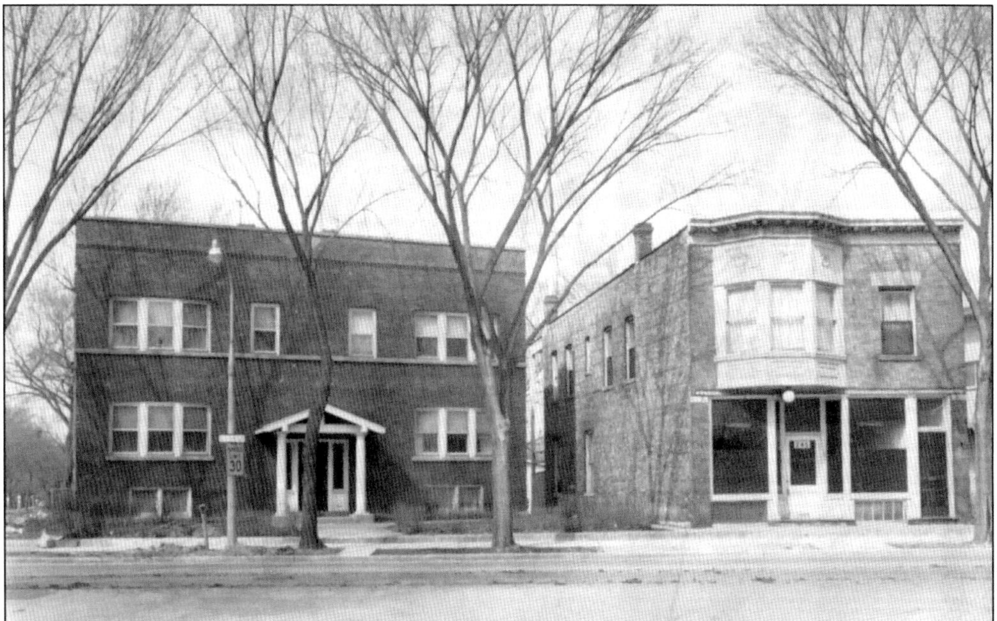

This photograph, taken around 1966, shows two buildings lost to "progress." The buildings, located on the west side of Des Plaines Avenue at Washington Street, were demolished to make parking lots for large apartment buildings, built at 241 and 303 Des Plaines Avenue during the apartment-building craze of the late 1960s and early 1970s. (Courtesy of Village of Forest Park.)

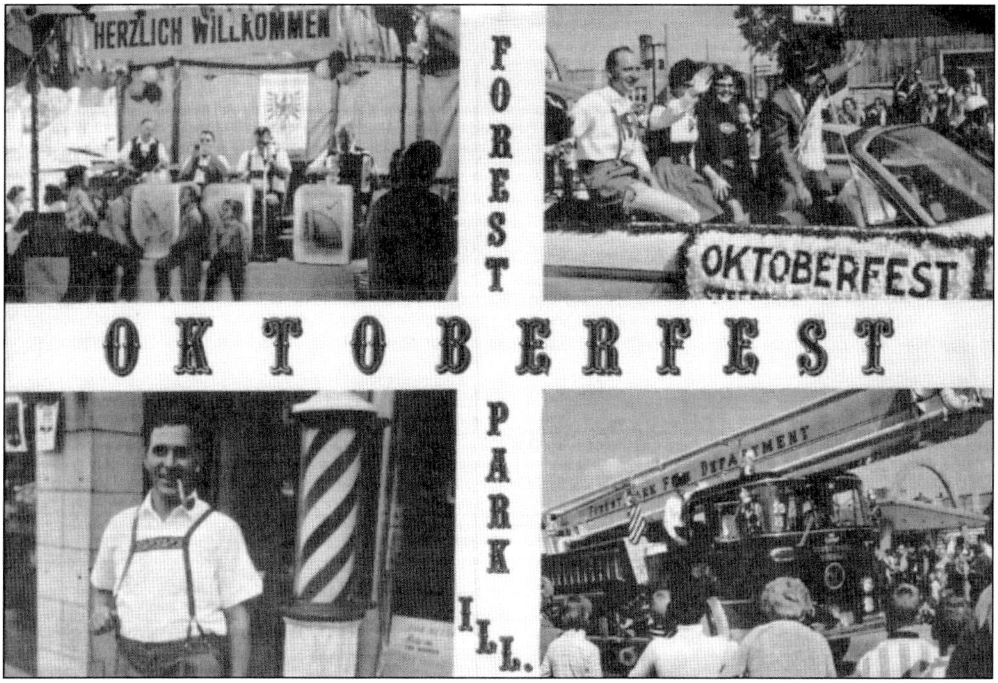

In 1966, Forest Parkers, led by the Harlem Mannerchor, strapped on their lederhosen to celebrate German heritage with bratwurst and beer at the inaugural Oktoberfest celebration. What began as a Madison Street event eventually grew to include parades, carnival rides, and games. It reached its height of popularity in the mid-1970s to the early 1980s, first moving to a parking lot north of Harrison Street at Elgin Avenue and then moving to the naval reserve center on Roosevelt Road.

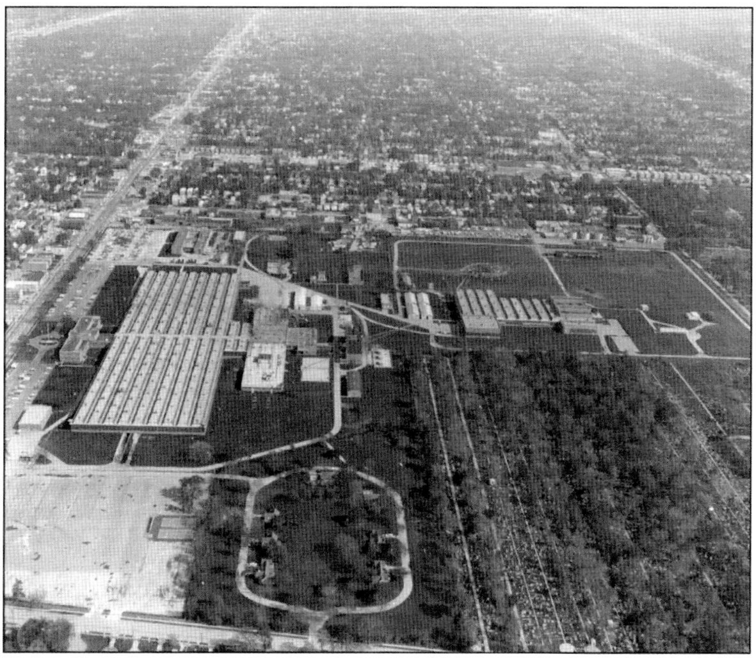

This 1967 aerial photograph shows the extensive layout of the naval ordnance plant, which is facing east from Des Plaines Avenue. The U.S. Postal Service acquired the section east of the Jewish cemeteries. The circular section in the foreground housed the officers' quarters. The homes were razed in the 1990s to make room for a Wal-Mart. (Courtesy of Village of Forest Park.)

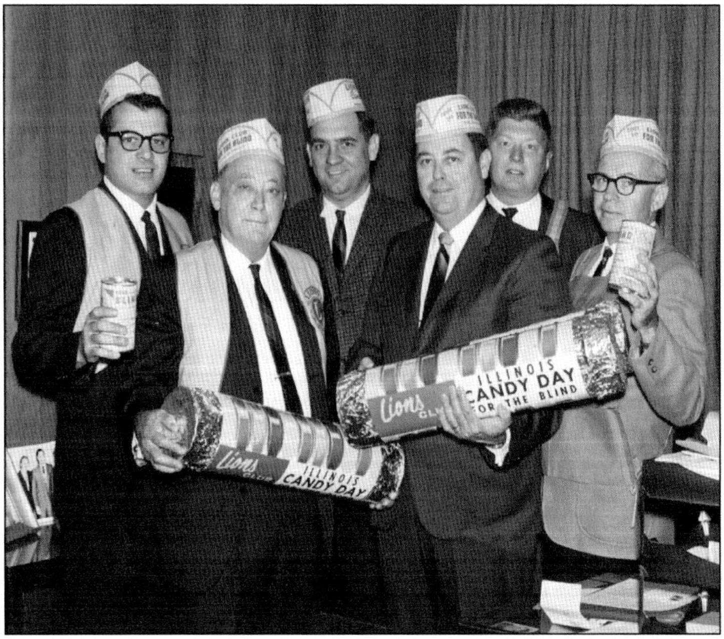

One long-standing service organization in Forest Park has been the Lions Club. Helen Keller urged the organization to crusade against blindness back in 1925. Since that time, Candy Day sales have helped raise funds for the Hadley School for the Blind and other institutions. From left to right in this 1966 photograph are Herman Milas, Roy Mohr, Edwin Miklas, Mayor Howard Mohr, Ed Schneider, and Ed Epstein. (Courtesy of Village of Forest Park.)

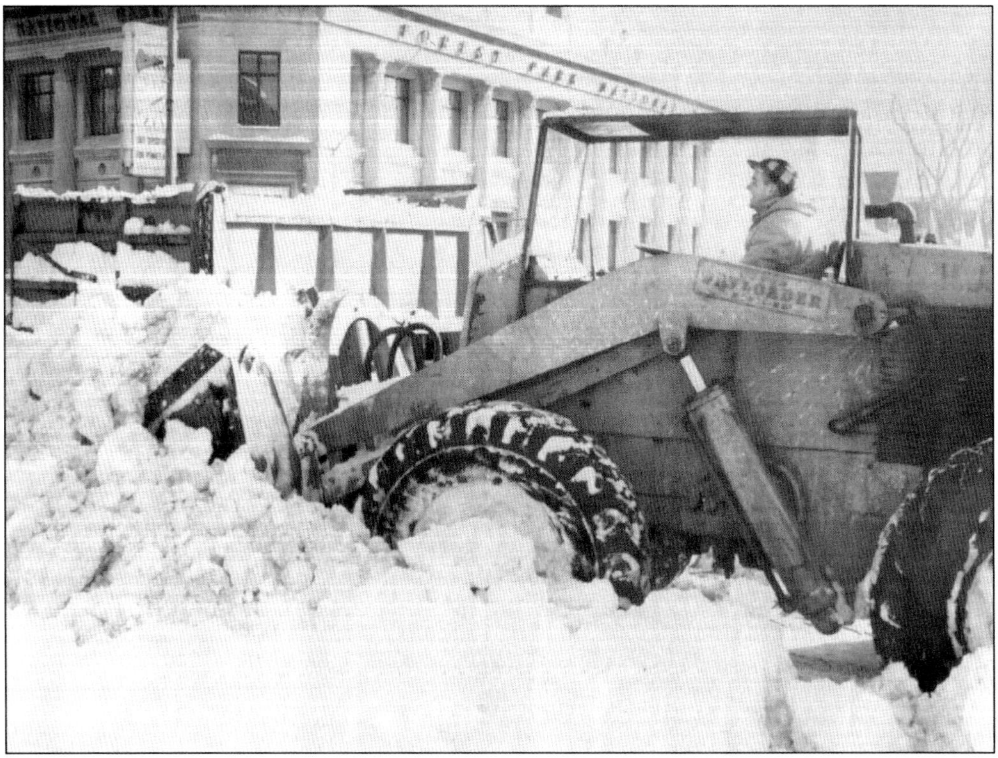

On January 26–27, 1967, the Chicago area was hit by a record-setting snowstorm. Although the temperature had been 65 degrees two days before the storm, a record 23 inches of snow fell, crippling the area. Many local businessmen came to the rescue. Here is Henry "Bud" Mohr of H. J. Mohr and Sons using his payloader to clear Madison Street in front of the Forest Park National Bank. (Courtesy of the Mohr family.)

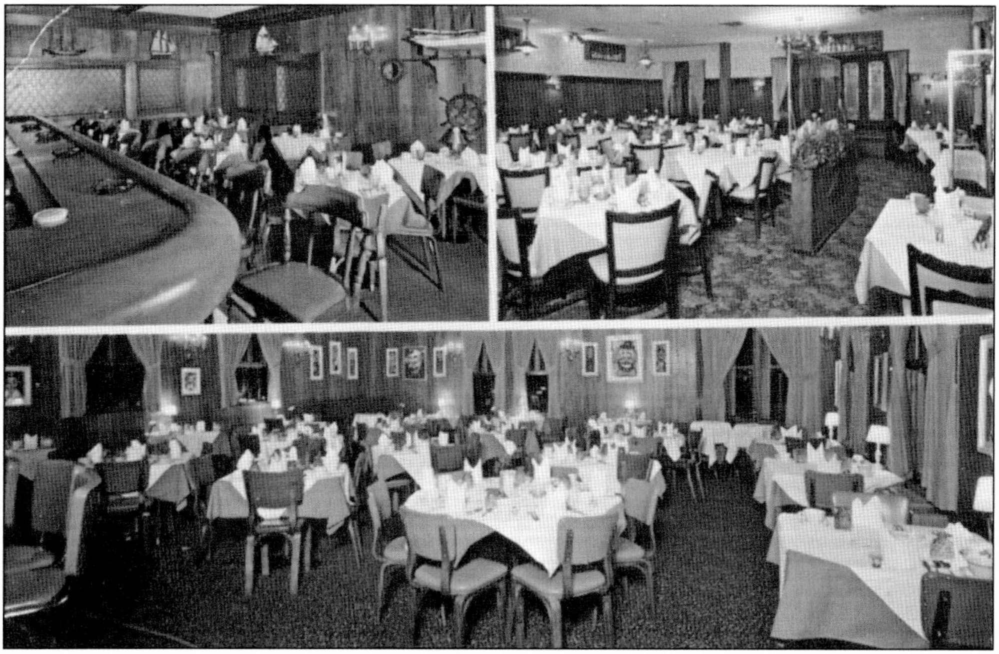

This postcard features the Marine Room, the main dining room, and the Club Room of Otto's Restaurant. The authentic German restaurant, located at Washington Street and Elgin Avenue, was started by Otto Schneider to cater to the funeral crowds. The Victorian-era building was destroyed by fire April 7, 1986, after being shuttered for some time.

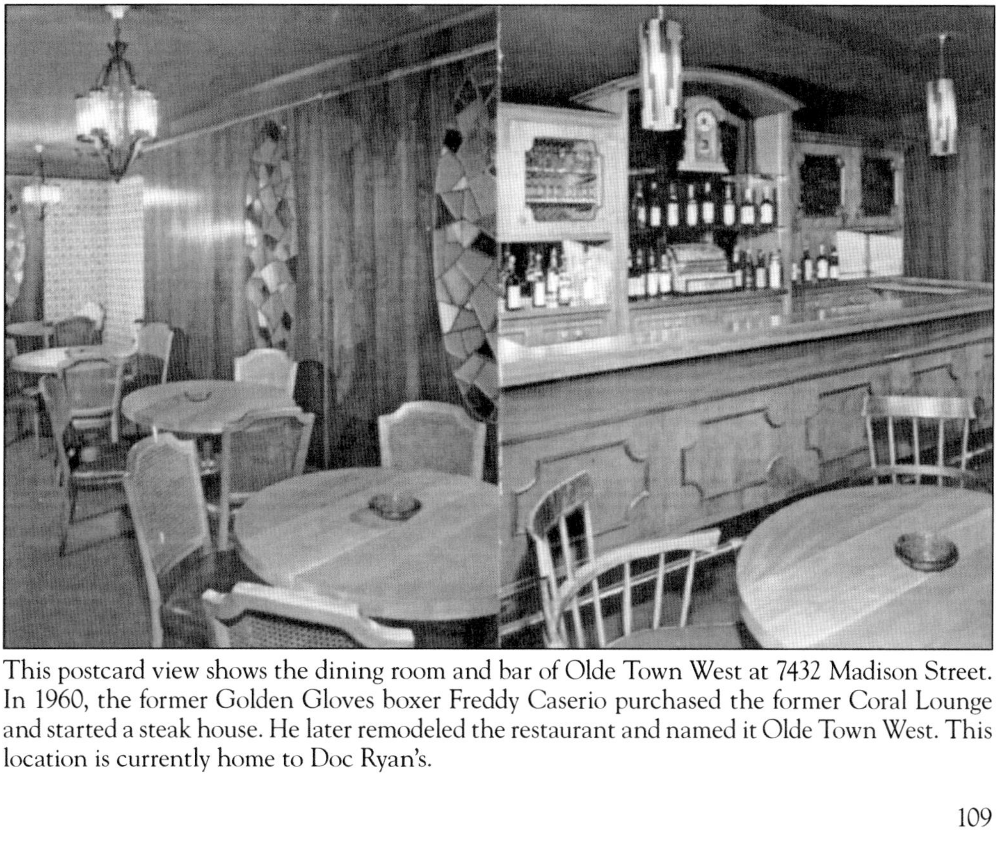

This postcard view shows the dining room and bar of Olde Town West at 7432 Madison Street. In 1960, the former Golden Gloves boxer Freddy Caserio purchased the former Coral Lounge and started a steak house. He later remodeled the restaurant and named it Olde Town West. This location is currently home to Doc Ryan's.

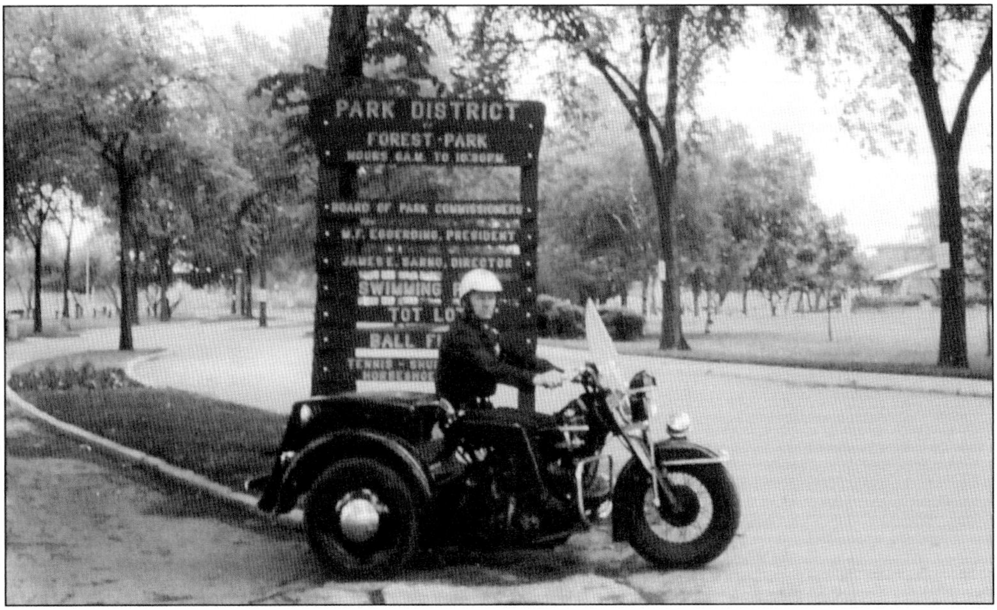

Maintaining the peace at the park is challenging during events like the annual No-Glove National Softball Tournament and Fourth of July celebration. Over the years, auxiliary police officers (also called police reserves) have patrolled the park. From 1968 until around 1990, the park maintained its own police department. In the early 1970s, the police utilized a three-wheeled motorcycle, as seen in this c. 1968 photograph of Officer Robert Maren. (Courtesy of Park District of Forest Park.)

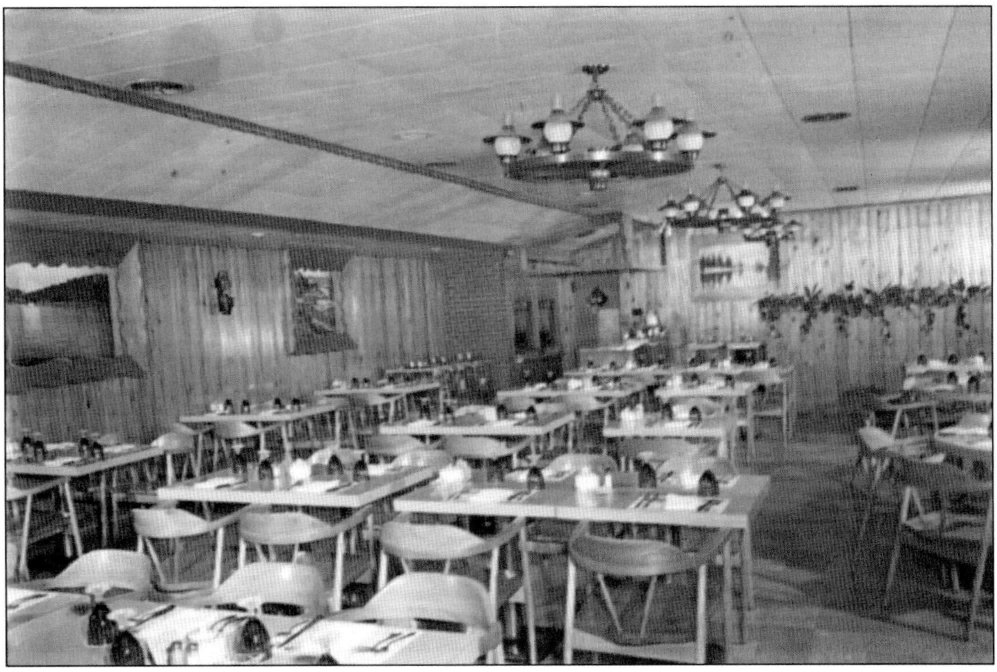

This postcard features the interior of the Pines Steak House. This restaurant at 7412 Harrison Street opened in the early 1930s and only recently closed. The knotty pine paneling and rustic decor gave the restaurant a north woods feel. Many civic groups, including the Kiwanis Club, held meetings in the spacious dining room.

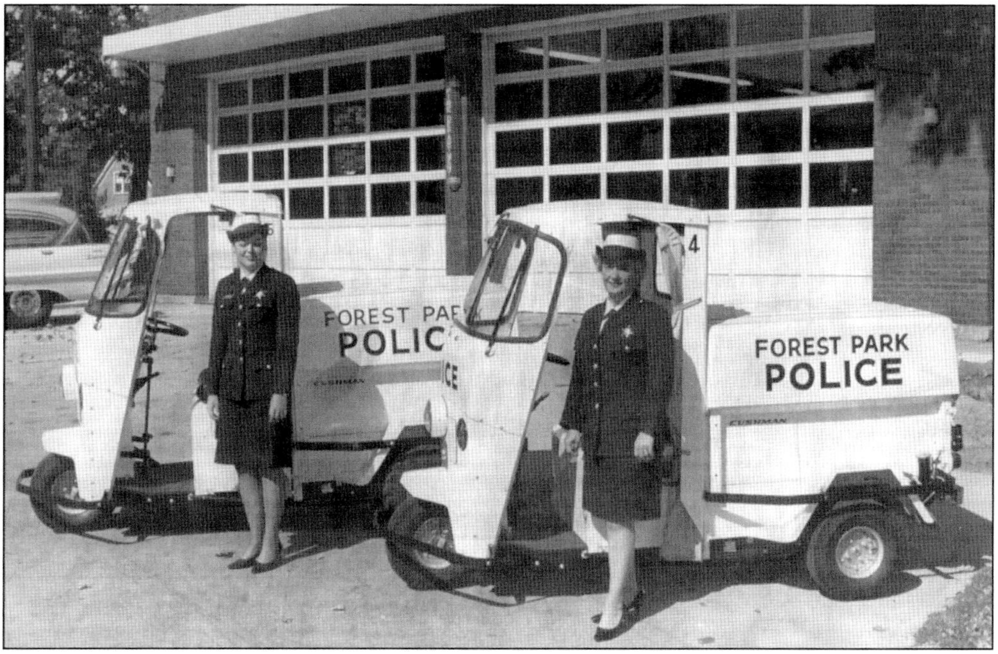

From 1965 until 1972, Forest Park employed meter maids. Mary Schnurstein (left) and dispatcher Rose Kletecka are standing alongside the Cushman three-wheel vehicles, parked in front of the firehouse. In addition to giving tardy shoppers tickets for expired meters, they did double duty as crossing guards. (Courtesy of Village of Forest Park.)

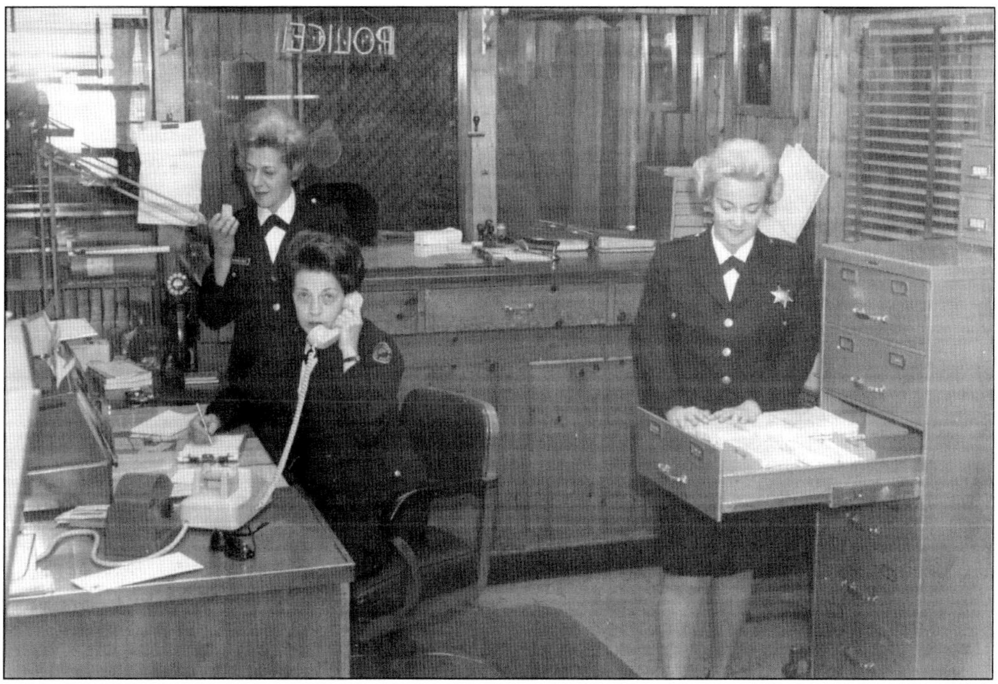

Police administrative personnel have always played an important role in the functioning of the department. From left to right, Ann Manone, Esther Hardtke, and Rose Kletecka are busy at work filing and answering phones. (Courtesy of Village of Forest Park.)

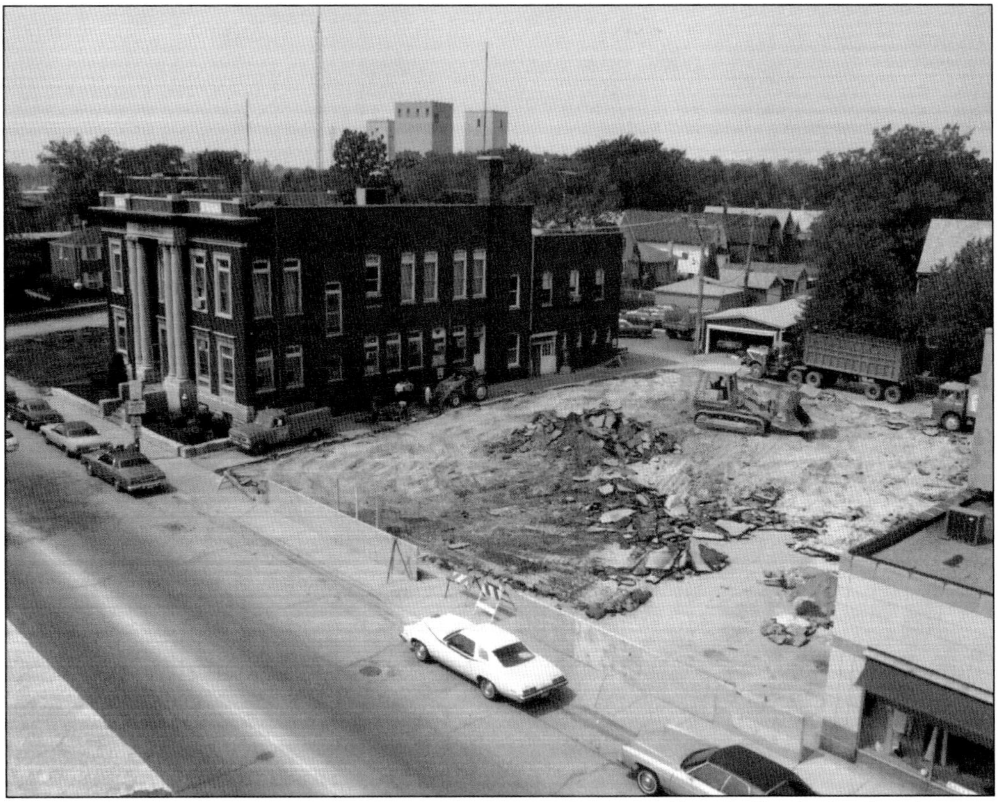

This 1974 bird's-eye view shows land being cleared for the new village hall. The landmark Acme Feed towers can be seen in the background. Abandoned for many years, the location of the grain towers would be the scene of a spectacular fire on September 9, 1980. Upon demolition, one of the towers proved to be too stubborn for dynamite, which resulted in a leaning tower that had to be taken down with a wrecking ball. (Courtesy of Jeff Oswalt.)

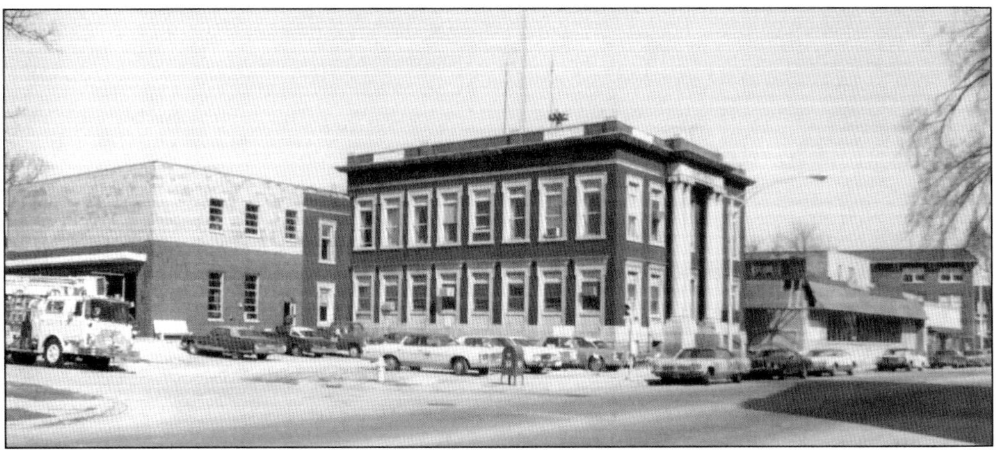

This photograph shows the new village hall being built just north of the old one, while the firehouse received a second addition. It would eventually be covered with stucco to match the new building. The back half of the firehouse is the original 1915 structure. The old village hall was demolished July 23, 1975. A portion of the original pillars can still be seen today holding up the sign in the parking lot. (Courtesy of Jeff Oswalt.)

The homes in this picture are being moved down the 7700 block of Monroe, from 414 and 418 Circle Avenue. They were moved to make way for a municipal parking lot in April 1976. This was a common sight in Forest Park during the late 1950s, when several homes were moved to make way for the Congress Expressway. (Courtesy of Harold Stover.)

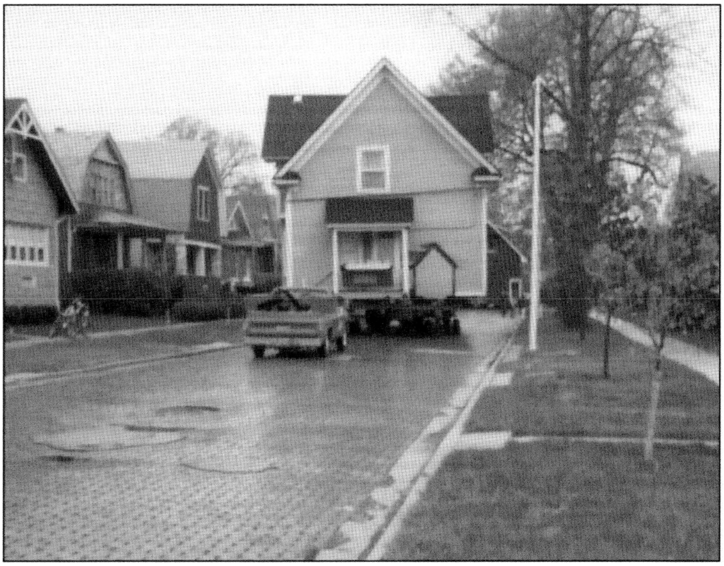

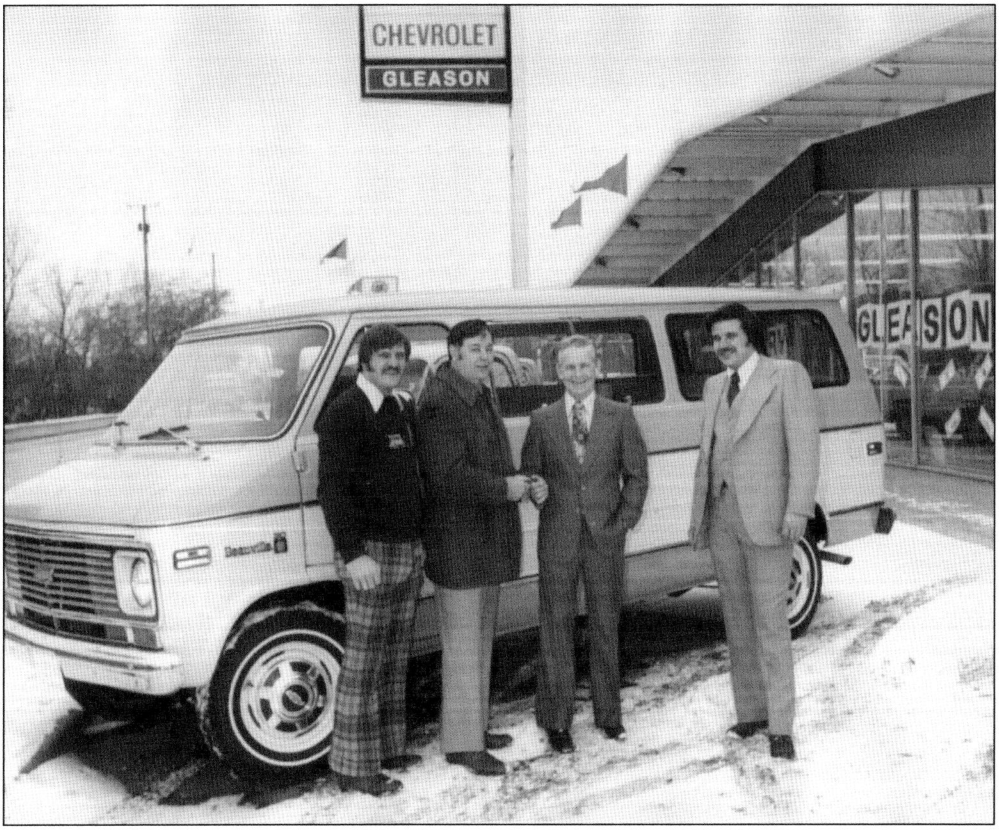

The Forest Park Community Center was championed by Mayor Howard Mohr in the early 1970s. It would later be named in his honor. In 1977, Jerry Gleason donated a new 12-passenger van to the center. Jim McCoy, Mayor Mohr, Jerry Gleason, and Roy Allen are pictured from left to right. The community center was started in 1973 in the old water works garage on Jackson Boulevard, near Des Plaines Avenue. (Courtesy of Village of Forest Park.)

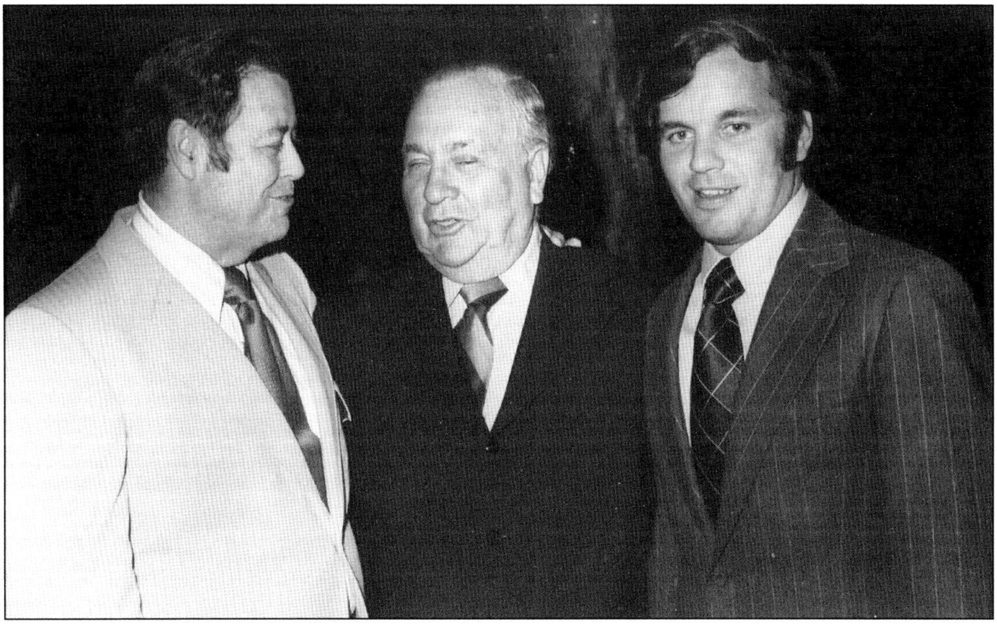

Mayor Howard Mohr, who was also a state senator at the time, is seen with Chicago mayor Richard J. Daley and then senator Richard M. Daley. Howard Mohr would suffer a fatal heart attack on the morning of January 12, 1977, three hours before his retirement from the Senate at the age of 55. This was less than a month after Richard J. Daley succumbed to a heart attack of his own on December 20, 1976. (Courtesy of Mike Mohr.)

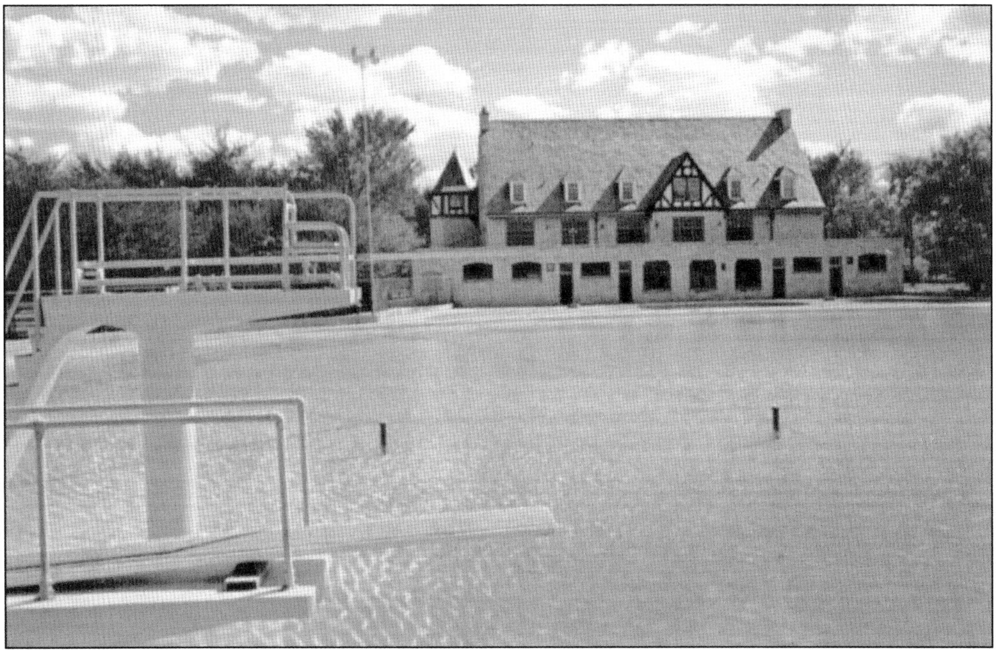

Generations of Forest Parkers cooled themselves during the dog days of summer in the refreshing oasis that is the Forest Park pool. The pool seen here was actually built within the original pool. Many people fondly recall trying to catch trout when the pool would be temporarily stocked after Labor Day in the 1960s and 1970s.

Eight

Same Place, Different Time

Much of Forest Park's past has disappeared—be it due to neglect, weather, the arsonist's match, or just for the sake of "progress." Some changes were forced upon the community such as the expressway, and others happened more gradually. Some places have changed so much that it is difficult to visualize how a place looked or where a building stood. Sometimes a building or location has changed significantly, while a familiar neighboring landmark remains much as it was.

In many cases, buildings simply become outgrown or so outdated that they become a danger or too costly to repair. In other cases, like the Park District Administration Building, care is taken to preserve the aesthetic beauty of the structure, while adapting it to meet the needs and requirements of today's society.

At the time of this writing, several historic places are in jeopardy. The Roos building faces an uncertain future, as does the post office on Des Plaines Avenue and the old chapel at Altenheim. Many of the churches and clubs are seeing declining memberships. Groups like the Eagles, the Moose, and the Mannerchor and Damenchor are shrinking or disappearing. The buildings that housed these organizations are in danger or already gone.

This final chapter will attempt to put some long vanished landmarks into proper perspective or perhaps reacquaint the reader with a place or location that they have not thought about in many years.

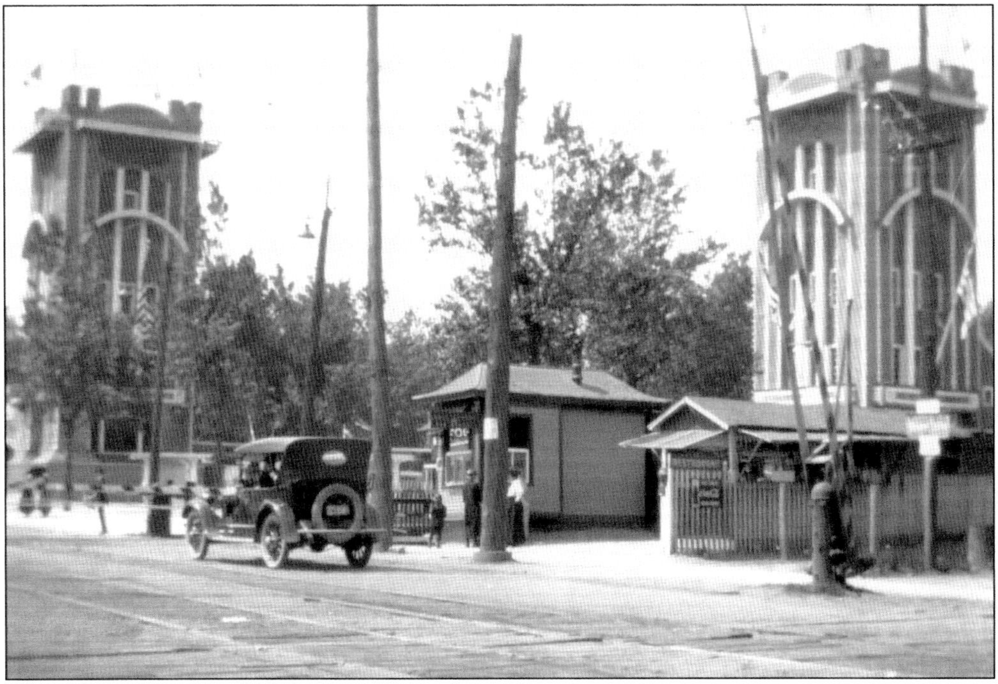

The photograph above shows the entrance to the amusement park and the towers that flanked the entrance. Most of the old location was excavated and regraded when the expressway was built. The approximately 12-acre site bordered Harrison Street to the south. The boundaries can be clearly seen on the 1910 map. (Above, photograph by Fred Borchert; courtesy of Bruce G. Moffat.)

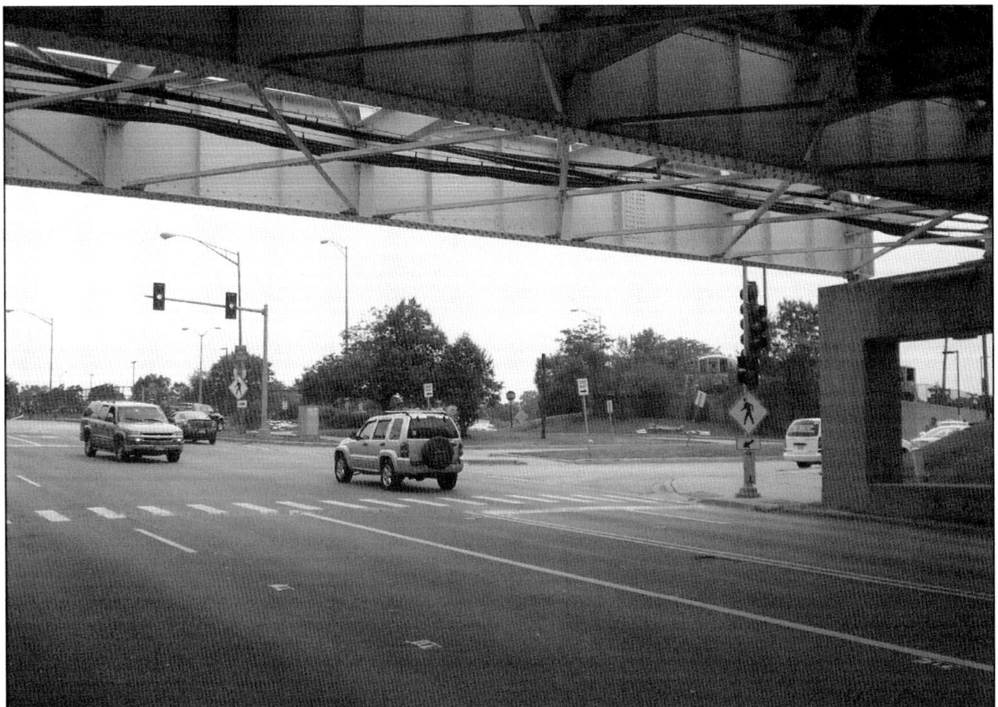

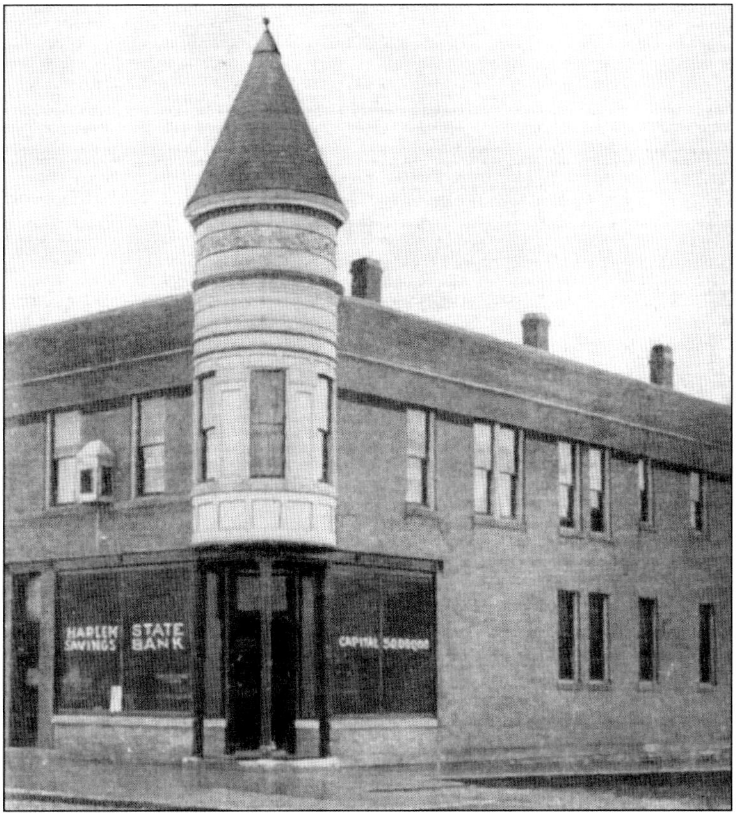

The Harlem State Savings Bank opened in 1904 and located at the southeast corner of Madison Street and Hannah Avenue. The bank was so successful that it built a new structure in 1925. The new bank was built with marble and ornamental iron in the lobby and had a 20,000-pound vault door. The Harlem State Savings Bank failed in 1931. In 1945, the First State Bank of Forest Park took over the location. It became the Forest Park National Bank the following year. (Courtesy of Forest Park Baptist Church.)

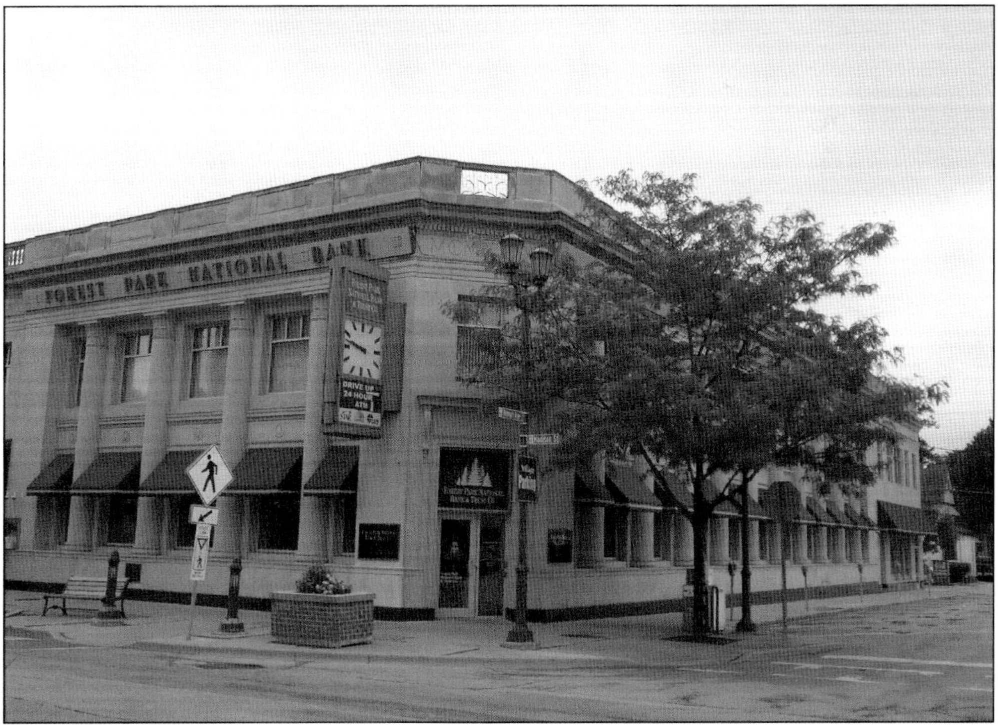

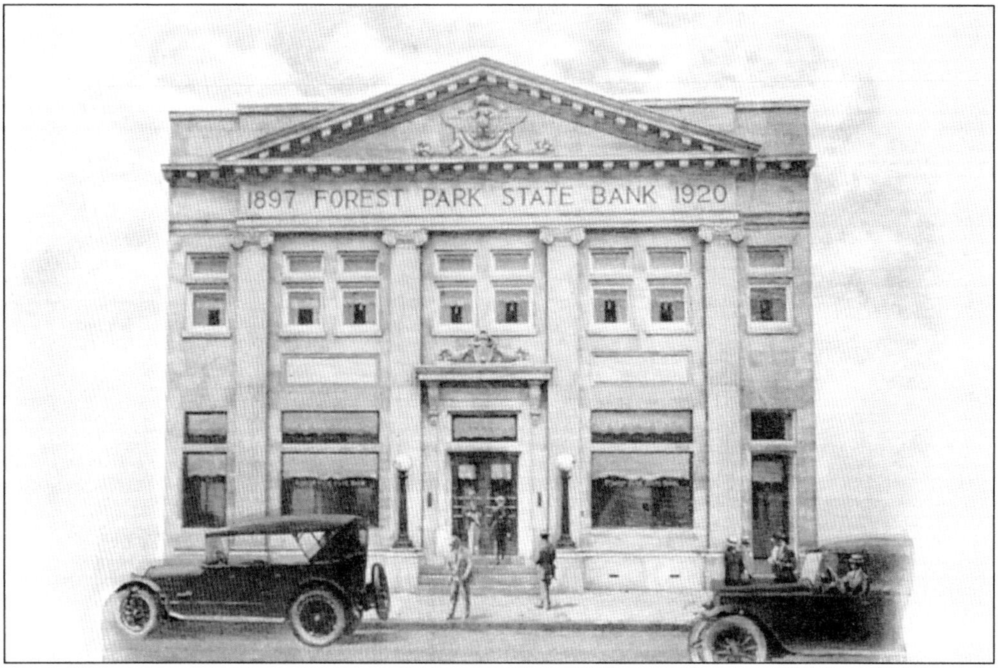

The building at 7401 Madison Street originally started as the A. Roos and Sons Bank, which became the Forest Park State Bank in 1917. Once home to the office of Dr. Clarence Hemingway (Ernest Hemingway's father), the building was renovated in 1920 and received a new limestone facade. The bank fell victim to the Great Depression. The building was the longtime home to Krest Uniforms and currently houses Two Fish art gallery and Flavour Cooking School.

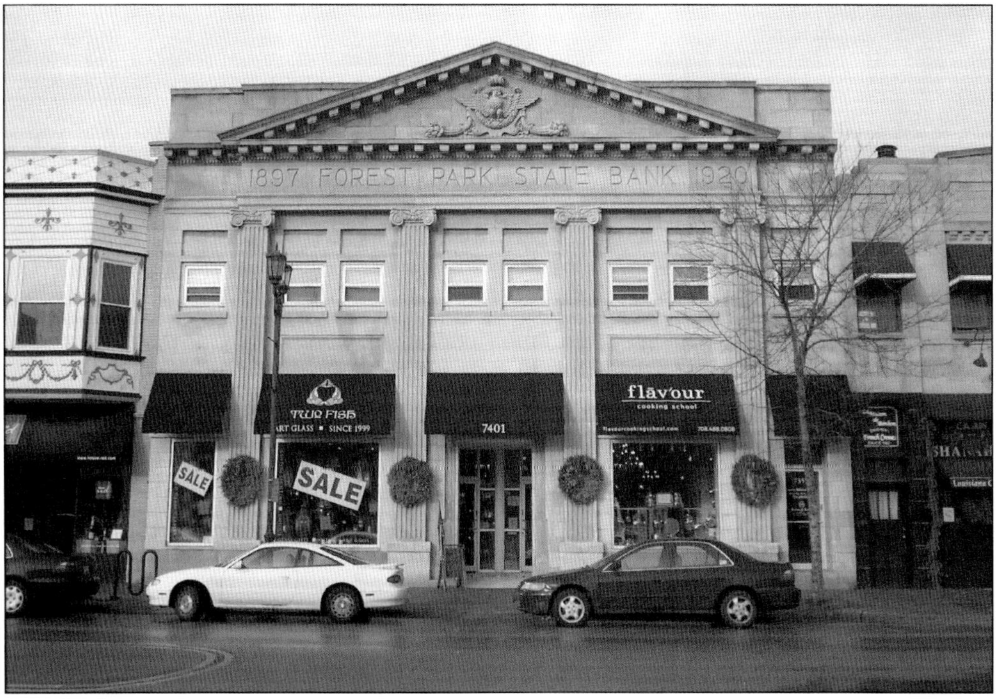

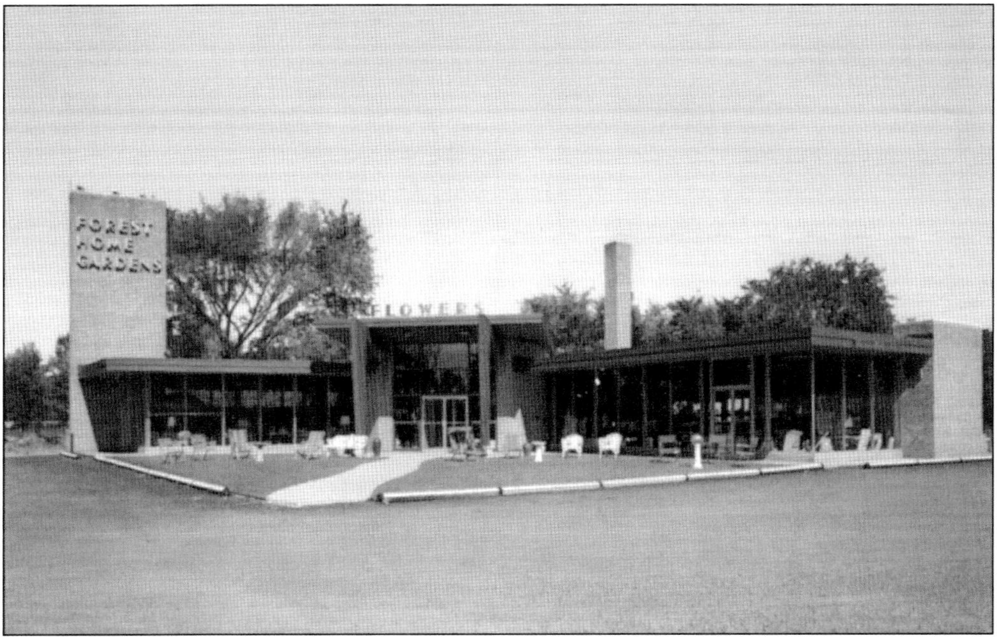

Forest Home Gardens began as a florist shop at 1111 Des Plaines Avenue. In 1952, they moved to the corner of Roosevelt Road and Des Plaines Avenue. In 1956, they opened this large, state-of-the-art garden center at that location. In 1959, the business became an Amlings. Jerry Gleason purchased the land in the 1980s, and a fire destroyed the building on January 5, 1989. In 1990, Jerry Gleason built the showroom currently at the location. The building and showroom are currently vacant.

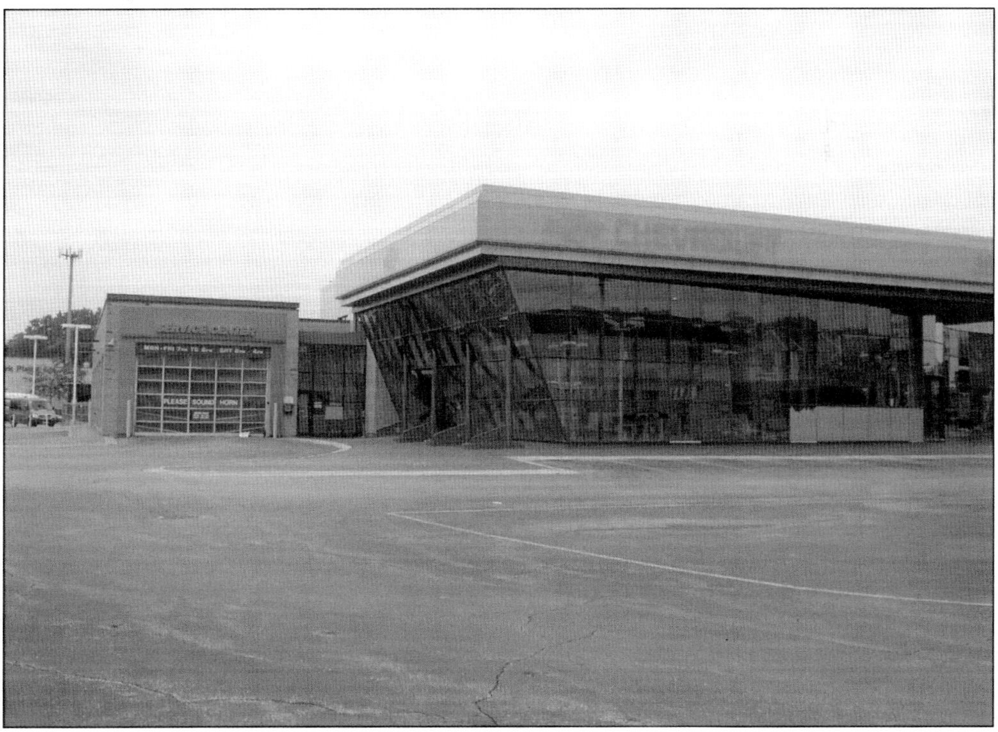

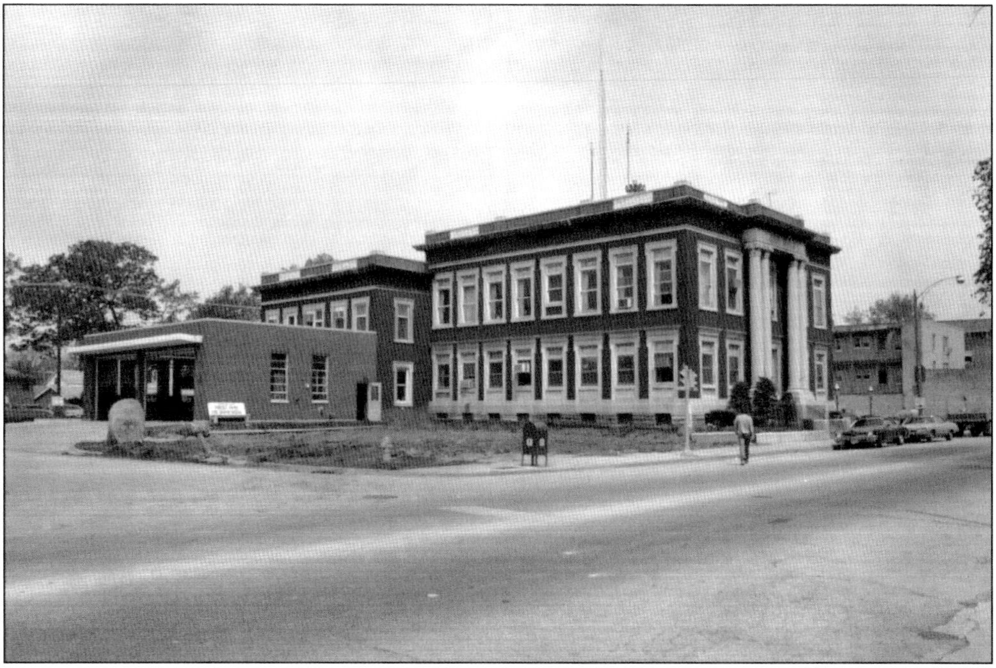

The 1974 photograph above shows the village hall as the parking lot was being shifted to the southeast portion of the property in preparation for the new village hall, which was being constructed. The upper addition to the firehouse also had yet to be completed. With its ramps and elevator, the new village hall was a vast improvement for handicapped and disabled residents. The building has undergone several renovations, including major upgrades to the communication center. (Above, courtesy of Jeff Oswalt.)

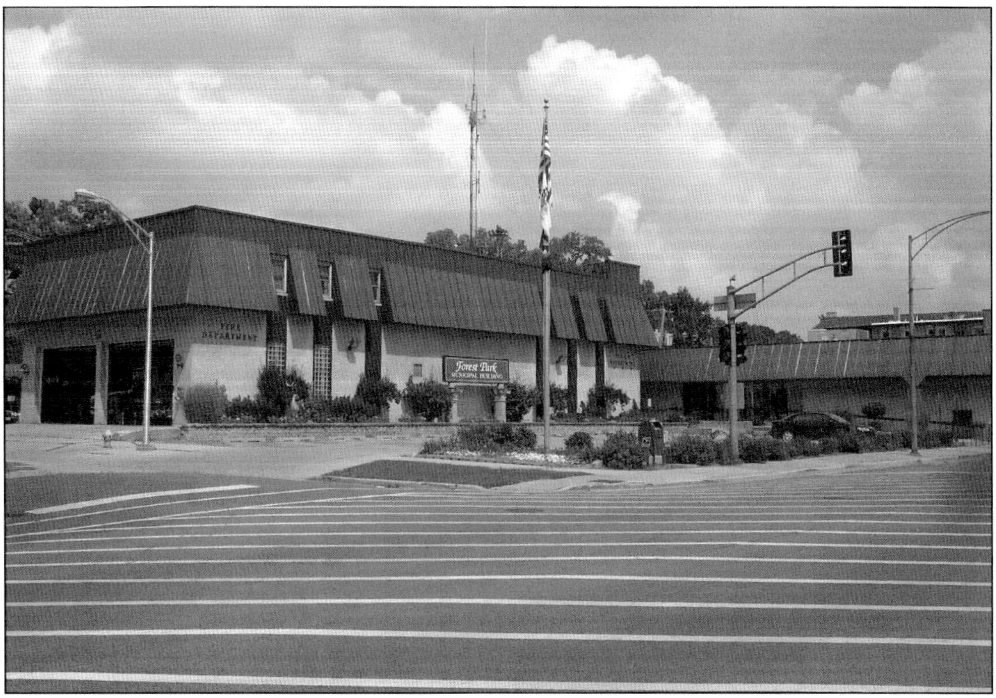

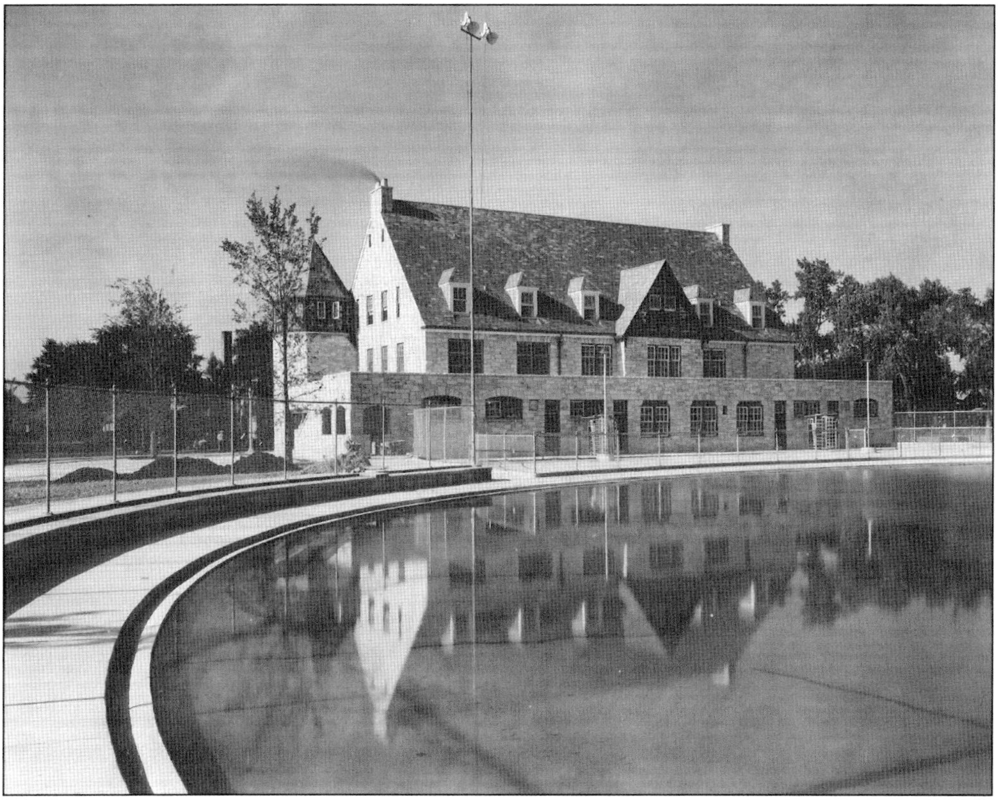

The original Forest Park pool was dedicated August 7, 1938, and at the time it was one of the largest pools in the area. It measured 230 feet by 180 feet, holding around 800,000 gallons of water. The pool was almost scrapped in the 1960s, when extensive repairs were needed. The renovations included a new pool, which was constructed within the old pool, and enlarging the deck area, which reduced the overall size of the pool. The Forest Park pool was entirely rebuilt in 1995. In 1996, the new aquatic center was opened, featuring two drop slides, two flume slides, and a sand volleyball court. The pool was also deepened to 12 feet from the previous 10-foot depth. (Above, courtesy of Park District of Forest Park.)

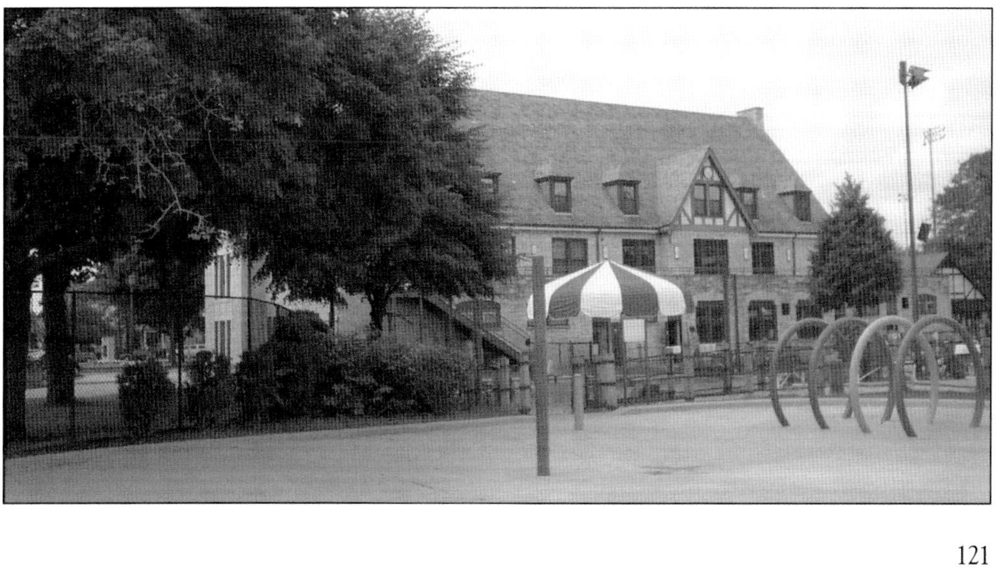

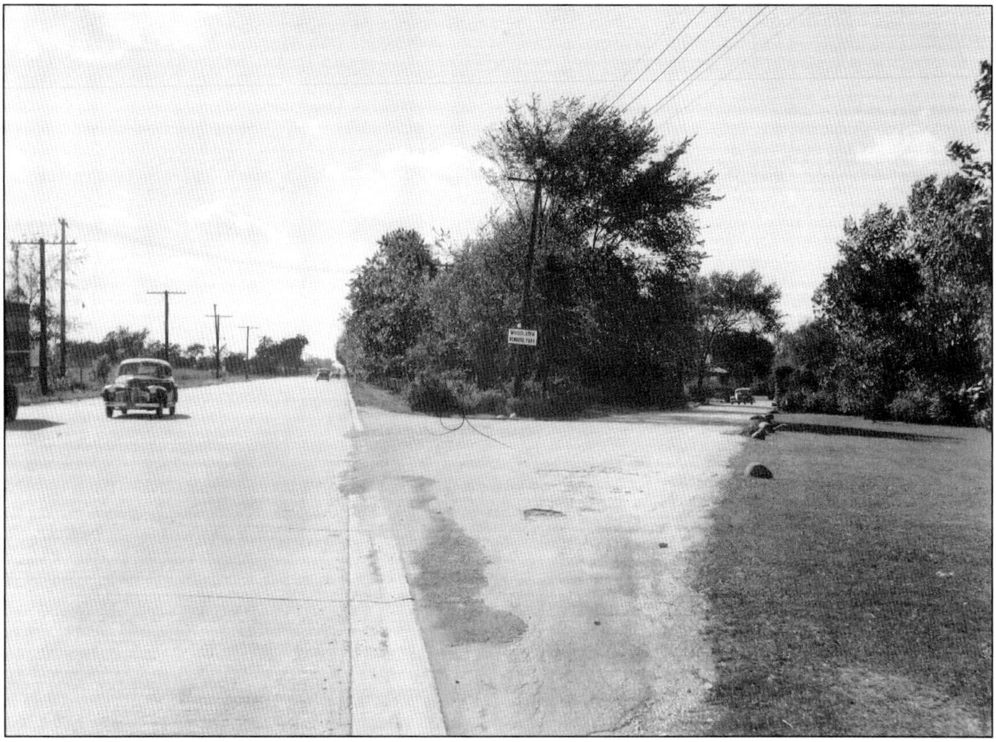

A photograph from the 1940s shows the view looking west on Twenty-second Street at the Woodlawn Cemetery entrance. As part of the parklike design of the cemetery, the office was set back from the main entrance. Many of the cemeteries have their own greenhouses, but Woodlawn featured an ornamental palm house for the growing of tropical plants. The cemetery's offices were moved when the new funeral home was opened at Twenty-second Street and Des Plaines Avenue in 2006. (Above, courtesy of Woodlawn Cemetery.)

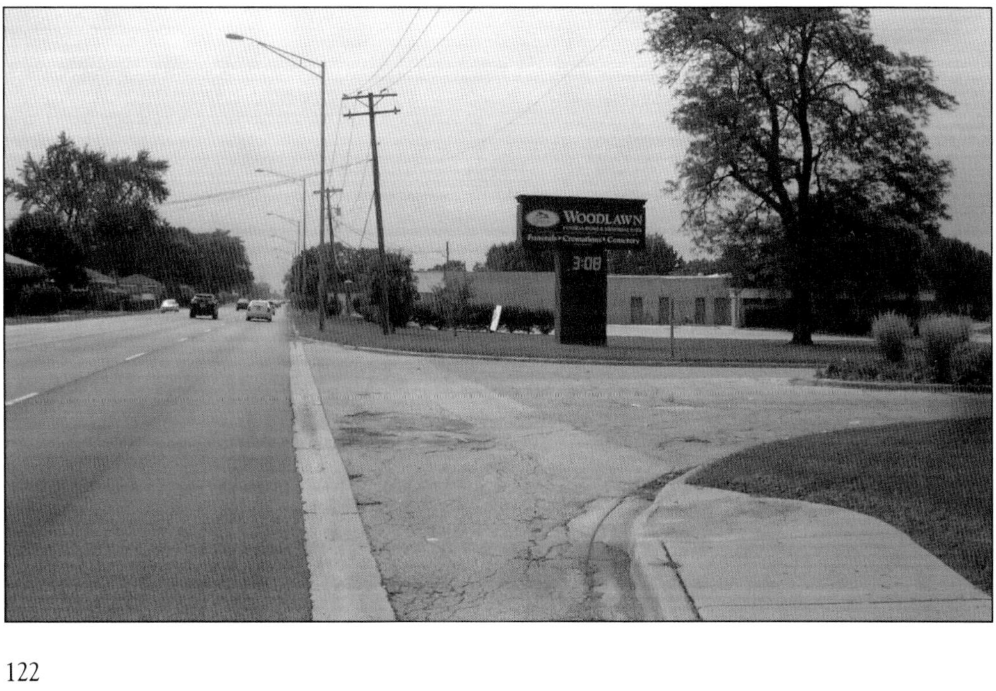

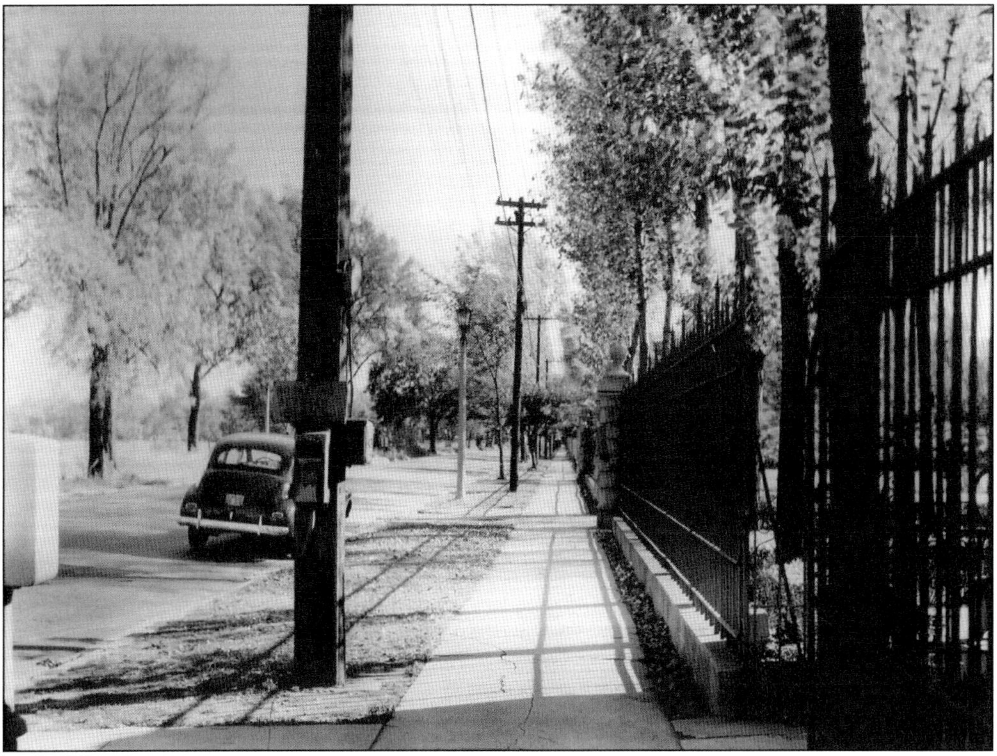

Des Plaines Avenue south of Roosevelt Road was once a quiet, tree-lined street, as seen in the 1940s photograph above. When the brick road was paved in 1925, the street was widened three feet on each side. The street has been widened again since then, but the biggest change has been the arrival of Wal-Mart in 1994. The discount retail giant purchased the land that once included eight military residences, along with the Child World, which is where a few scenes from the Tom Cruise movie *The Color of Money* were filmed. An aerial shot of the location can be seen on page 107. (Above, courtesy of Woodlawn Cemetery.)

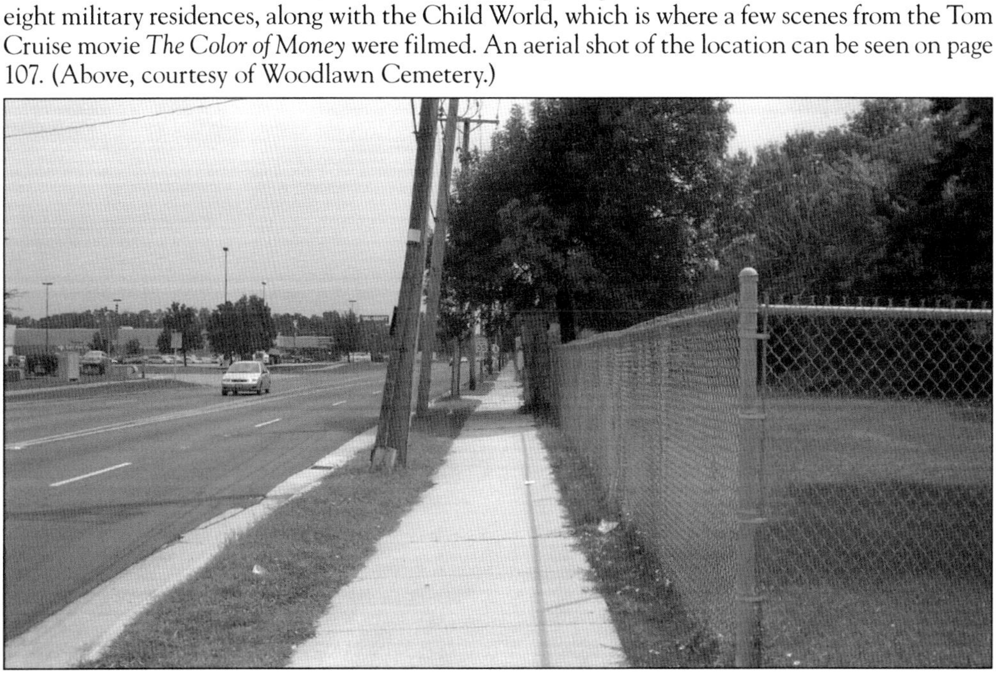

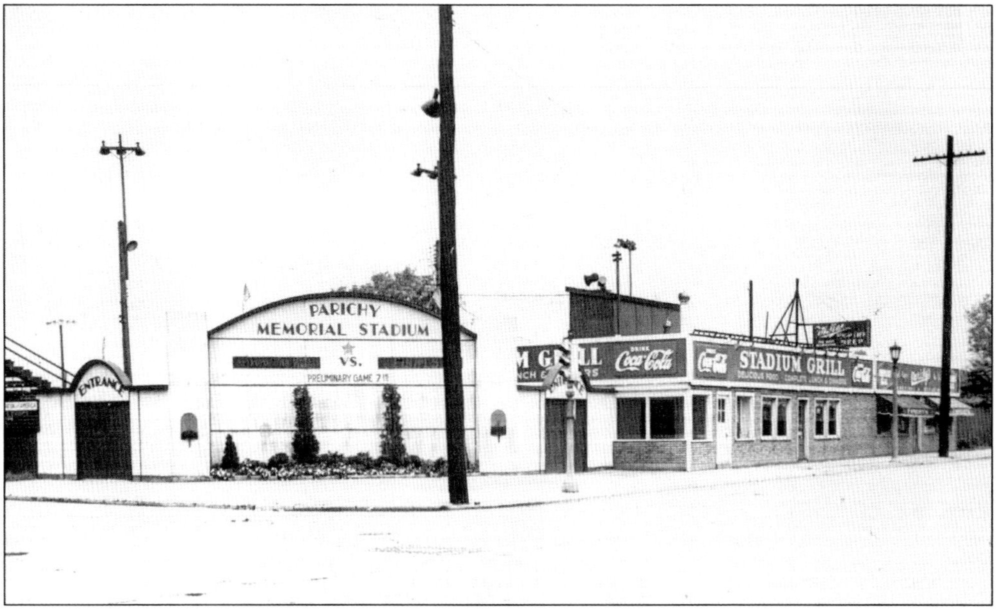

Parichy Memorial Stadium was home to the Parichy Bloomer Girls of the National Girls Baseball League during the 1940s and 1950s. The stadium also provided a new home for the country's first baseball museum, which Parichy began in 1933. When the girls were not playing, the stadium was home to wrestling and boxing matches, as well as the occasional donkey baseball game. The stadium was yet another casualty of the expressway construction. In the mid-1960s, a Dodge dealership purchased what remained of the lot, along with the Vogel tavern and bowling alley on the south side of Harrison. A showroom was built on the south side of the property and a service department on the north. In 1978, U-Haul purchased the properties, and they continue to use the buildings today. (Above, courtesy of Historical Society of Forest Park.)

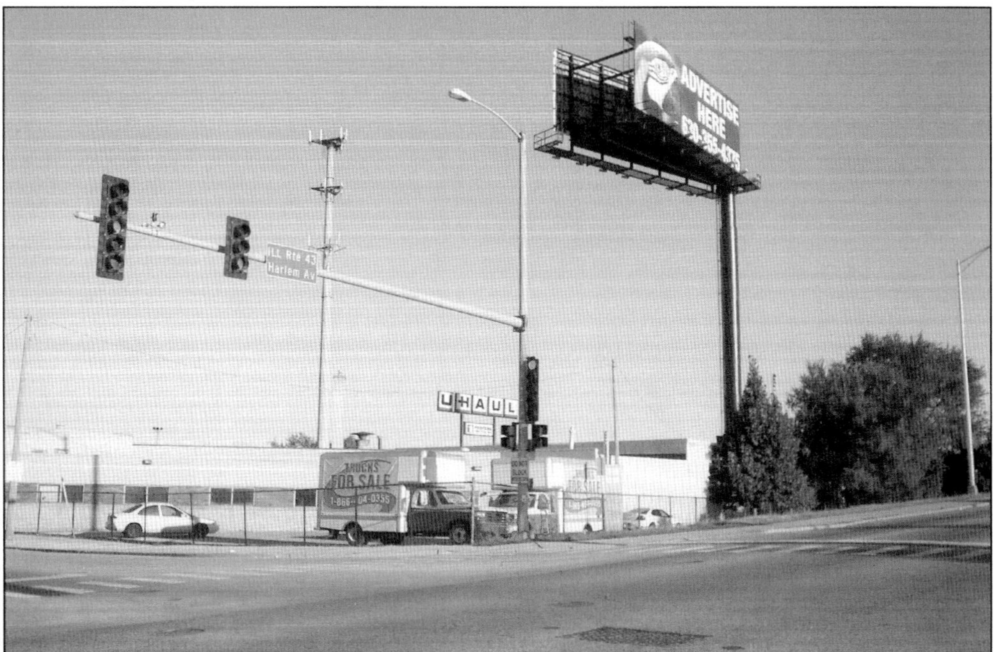

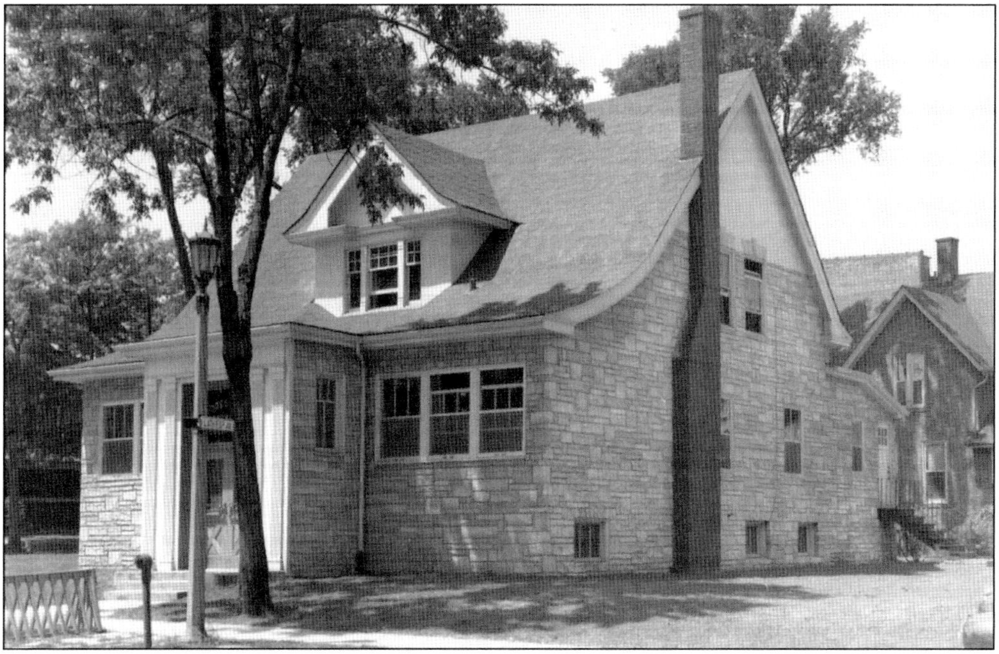

The image above shows the Forest Park Library around 1958 as viewed from Lathrop Avenue and Jackson Boulevard. For many years, the library had been located on the second floor of the old municipal building. The library board purchased the home of Polly Haase Thomas in 1946. The former residence would be expanded in 1960 with the Mathilde Petersohn addition and then again in 1972 with the Viola Gitzel addition. The building was leveled in 1994 to allow for construction of the current library. The original plan was for a three-floor building, but funding did not pass. A second proposal for a two-floor building was approved. Ground was broken August 17, 1994, for the building seen below, which opened October 8, 1995. (Above, courtesy of Village of Forest Park.)

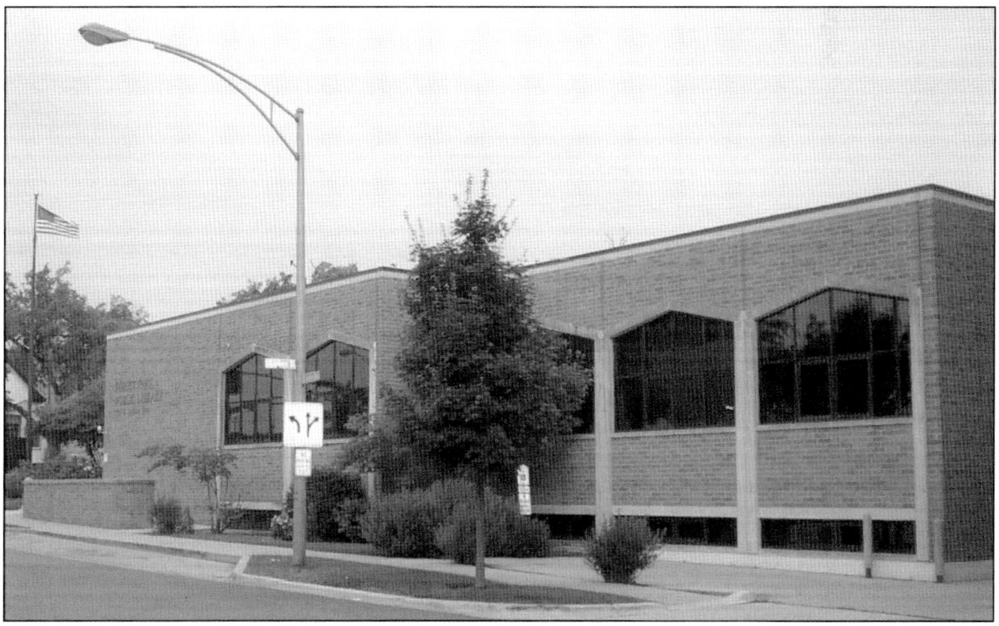

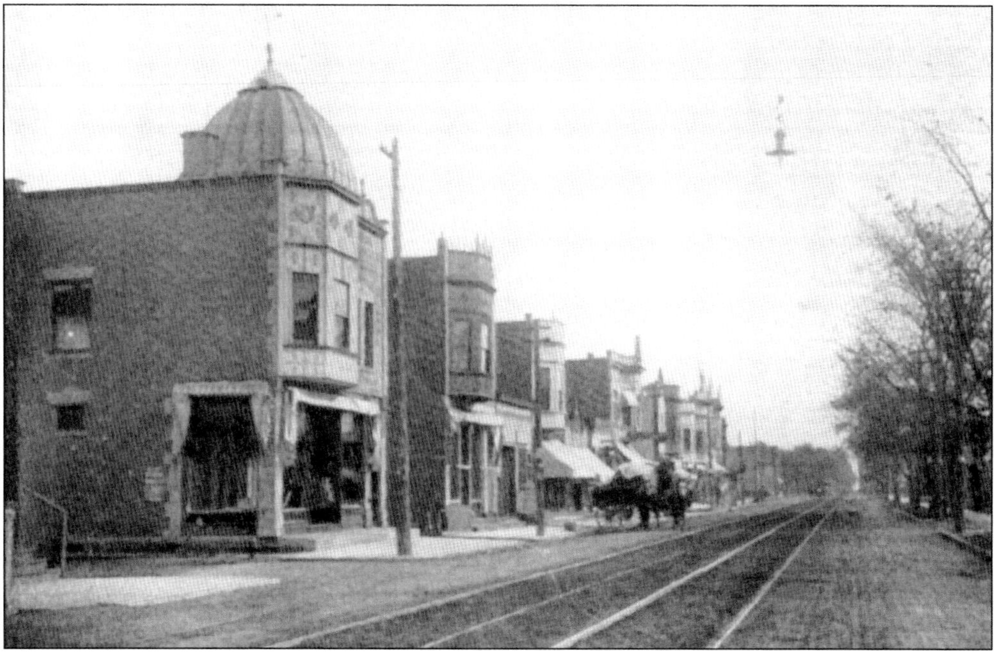

The c. 1906 photograph above looks east from Burkhardt Court along Madison Street. Burkhardt Court may have been named after the longtime principal of St. John's Parochial School, M. J. S. Burkhardt. Many of the buildings seen are still standing. The building on the left has been the home of Forest Park Liquors for some time, although the dome was removed many years ago. Madison Street has undergone some face-lifts over the past decade. Old-fashioned streetlights were installed, along with brick planters and a fountain in Constitution Court. (Above, courtesy of Forest Park Baptist Church.)

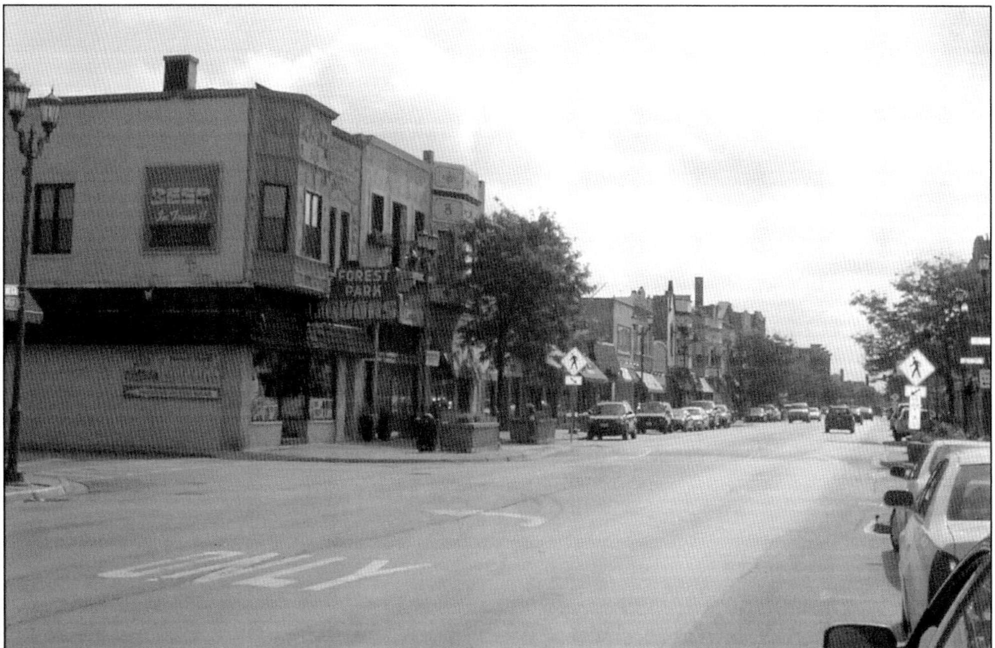

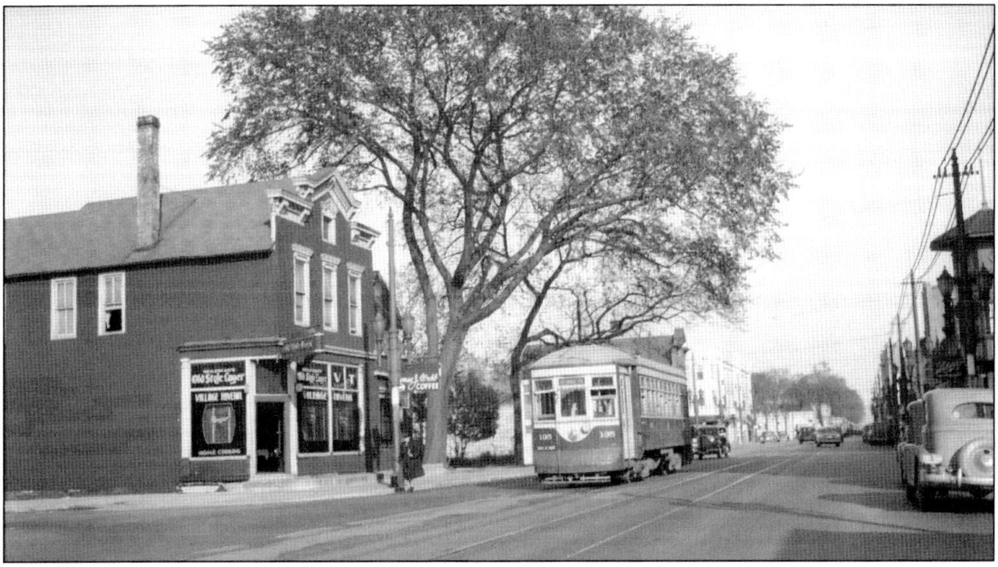

The photograph above, taken on October 6, 1946, shows a streetcar passing 7301 Madison Street. The building was the longtime home of Ernst Fichtler's shoe store. It later become a beauty parlor and then served as the home for several taverns. The Village Tavern was located here for five years before the building was condemned and demolished in 1951. On the far right, the turret of the building that currently houses O'Sullivans can be seen on the southeast corner of Madison Street and Marengo Avenue. The photograph below shows the scene today. Madison Street Commons was built in 2005 on the north side of Madison Street between Elgin and Marengo Avenues. The large commercial and residential building was constructed on the spot where Brown's Chicken and the Inne Towne Pet Motel once stood. The building currently counts the Original Pancake House and a Starbucks among its tenants. (Above, photograph by Robert Gibson; courtesy of Walter R. Keevil.)

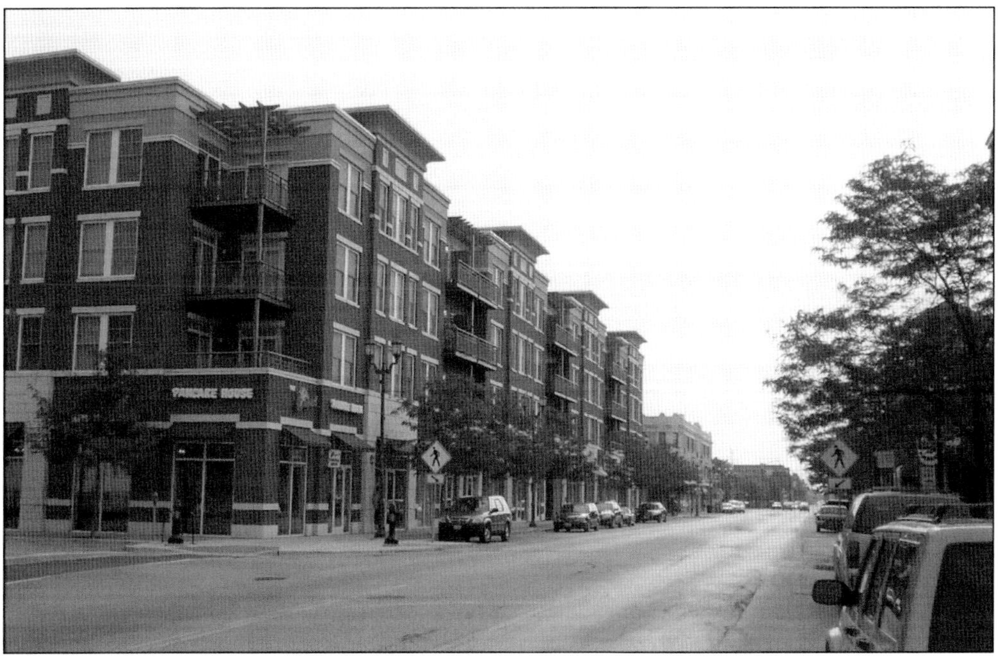